CRISIS AND CHANGE IN THE BRITISH AND DUTCH PRISON SERVICES

To my parents

Crisis and Change in the British and Dutch Prison Services

Understanding Crisis-Reform Processes

SANDRA L. RESODIHARDJO
Leiden University, The Netherlands

Routledge
Taylor & Francis Group
LONDON AND NEW YORK

First published 2009 by Ashgate Publishing

2 Park Square, Milton Park, Abingdon, Oxfordshire OX14 4RN
52 Vanderbilt Avenue, New York, NY 10017

Routledge is an imprint of the Taylor & Francis Group, an informa business

First issued in paperback 2020

British Library Cataloguing in Publication Data
Resodihardjo, Sandra L.
Crisis and change in the British and Dutch prison services
: understanding crisis-reform processes.
1. Prison administration--Great Britain. 2. Prison
administration--Netherlands. 3. Crisis management--Great
Britain--Case studies. 4. Crisis management--Netherlands--
Case studies.
I. Title
365.9'41-dc22

Library of Congress Cataloging-in-Publication Data
Resodihardjo, Sandra L.
Crisis and change in the British and Dutch prison services : understanding crisis-reform processes / by Sandra L. Resodihardjo.
p. cm.
Includes bibliographical references and index.
ISBN 978-0-7546-7549-5
1. Prisons--Great Britain. 2. Prisons--Netherlands. 3. Prison administration--Great Britain. 4. Prison administration--Netherlands. I. Title.

HV9647.R45 2009
365'.70941--dc22

008053458

ISBN 978-0-7546-7549-5 (hbk)
ISBN 978-0-367-60315-1 (pbk)

Contents

List of Figures and Tables

Figures

Tables

Acknowledgements

This book is by no means the result of a solo project. Many people have contributed by providing information, advice, and support – though naturally any mistakes in this book are mine and mine alone.

The book could not have been written without the help of the people working in the Dutch and British Prison Services – both in headquarters as well as in the field. Without their willingness to let me into their prisons, show me around, let me follow them for one or more days and tell me about current and past events, I would not have been able to understand the difficulties involved in running a prison. Although I cannot thank you by name (a consequence of the policy of anonymity), I would like to thank everyone I interviewed for their willingness to share their knowledge with me.

I would like to thank the following people for their valuable feedback: Fleur Alink, Arjen Boin, Gerard Breeman, Henk van de Bunt, Francesca Gains, Paul 't Hart, Liesbet Heyse, Frans Jorna, Roy King, Sanneke Kuipers, Mathilde Meijers, Paul Nieuwenburg, Jörg Noll, Christopher Pollitt, Michiel de Vries, Kutsal Yesilkagit and Frank de Zwart. I would especially like to thank Andrew Coyle for letting me stay at ICPS (International Centre for Prison Studies) for almost six months to investigate the British cases.

The book could not have been published without the help of various organizations. I would like to thank the Netherlands Organization for Scientific Research (NWO 41560013 and 2002/00676/MaGW), the British Council (grant-in-aid), the Leiden University Fund (7509/29-01-02\F, vW), the Netherlands Institute of Government (N01-076-so) and the Hallsworth Committee of the University of Manchester (Hallsworth Visiting Professorship) for their financial support.

This book could not have been written without the support of my friends and family. I would like to thank them for listening to my stories while I was trying to figure out how to write it. Last, but certainly not least, I would like to thank Alison Kirk, my commissioning editor at Ashgate, for her helpful comments and suggestions.

Chapter 1
Crisis and Reform in the Public Sector

Reform is difficult to accomplish. Political science and public administration literature is rife with examples of the barriers that hamper reform. If one would want to reform a policy sector, one could stumble over a number of obstacles, including budgetary obligations (which limit options because there is no money), goals set by outsiders (if parliament passes a law with new goals for the organization, the organization has to use its resources to obtain these goals), the paradigm of the policy sector (which includes values that dictate how to achieve goals, how to deal with certain problems and how not to) and reluctant civil servants (who could decide not to implement reform ideas).

Despite these many obstacles, reform – defined in this book as intended fundamental change of the policy and/or administration of a policy sector – does occur (cf. Heyse et al., 2006).[1] Departments in ministries become agencies (for instance, the Dutch Immigration Services or the Child Support Agency in England), new ministries are created (the Department of Homeland Security in the United States of America), government's monetary policy changes (from a Keynesian model to a monetarist model; cf. Hall, 1993), constitutions are amended (Germany's article 16 concerning asylum; cf. Alink, 2006), armed forces change their recruiting systems from conscription to all-voluntary forces (cf. Noll, 2005) and policies are changed (such as the social security policy changes in the Netherlands and Belgium; cf. Kuipers, 2006). These are just a few of the many examples of reform that occur regularly in the domain of public administration. Yet, if literature claims that reform is so difficult to obtain because of the many obstacles hampering reform, how does it come about?

Three answers are possible. First, political and bureaucratic leaders may introduce reform (Doig and Hargrove, 1990; 't Hart, 2000; Terry, 2003; Noll, 2005; Heyse et al., 2006). Second, reform is stumbled upon through the incremental policy process. Policy makers change policies by taking small steps that hardly deviate from existing policies (Lindblom, 1959, 1979; Harrison et al., 1990). These small changes, however, can add up over time and result in drastic change that may surprise policy makers (Lindblom, 1979: 521; cf. Rose and Davies, 1994: 36). The third manner in which reform can come about is interesting because incremental policy making, which is the standard method of making policy, is actually disrupted. Crises disrupt policy-making processes and present opportunities for reform. It is this last assumption – that crises can lead to reform – which is investigated in this book.

Although there is no such thing as an official crisis-reform thesis in the crisis or reform literature, it is possible to group the works of several authors together under this banner because these authors basically advocate the same argument (cf. Keeler, 1993; Kingdon, 1995; Cortell and Peterson, 1999). Their line of argument runs as follows. During crises, the policies, paradigm (which dictates how to achieve goals and implement policies), goals and functioning of a policy sector come under attack. The crisis poses a severe threat to the core values of a social system. Actors have to decide quickly how to deal with the crisis while the situation is highly uncertain (Rosenthal et al., 2001: 6–7). A crisis has two effects. First, actors – policy makers in this book – are under extreme pressure to find solutions to end the crisis. Media and Members of Parliament (MPs) question the functioning of the policy sector and demand better performance. Their message is clear: policy makers either have to deal with the crisis or resign. The second effect is that questioning the policies, paradigm, goals and functioning of a policy sector results in a declining support for these policies, paradigm, goals and functioning. Normally, these policies, paradigm and goals act as constraints because they limit what policy makers can do in terms of reform. Goals, for instance, are difficult to change, and so is the paradigm that dictates how to achieve these goals. However, as support for the paradigm, policies and goals declines, such constraints diminish. Consequently, it will be easier for people to push for reform as they can introduce new policies and goals that differ from the old ones. Moreover, other constraints, such as money, will also diminish as MPs will increase policy makers' budgets to deal with the crisis.

As a result, or so the line of inquiry suggests, policy makers looking to end the crisis will have more leeway to suggest measures that were hitherto unacceptable or even unheard of. Moreover, so-called entrepreneurs can use the situation of lessened constraints to get a certain problem on the agenda, change the way a problem is defined – which will have consequences in determining the appropriate measures to deal with the problem (cf. Rochefort and Cobb, 1994) – or push for a favourite solution (Kingdon, 1995; Cortell and Peterson, 1999).

In short, the crisis-reform thesis postulates that policy makers are not only under pressure to find solutions to end the crisis, they also have increased freedom to suggest alternative measures. Crises present opportunities as the incremental policy-making process is disrupted.

Although the authors of the crisis-reform thesis claim the same thing (a crisis is an opportunity because constraints diminish, allowing policy makers to deal with the crisis and entrepreneurs to push for favourite solutions), a certain vagueness remains in the thesis. For starters, the authors do not employ a clear and widely shared body of concepts and terminology. Neither crisis, constraints, diminishing constraints, entrepreneurs nor reform are defined clearly. Definitions vary or do not exist at all. Moreover, the assumptions underpinning the model are not clearly expressed. Authors do not proceed beyond, for example, stating that constraints will diminish as a consequence of pressure, urgency and need. Exactly how this process works remains unclear. Which constraints are to diminish remains unclear as well. Furthermore, nothing is said about the broader framework in which crises occur. The theory states that crisis will lead to reform as actors can use the situation of diminished constraints to push for reform. It is as if the crisis occurs in a vacuum – only the crisis matters, not its context. As a result, no attention is paid to the possibility of a crisis as an accelerant of trends already occurring in the larger societal and political context of a policy sector.

Existing theory contains interesting ideas on the crisis-reform process, but lacks empirical findings to construct a coherent crisis-reform thesis. Empirical research conducted in this study should help to streamline current theory on the crisis-reform process. This study therefore takes a first step in opening the black box of the crisis-reform process by answering the following question: Under what conditions do crises in policy sectors lead to reform?

To answer this question, it is necessary to focus the research by studying a single type of crisis (instead of the many types of crises mentioned in the literature) in a single policy sector. Such a focus will ensure that the selected cases generate results which can be compared in order to determine the conditions under which crises lead to reform.

The type of crisis selected for this book is one which occurs in policy sectors: the institutional crisis. Such a crisis occurs when the institutional structure of a policy sector 'experiences a relatively strong decline in (followed by unusually low levels of) legitimacy' (Boin and 't Hart, 2000: 13). In other words, incidents show that a policy sector is not functioning as it ideally should. As a consequence, media and MPs start to question the functioning of the policy sector. They demand better performance of the policy sector, while questioning the policy sector's rules, regulations, policies, goals and paradigm. This increase in negative attention from media and MPs towards the policy sector indicates that the policy sector's legitimacy is in decline. Hence, actors working in the policy sector face an institutional crisis.

The selected policy sector is the prison service. The prison service is a clearly demarcated policy sector where only one ministry is in charge, the prison service is a clear and distinct organization within this ministry and the number of actors is limited and well known. This makes building case studies easier, as it is clear which actor to focus on while the number of actors one has to collect data on remains manageable.

By selecting cases from two countries, it is possible to conduct a comparative case analysis which takes the context and events of the various cases into consideration (Kaarbo and Beasley, 1999; Yin, 2003; Rueschemeyer, 2003). The two countries differ markedly on two accounts: parliamentary system and media. The Dutch parliamentary system can be labelled a consensual system where building consensus is key. The emphasis on consensus building is not only found in the parliamentary tradition of the Netherlands, but also between government and other organizations (cf. Bovens et al., 2001: 19). The British parliamentary system is more adversarial and characterized by a dominant Cabinet (Gallagher et al., 1992: 54; Hague and Harrop, 2001: 239–40; Hueglin, 2003). In addition, Dutch media attention towards the prison service is usually low key and nonexistent (unless something happens such as an escape), while the British media addresses the prison service almost daily in their newspapers. When there are no incidents to pay attention to (such as escapes), topics in the British media range from pleas to either cut or increase jail sentences to privatization of prisons and court escort services. Moreover, the British media are much more outspoken and judgemental when it comes to the prison service than their Dutch counterparts. Despite these dissimilarities, cases from these two countries can be selected for comparative analysis because of the similarities within the two prison services: the structure of prison services is quite similar and both prison services face similar problems and constraints as they need to keep prisoners contained and treat them properly on a small budget. In addition, the selected cases all focus on matters related to security and prison conditions.

For this study, the following three cases were selected: escapes and cell shortage in the Netherlands (1992–1993), and escapes (1994–1995) and riots (1990–1991) in Britain. The three cases are characterized by an institutional crisis with reform as the end result. The cases diverge, however, in the paths taken to this outcome making it possible to further our understanding of how and when crises lead to reform.

In order to understand the different paths taken to reform, the literature concerning the crisis-reform thesis will be discussed in Chapter 2. Following a description of the barriers normally hampering reform, the basic functions of the crisis-reform thesis is explained as well as the crisis-reform patterns one should be able to discern in a case if the theory is correct. In order to be able to discern these patterns, we need to know what to look for in a case. Chapter 2 ends with a clarification on how to find the most important concepts of the thesis in reality. Chapter 3 provides a brief introduction to the two prison services and describes the status quo prior to the outbreak of the crises. As such, this chapter offers background information for the reader and provides the information needed to determine the occurrence of reform following the crises. The three cases are presented in Chapters 4, 5, and 6. Each case chapter contains a description of the events. For each case, the existence of an institutional crisis and reform is established. The extent to which the theoretical patterns of reform can be discerned in the three cases is discussed in Chapter 7. In this chapter, it becomes clear that the crisis-reform thesis does not completely explain the crisis-reform processes in these three cases. Other conditions are at work which are currently not addressed in the crisis-reform thesis. Chapter 8 provides an explanation of these additional conditions and introduces alternative paths to reform.

Note

1. Please note that the definition of reform used in this study is neutral. Consider, for instance, the effects of the escapes in 1994–1995 on the Prison Service of England and Wales: a massive redirection from Woolf's need to balance justice, security and control to an overwhelming focus on security. In general, criminologists will not label this change in direction as reform because of the negative effects it created for the prisoners. In this book, however, the change is labelled reform because it fits the definition. Moreover, no normative stance is taken towards the effects – be they positive or negative – of reforms described in this book.

Chapter 2
The Crisis-Reform Thesis: How Crises Can Lead to Reform

Introduction[1]

Most scholars of public administration and political science tend to agree that re-designing policy and organizations within a policy sector is difficult. Their research shows that it is hard to get reform proposals on the political agenda (Kingdon, 1995) and even harder to overcome barriers such as vested interests and sunk costs that prevent reform proposals from being accepted by parliament (Wilsford, 1994; Shepsle, 2001). In the unlikely event that parliament does accept them, successful implementation of these proposals often proves a challenge in itself (Caiden, 1991; Cortell and Peterson, 2001; Patashnik, 2003).

In spite of all these difficulties, reform – that is, intended fundamental change of the policy and/or administration of a policy sector – does occur (Heyse et al., 2006). The Dutch Minister of Agriculture, for example, restructured the agricultural sector in the late 1990s. This sector was infamous for the way farmers were able to block any reform (Breeman et al., 2000). In the Dutch Prison Service, a long tradition of one person to a cell, supported by a coalition of governors, prison officers and Members of Parliament, was abandoned when double-bunking was introduced in 2002 (Dekker et al., 2003). In Germany, the right to asylum had traditionally been a sensitive subject due to Germany's Nazi past and the effects of unification. In the early 1990s, a coalition of CDU/CSU, FDP, and SDP managed to reform article 16 of the Basic Law in order to limit the influx of asylum seekers (Alink, 2006). If reform is really as difficult as conventional wisdom has it, the question arises how and why it can sometimes happen.

All the above mentioned examples of reform were preceded by crises. Crisis is an interesting phenomenon because it is often identified as a necessary catalyst for reform (cf. Keeler, 1993; Kingdon, 1995; Cortell and Peterson, 1999).[2] Crises create possibilities and opportunities. Constraints that normally limit policy makers when they want to propose reform tend to lessen in times of crisis. As a result, policy makers can formulate reform proposals that were unacceptable or even unheard of before the crisis. In short, crisis presents an opportunity for reform, or so these authors claim.

The idea that crisis facilitates reform will be referred to in this book as the crisis-reform thesis. In reality, there is no such thing as an official crisis-reform thesis, but it is possible to group the works of several authors on crisis and reform together under this banner because these authors basically advocate the same argument. They argue that a crisis can overcome the barriers that normally halt reform. Solutions that were hitherto unthinkable become acceptable. Crisis presents an opportunity, which can be exploited to push for reform. The thesis is often suggested and intuitively accepted as one way in which reform actually comes about. This book aims to explore under what conditions crises lead to reform.

In order to do so, this chapter presents the crisis-reform thesis and explains which patterns one may expect to occur if crisis is to lead to reform.[3] Starting with a description of the barriers blocking reform, the chapter then continues to explain how these barriers can be overcome by describing the most important concepts of the crisis-reform thesis. Having described the patterns of the crisis-reform process, the chapter concludes with an explanation how these crisis-reform patterns can be discerned in reality and which data are needed for this research.

Barriers to Reform: A Review of the Literature

Conventional wisdom dictates that it is difficult to reform policy and organizations within a policy sector. It suggests, and empirical research tends to bear out, that policy makers are constrained in their actions and many hurdles have to be overcome if reform is to materialize (Bannink and Resodihardjo, 2006). The constraints can be roughly divided into three categories: individual, organizational, and political constraints.[4]

The first type of constraint flows from individuals either inside or outside the public organization. An example of such a constraint is the individuals' interests in the current status quo because they either benefit from the status quo and/or have invested their resources in order to create and maintain the current status quo. The second, that is, the organizational constraint, refers to the constraints arising from the way an organization is structured, such as rules and decision-making procedures. Finally, political constraints flow from actions taken by the political masters of a public organization that affect the organization. Such actions could consist of setting the goals that have to be achieved and deciding how much and where to invest scarce resources.

Together, the individual, the organizational and the political constraints can hamper or even block reform. The purpose of this book is not to study constraints. Therefore, only the most salient constraints that create the conditions under which policy makers have to accomplish reform in policy sectors in order to give an idea what these constraints are about, how they operate, and what their effects can be will be discussed (cf. Leemans, 1976a: 10–13; Wilson, 1989; Caiden, 1991; Wilsford, 1994; Rose and Davies, 1994; Kingdon, 1995; Kaufman, 1995; Shepsle, 2001; Cortell and Peterson, 2001;

Patashnik, 2003; Terry, 2003; Bannink and Resodihardjo, 2006; see also Table 2.1).

Individual Constraints

The so-called policy legacy creates individual constraints because once policy is in place it creates, for example, benefits for a number of people. These benefits may range from receiving subsidies to having access to certain resources or having gained access to the decision-making process. Any change in policy may affect these benefits. As a result, the people who are currently benefiting from the status quo will try to prevent change (Kaufman, 1995: 11–12; Korsten, 1993: 205).

Another example of individual constraints is created by those who work in the policy sector. Even though they may be aware that the current system of rules has negative side effects, at least these side effects are known. Changing the rules might produce even worse side effects, so why not stick with the known evils (Kaufman, 1995: 10)? They may also perceive reform proposals as uprooting the predictable way of doing things. Adjusting to new patterns is a very difficult process and the outcome of the reform may affect their position and resources in a negative way (Leemans, 1976b: 88–9; Gains, 2006).

Lastly, people have an interest in the status quo. They have, for example, invested time and money to reach their current position. As a result, they have a stake in maintaining the current status quo (Wilson, 1989: 131; cf. Leemans, 1976b: 88; Rose and Davies, 1994: 14; True et al., 1999: 102). Consider, for instance, incumbent politicians who have invested in the present political system. Changes to the political system of which they are part of could endanger their investments. An example of such an investment is familiarity with local political conditions. All the time and energy used to get to know the local political conditions would become almost worthless if the electoral institution changed from a regional first-past-the-post system to a single district proportional representation electoral system. As a result of losing invested resources when political systems change, politicians will oppose reform in general and only accept cosmetic change if they have no other choice (Shepsle, 2001: 324).

Organizational Constraints

In terms of organizational constraints that hamper reform, one can think of routines, standard operating procedures and decision-making rules that characterize a policy sector. These decision-making rules affect the policy-making process. A reform proposal has to go through a number of veto points. The more veto points a proposal has to go through, the more difficult it is to get a proposal accepted, because each veto point is also an opportunity for someone else to stop or change the proposal (Cortell and Peterson, 1999: 190).

The rules, routines and standard operating procedures are only one side of the policy sector. The other side consists of the norms, values and ideas with regard to what the organization should do and how this should be done; in other words, its paradigm (Hall, 1993: 279). The paradigm determines what is acceptable and what is not when dealing with a problem or achieving a goal. As such, it constrains the actions of ministers because it is difficult for them to suggest changes that do not fit the paradigm (Kaufman, 1995: 15–23; Boin and 't Hart, 2000: 13; 't Hart, 2000: 26–7).

Political Constraints

The actions of the policy sector's political masters, such as the minister, cabinet and parliament, create political constraints. These political masters, for example, set the budget for a policy sector. The budget, in turn, limits the kinds of changes that are possible. Some options are just too expensive. As a result, policy makers will not suggest some measures or will tone down the measures severely in order to make them monetarily acceptable (Kingdon, 1995: 106). These same political masters can set the goals a policy sector has to achieve or the means with which to achieve them. Again, these act as a constraint because actors working in a policy sector have to fulfil these goals and/or use a certain kind of means to achieve a goal (Wilson, 1989: 113–36; Kaufman, 1995: 23–9).

This type of constraint is not only created by incumbent political masters, but also by previous ones who leave behind the policy that incumbent political masters and leaders of public organizations inherit (Wilsford, 1994). The incumbent political masters and leaders of public organizations are bound to uphold existing laws and policies and, as a result, there is usually not much leeway for them to add, adjust, or terminate public policies (Rose and Davies, 1994: 1–4, 15–16). Leaders of public organizations coming into office, for instance, can usually do little other than accept the budget allocated to their government agency. At the same time, they will have to accept the manner in which they can dispense the budget because they also inherit obligations (Rose and Davies, 1994: 12).

Political, organizational and individual constraints do not operate separately. They are linked. A political constraint such as policy inheritance affects the advantages people receive from the organization. Budget is not only limited because outsiders, such as MPs, determine the budget, but also because of sunk investments (that is, money tied up in investments). Policy makers wishing to change their organization or policy sector face tremendous obstacles and consequently they cannot change everything they would like to change. Moreover, even if they are capable of changing an aspect of policy or of the administration, they have to consider all the actors with vested interests

Table 2.1 Constraints hampering reform

Type of constraint	Examples
Individual	Benefits Stick with the evils you know, uprooting Invested in status quo
Organizational	Routines, standard operating procedures, and decision-making rules Norms, values, and ideas
Political	Budget Goals Policy inheritance

in the status quo. Even if policy makers are able to get reform proposals on the agenda, this will not automatically lead to a successful outcome in terms of reform. Actors whose interests may be adversely affected by reform proposals can obstruct the acceptance of the reform or, if they were not strong enough to stop the reform proposal from being accepted, they may attempt to hamper the implementation of the reform (Caiden, 1991; Cortell and Peterson, 2001; Patashnik, 2003; cf. Bachrach and Baratz, 1970: 44).

Yet Reform Does Occur

In short, constraints to reform are numerous and as a result reform seems to be a very difficult aim to achieve. Nevertheless, reform does occur. In the summer of 1997, for instance, the Dutch Minister of Agriculture introduced a law into Parliament that aimed to restructure the pig farming industry. The law was presented at a time when an outbreak of classical swine fever was holding the pig-breeding industry in a deadly grip. The fever broke out on 4 February 1997. It resulted in the slaughter of approximately 11 million pigs and cost about €1.36 billion. Since 1984, the high and ever-growing number of pig farms in the Netherlands had been put firmly on the political agenda as the associated manure caused severe environmental problems. Politicians and civil servants wanted to do something about the problems caused by the pig farming industry. Decreasing the number of pigs and dealing with the problems concerning manure turned out to be very difficult: farmers were reluctant to cooperate, agreements between farmers and the Ministry were watered down during the implementation stage or even after an agreement had just been made and farmers organized roadblocks to express their dissatisfaction with the new measures. In 1997, however, it was possible to restructure the pig farming industry, which included a decrease of the livestock by 25 per cent. The Minister of Agriculture seized upon the outbreak of classical swine fever and used it as an argument to restructure the pig farming industry in the Netherlands. He was able to link the swine fever with the pig farming industry by arguing that it was of vital importance not only to deal with the swine fever itself but also to focus on ways to prevent another outbreak in the future. He argued that the only way to prevent such a future outbreak was to restructure the pig farming industry (Breeman et al., 2000).

An equally drastic reform occurred in the Dutch Prison Service in October 2002, when the tradition of one person to a cell was abandoned. In the previous year, security checks to catch drug mules had been intensified at Schiphol airport. Consequently, more people were caught carrying drugs. There were, however, not enough cells to accommodate these drug runners. In January 2002, the press got wind of a letter from the Haarlem chief public prosecutor calling for drug runners who were caught with less than one kilo of cocaine to be sent home. MPs and the media perceived this proposal as yet another example of the Dutch practice of tolerating people breaking the law instead of strictly upholding it.[5] The media interpreted the sending home of drug runners as allowing people to smuggle cocaine. As national elections were coming up, opposition MPs used the incidents to draw attention to and attack the Minister of Justice. Media attention soared as new facts became public knowledge. Two weeks after the letter had become public, the Minister of Justice presented a plan to deal with drug running at Schiphol airport. A temporary emergency law enabled the Minister to increase cell capacity and to put more than one drug runner in a cell. However, cell capacity in general, not just for drug runners, had started to become a problem by the end of 2002. According to the newly elected Minister of Justice cell shortages could not be solved with the conventional solution of building new prisons. In October 2002, he therefore announced that double-bunking would be possible for other offenders as well. The combination of cell shortages, the drug runners caught at Schiphol airport and a newly elected government that had no qualms where double-bunking was concerned proved sufficient to change the Dutch policy tradition of one person to a cell (Dekker et al., 2003).

Reform does not just occur in the Netherlands. It occurs in countries all around the world. Following 9/11, for instance, the Department of Homeland Security was created under the Bush administration; the German constitutional law was changed to limit immigration (Alink, 2006); and the New Zealand government introduced economically oriented (free market, deregulatory) reform to cope with the country's unsustainable economy and the exchange crisis (Aberbach and Christensen, 2001).

The Basics of the Crisis-reform Thesis

Crises as Catalysts

In all the above-mentioned instances, reform became suddenly possible when a crisis broke out. The cases exemplify the idea that policy makers often propose reform at times when normal policy making is disrupted (Hall, 1993: 279–80).

Reform, in other words, seems to become possible when the routine policy-making process is disrupted.

In normal times, the policy-making process is characterized by incrementalism. It advances in small steps and new policy differs only marginally from old policy (cf. Lindblom, 1959, 1979; Harrison et al., 1990: 9). According to Baumgartner and Jones and their punctuated equilibrium model, these long periods of stability and incrementalism are punctuated by short, violent periods of change (Baumgartner and Jones, 1993: 4).[6] Stability is disrupted as new problems catch the attention of the media and demand the immediate attention of policy makers. Political action is required to address these problems. This political action 'will not flow incrementally' but more abruptly because the normal policy-making process is disrupted (Baumgartner and Jones, 1993: 10).

During this disruption, policies are questioned at the most fundamental levels. This, in turn, creates opportunities to change dramatically that which is being questioned; in other words, exactly because something is being questioned, it is possible to change it. If a policy is not questioned or challenged, it will be difficult to change the policy radically – although small adjustments may be possible (True et al., 1999: 97–8; cf. Boin and 't Hart, 2000: 12). After policy makers have adequately dealt with the problems that caused the disrupted policy-making process in the first place, a new long era of stability can begin (Baumgartner and Jones, 1993). In short, long periods of stability are governed by incrementalism; the short unstable periods are governed by disrupted policy making that opens the doors to reform (True et al., 1999: 97).

The Crisis-reform Thesis in Brief

What explains these short unstable periods? In a later work, True, Jones, and Baumgartner (1999: 97–9) argue that disrupted policy making is the result of an issue catching fire. Other authors report similar findings (cf. Leemans, 1976a: 16–17, 33; Heffron, 1989: 156; Hall, 1993; Rose and Davies, 1994: 105–6, 108–11, 178–9; Hay, 1999). These authors see crises as moments in time when change is finally possible. Crises are seen as turning points (Dogan and Higley, 1998: 7) when incrementalism is overcome and proposals for reform can be suggested (cf. Rose and Davies, 1994: 178; Wilsford, 1994: 258; Goldfinch and 't Hart, 2003: 237). But how exactly can a crisis be a turning point for reform?

The crisis-reform thesis presents us with an explanation of how crisis can lead to reform. This thesis states that at times of crises, barriers normally hampering reform will diminish, which provides two advantages. Policy makers who are under immense pressure to end the crisis will experience an increase in their leeway. The range of solutions they can suggest expands as the crisis increases. Solutions that were hitherto unacceptable or even unheard of can now be suggested to end the crisis. At the same time, the situation of diminished constraints allows entrepreneurs to define a problem (and thereby determine its solution) or push for a pet solution. This favourite solution can range from small changes to elaborate reform proposals. Entrepreneurs can use the crisis to push for reform. In short, the momentum created by the crisis can lead to reform. In the remainder of this section, each element of the crisis-reform thesis – the crisis, diminishing constraints, policy makers and entrepreneurs – will be described.

The Institutional Crisis

There are several types of crisis, such as aeroplane accidents, war, economic depression, social conflict and threats to national security. In general, a crisis can often be characterized in terms of a severe threat to the core values of a social system and the perceived need for actors to decide quickly even though the situation is highly uncertain (Rosenthal et al., 2001: 6–7). In this study, the effects of a crisis in the prison service (a policy sector) are investigated. We therefore need a concept that captures the notion of a policy sector in crisis as well as portraying the general characteristics of a crisis. Both requirements are met in the concept of an institutional crisis.[7] Such a crisis occurs when the policy sector's institutional structure 'experiences a relatively strong decline in (followed by unusually low levels of) legitimacy' (Boin and 't Hart, 2000: 13).

The focal point of an institutional crisis is the policy sector. Policy sectors, such as security or social welfare, are the areas around which governments are organized (Rayner et al., 2001: 319). Each policy sector consists of an 'institutional [structure] of actors, rules, and practices associated with state efforts to address a particular category of social issues and problems' (Boin and 't Hart, 2000: 11). As time progresses, policy sectors become institutionalized to a certain extent as these rules, organizational structures, practices, norms and values become part and parcel of the way people in a policy sector function.

A stable policy sector is characterized by a fit between the way the policy sector performs its tasks and the wishes generated in its environment (Alink et al., 2001: 290). A good fit means that the policy sector's goals and performance are congruent with the demands of its environment (i.e., politicians, the public in general, clients, semi-public and private organizations).

However, over time and as the policy sector becomes more and more institutionalized, this fit between the policy sector and its environment may become endangered. There is a risk that the people working in a policy sector become so accustomed to the way they work that they no longer look around to see if what they do is consistent with the wishes of the general public (Miller, 1999).[8] If this is the case, the policy sector will probably (slowly) drift away from its environment (Senior, 1997: 36–7; cf. Kaufman, 1995: 20; Alink et al., 2001; Kuipers, 2004: 207–8). A division develops between the actual actions of the policy sector and the way the policy sector should function according to the general public.

Such a division by itself does not create an institutional crisis. This only happens when one or more incidents attract the attention of media and MPs to the malfunctioning of the policy sector. Media and MPs will then start to raise questions about the functioning of the sector (cf. Rose and Davies, 1994: 38, 178). They may suggest changes and demand the resignation of those politically responsible. When they scrutinize and question the policy sector's functioning, a rapid decline of the policy sector's legitimacy[9] is in the offing (cf. Terry, 2003: 138).

Note, however, that the media's and MPs' attention during an institutional crisis is not the same as the daily banter used in politics and news reporting. During an institutional crisis, this scrutiny is much more severe and negative in tone – widespread, sustained and extensive. In other words, we are looking at media and MPs whose attention was triggered by incidents that show that the policy sector's performance is not in accordance with the wishes of its environment and public. Moreover, this attention is more intense than usual, negative as the policy sector's functioning is questioned severely, increases significantly and continues unabated for quite some time.

The effects of an institutional crisis can be quite severe. Valuable structures and ideas within the policy sector become delegitimized. The structures and ideas that normally form the policy sector's institutional structure are questioned. The media and MPs will, for example, question the policy instruments that are used to implement policy. Or they will demand a completely new way of dealing with certain problems (Heffron, 1989: 153). Policy makers will face enormous pressure to come up with solutions to end the institutional crisis and stop the delegitimization of their policy sector.

At the same time, the questioning of the way a policy sector functions at its most fundamental levels creates opportunities for reform (True et al., 1999: 97–8). Exactly because certain practices and policies are questioned, it is possible to replace them by new ones.

The Opening of Windows

Replacing existing practices and policies will also be easier because institutional crises lead to a situation of diminished constraints, that is, a window of opportunity opens. Kingdon (1995) uses the window metaphor to describe this situation of diminished constraints. The window metaphor is derived from NASA terminology, where the term is used to describe the opportunity created by good weather, the alignment of the planets and other conditions to launch a space flight (Kingdon, 1995: 166; cf. Cortell and Peterson, 1999: 185). The window metaphor refers to the sudden lessening of constraints and the limited amount of time actors have to seize the moment and push for reform before the window closes.

According to Keeler (1993), there are two types of windows: a mandate-driven window and a crisis-driven window.[10] A mandate-driven window is opened by elections and national mood swings; a crisis-driven window occurs when pressing policy problems come to be perceived as a crisis (cf. Rochefort and Cobb, 1994). Both windows refer to a disrupted policy-making process, where constraints diminish and reform is possible. As this book focuses on the crisis-reform process, however, only the crisis-window will be described.

There are three mechanisms that can open a crisis-driven window. First, there is the *crisis-mandate mechanism*: a crisis discredits current governing parties after which an election puts opposition parties in charge. The new government parties have a crisis mandate to push for reform. Second, there is the *urgency mechanism*: a crisis results in an urgent feeling within government and/or legislature that something must be done because inaction will exacerbate the situation. The third mechanism is the *fear mechanism*. Serious socio-economic problems combined with large public unrest may instil fear in government leaders that doing nothing will result in death, destruction of property, or even a revolution (Keeler, 1993: 440–42).

The last two mechanisms will not only pressure government to act, but also result in 'the political opposition and the social opposition [being] too intimidated to resist or even feeling compelled to lend at least reluctant support to the government's proposals designed to defuse protest and restore order' (Keeler, 1993: 442). Consider, for instance, the following quote from *The Washington Post*:

> On Sept. 11 politics died. Contemporary American partisan politics as we have come to know it, full of thrusts and parries, charges and counter-charges, simply stopped. Without any polls or focus groups telling them what to do, Democrats and Republicans instinctively stopped quarrelling among themselves, rallied behind a president whose very legitimacy had been questioned and pledged to give him whatever he wanted to fight a war on terrorism. Budgets did not matter. Protecting the 'lock box' of Social Security did not matter. Political positioning did not matter. Elections did not matter. Only America mattered.[11]

In other words, after the 11 September 2001 events Democrats supported the actions of Republican President Bush while opposition to Bush's actions was widely seen as unpatriotic.

Policy Makers' Response

Policy makers consist of the political leaders of the policy sector (the minister and junior minister) and the administrative leaders of the policy sector (cf. Alink et al., 2001: 289). They are the ones under pressure to come up with solutions to end the crisis.

Policy makers' response towards an institutional crisis can either be conservative or reformist. A conservative response is aimed at restoring the status quo before the crisis broke out. Policy makers will try to end the institutional crisis by proposing solutions within the context of the policy sector's existing institutional structure. There will be no proposals for fundamental reform, but rather small-scale adjustments within the institutional structure of the policy sector. In contrast, a reformist approach aims to create a new fit between the policy sector and its environment by reforming the policy sector (Boin and 't Hart, 2000: 21; cf. Terry, 2003).

If policy makers opt for a reformist approach right from the start, then they can be labelled entrepreneurs (see next subsection). The literature on crisis management, leadership and reform, however, states that the odds for policy makers to be reformist from the start are slim (Staw, 1976; Fox and Staw, 1979; Staw et al., 1981; Boin and 't Hart, 2003; Terry, 2003). Instead, the initial response towards an institutional crisis is most likely to be conservative.

The reasons for an initial conservative reaction are threefold. First, a reformist response conflicts with policy makers' need to manage the crisis. A reformist response, for instance, requires exploiting the crisis, maybe even exacerbating the situation, and blaming the policy sector for the crisis. In contrast, a response that will end the crisis is aimed at damage control and restoring order, which 'requires the reaffirmation of existing values and structures' (Boin and 't Hart, 2003: 549). Moreover, policy makers pushing for reform by claiming that the current institutional crisis is the result of faulty existing policies and organizations may antagonize the stakeholders with whom they have to continue to live long after the crisis has ended (Boin and 't Hart, 2003: 550). Correspondingly, policy makers who use the crisis and the subsequent centralized decision-making process to push their reform agenda may expect a strong backlash from these same stakeholders (Boin and 't Hart, 2003: 550).

Second, policy makers have an interest in the status quo. On the one hand, they have invested resources in it and/or receive benefits from the current status quo. Policy makers, for instance, have invested their time and energy to obtain their current position (Wilson, 1989; cf. Leemans, 1976b: 88; Rose and Davies, 1994: 14; True et al., 1999: 102; Shepsle, 2001: 324). On the other hand, policy makers identify with the institutional structure that they are part of, that is, 'they are part of the norms and ways of working that they value' (Alink and Resodihardjo, 2002: 5; cf. Terry, 2003: 24).

Third, psychological studies show that people are committed to a set course of action. This commitment occurs, for instance, when decision makers are '*personally responsible for negative consequences*' (Staw, 1976: 39; italics in original), that is, decision makers have personally taken decisions that did not lead to the expected outcome. The reluctance to admit mistakes and the need to rationalize and justify prior behaviour results in even further commitment to existing policy by allocating more resources to it (Staw, 1976). This commitment to a set course of actions could also occur when administrators experience high job insecurity and encounter a lot of resistance to their actions (Fox and Staw, 1979). Consequently, 'administrators may become trapped in the defense of a failing program' (Fox and Staw, 1979: 467).[12] Adversarial situations can also induce rigidity in the behaviour of individuals (Staw et al., 1981: 505).

Combined, these reasons make a compelling argument that policy makers' initial response towards an institutional crisis will be conservative rather than reformist. Moreover, this argument is substantiated by case studies (Boin et al., 2000; Alink and Resodihardjo, 2002).

In short, it seems likely that policy makers will opt for restoring the status quo – and even allocate more resources to current policy and practices – instead of reforming it. Unless of course they wanted to reform the policy sector even before the institutional crisis broke out, in which case policy makers may be inclined to use the crisis to push for reform (see the description of entrepreneurs in the next subsection). In general, however, policy makers will opt for conservation.

It is possible for policy makers to end the crisis by proposing measures that correspond with their conservative inclination. If that is the case, then the policy sector's status quo is restored. It is equally possible, however, that conservative measures do not have the anticipated result. Instead, MPs and media may view the measures as inadequate. Moreover, incidents may continue to occur and, as a consequence, media and MPs may press policy makers into taking more radical measures. At the same time, these combining and increasing pressures during crisis situations will also create additional leeway for policy makers as constraints diminish. The same MPs who demand more radical action, for instance, will also be inclined to approve additional funding to realize these measures. Policy makers therefore face a predicament: should they hang on to their conservative response and face the wrath of MPs and media as the crisis continues or should they change their tune to a more reformist one?

As policy makers are the ones who set the plans for policy sectors and propose measures to improve the policy sector's performance to end the crisis, it would be logical to assume that reform will probably be the outcome of the crisis if policy makers adopt a more reformist stance towards managing the institutional crisis. Hence, if policy makers' conservative measures cannot end the crisis while pressure to do something more radical mounts, then it is possible that at some point the pressure will be too much and policy makers will abandon their initial reaction. Instead, they will propose reformist measures[13] in order to end the crisis (Rose and Davies, 1994: 109–11).[14]

The Role of Entrepreneurs

At times of crisis, policy makers are under tremendous pressure to end the crisis. Policy makers are able to appease angry MPs and media by introducing more radical measures because the crisis also creates an opportunity as constraints that normally hamper these radical measures diminish. Policy makers are not the only ones able to use this window of opportunity. So-called entrepreneurs can use it as well.

According to Kingdon's definition (1995: 122), entrepreneurs are people who are willing to invest their resources to push for their favourite solutions (that is, pet solutions) (for the definition of entrepreneur used in this book, see the last section of this chapter). These solutions can range from small policy changes to elaborate reforms.[15] In order to reach their goal, entrepreneurs could, for example, suggest to policy makers that their favourite solution is the best way to deal with the crisis or they could try to let their pet solution ride along with other measures initiated to end the crisis. Entrepreneurs can be found inside as well as outside the policy sector and include state officials (Cortell and Peterson, 1999: 183), ministers of departments (Richard and Smith, 1997), representatives of interest groups, and members of research organizations (Kingdon, 1995: 122).

In the case of the restructuring of the Dutch pig farming industry, it was the Minister of Agriculture who was able to use the classical swine fever to finally reform the Dutch pig farming industry. This minister can be labelled an entrepreneur as he was able to overcome obstacles that had hampered reform for years by grabbing the opportunity presented by the crisis. He managed to link the crisis to the need to prevent the occurrence of swine fever in the future. The only way, so he claimed, to prevent another outbreak was radically to restructure the pig farming industry. This proposal for reform had been an issue for the minister and the civil service for a long time, but had been impossible to implement or even suggest as farmers blocked any proposal for change. Thanks to the minister's ability to link the crisis to future outbreaks, this proposal could finally become law (Breeman et al., 2000).

As an example of outside entrepreneurship, we can use the American airline-industry lobbyists and the way they responded to the events of 9/11:

> After the terrorist attacks of September 11, 2001 forced a temporary suspension of flights across the nation, Congress passed a $15 billion assistance plan to rescue the airline industry. The speed with which Congress approved this generous aid package was a tribute not only to the economic importance of air travel but also to the political skill (and opportunism) of airline-industry lobbyists, who extracted more money from taxpayers than the industry lost during the brief shutdown. (Patashnik, 2003: 225)

Both examples show entrepreneurs taking advantage of the crisis to push for pet solutions. The central idea of the crisis-reform thesis is that entrepreneurs can skillfully use the window of opportunity to press for pet solutions. It will therefore be more likely that reform is the outcome of a crisis if there is an entrepreneur present pushing for reform solutions.

Crisis-reform Patterns

The crisis-reform thesis provides us with a pattern along which a crisis process is expected to evolve if reform is to be the outcome of the institutional crisis (Yin, 1993: 39). Each event provides us with a benchmark (or hypothesis) against which we can compare the three case studies. In other words, the crisis-reform thesis consists of events that we can use as benchmarks to see if these events occur in the three cases investigated in this study. If all benchmarks occur in a case, then reform should be the outcome. We can thus establish whether these benchmarking events occurred, whether the benchmarking events did result in reform and whether other events played a role in the crisis-reform processes in these three cases. The crisis-reform thesis provides us with five such benchmarks.

The first benchmark focuses on the constraints that normally hamper reform. During an institutional crisis, the structures and ideas that normally form the policy sector's institutional structure are questioned. The media and MPs question, for instance, the way a policy sector is trying to achieve its goals. The questioning of these practices and values indicates that support is low. Consequently, it will be easier to replace them with new ones. In other words, constraints such as existing policy and paradigms diminish because support for them has subsided. New policies and priorities can be suggested that radically deviate from these old policies and paradigms. Moreover, as the media and MPs put pressure on policy makers to do something about the malfunctioning policy sector, other constraints will diminish as well. MPs, for instance, will be more inclined to back up their demands for change with promises of monetary resources to deal with these problems. In short, *if an institutional crisis occurs, constraints that normally hamper reform will diminish*.

The second benchmark logically follows from the first one: *the more constraints diminish, the more likely it is that reform will be the outcome of the institutional crisis*. In other words, if a macro-window opens (that is, multiple constraints diminish at the same time), then reform is more likely to occur.

Policy makers' response to the institutional crisis will initially consist of attempts to restore (that is, conserve) the status quo. Policy makers' need to manage the institutional crisis instead of worsening it, their dependence on stakeholders, their investments in the status quo, their identification with the institutional structure that they are part of combined with psychological factors such as their reluctance to admit mistakes and the need to rationalize and justify prior behaviour result in a preference to adhere to the status quo. The third benchmark is therefore that *if an institutional crisis occurs, then policy makers' initial response will be to conserve the status quo*.

As time progresses and the crisis becomes worse, policy makers may not be able to hold on to their conservative approach towards managing the institutional crisis. If incidents continue to occur and MPs and the media are not satisfied with the suggested measures to end the crisis, policy makers may be forced to come up with more radical solutions to end the institutional crisis – even reform. As the policy makers are the ones who propose solutions to deal with the institutional crisis, it is assumed that their crisis management approach will be largely influential in determining the outcome of the crisis. Hence, *if policy makers switch from a conservative towards a reformist approach, then it is more likely that the outcome of the institutional crisis will be reform*.

The last benchmark central to the crisis-reform thesis is that reform will occur if so-called entrepreneurs are present. Entrepreneurs will skillfully use the window of opportunity to press for reform. Thus *if entrepreneurs are present, then it is more likely that the outcome of the institutional crisis includes reform*.

Taken together, these benchmarks form a pattern. Through pattern-matching (Yin, 1993), it is possible to determine whether the pattern described by theory is actually present in reality by carefully looking at a case to see whether the benchmarks occurred in reality or not. Additionally, process tracing (Bennet and George, 2004) allows a researcher to carefully trace a process to determine what happened while remaining open for alternative conditions which might have influenced the crisis-reform process. But what exactly do researchers need to look for if they want to be able to do all this? How can this crisis-reform pattern be discerned in reality and which data do you need to do so? These issues will be addressed in the remainder of this chapter.

Clarifying Concepts

Policy Sector

This book focuses on institutional crises in policy sectors. According to Alink, Boin and 't Hart (2001) a policy sector is 'an institutional field of actors, rules and practices associated with state efforts to address a particular category of social issues and problems' (p. 289; cf. Rayner et al., 2001: 319). Sometimes the lines between policy sectors can be blurred. In the Netherlands, for instance, the policy area of fighting crime is divided between the Ministry of Internal Affairs (police) and the Ministry of Justice (prosecution and prisons). This division of responsibilities is not problematic for this study as it focuses on institutional crises in the prison service. This policy sector is limited in the number of actors and is distinct from any other policy area of interest to government. In terms of government actors, the prison policy sector consists of the Home Office and the Prison Service of England and Wales in Great Britain; the Ministry of Justice and the Dutch Prison Service make up the Dutch prison policy sector. In terms of non-government actors, the prison policy sector consists of prison officers' unions, governors' unions, prisoners' unions and interest groups (for instance, the Prison Reform Trust in England).

Institutional Crisis

An institutional crisis occurs when the policy sector's institutional structure 'experiences a relatively strong decline in (followed by unusually low levels of) legitimacy' (Boin and 't Hart, 2000: 13). This drop in the policy sector's legitimacy is indicated by an increase in negative attention from the public and MPs. One can determine an increase in negative attention from the public by examining the statements and actions of the media. The media can be used as an indicator of public support for a policy sector, because 'media attention is expected to translate or prompt public attention, it can be used as a reasonable measure of public interest and thus help the analysis by somewhat lengthening the lag expected to be found between "public" outcry and government response' (Howlett, 1997: 14).[16]

Thus an institutional crisis only occurs if this attention increases and is negative in tone. Change in media attention is considered an increase when the number of media articles on the prison service doubles. An increase in MPs' attention occurs when the following events take place: (1) long debates are held on the topic; (2) the topic is addressed on occasions where time is short, that is, budgetary debates in the Netherlands and Prime Minister's Questions[17] in England. When MPs use the short time available to them to address the prison service, it shows that this topic is important to them; (3) emergency or *interpellatie* debates take place; and (4) the number of written questions increases. These four events do not all have to occur to establish the existence of an institutional crisis because the two parliamentary systems differ too much. In the British parliamentary system, for instance, MPs use the tool of written questions much more frequently than their Dutch counterparts do. In contrast, Dutch MPs ask for an *interpellatie* debate[18] more often. Hence, if three out of four events occur, an increase in MPs' attention can be established.

The mere description of the events in the media and parliament is not considered to be negative attention. Instead, negative attention only occurs when journalists and MPs question the functioning of the prison service by, for instance, stating that the events are embarrassing and undermine law and order in the country, measures need to be taken as the current situation obviously cannot continue, the prison service is not up to its task, ministers and/or the prison service are malfunctioning and something needs to be done.

Constraints

For this book, it is not important to exactly understand *how* crises affect constraints; it is more important to determine whether crises *do* affect them. Once it has been determined that crises do lead to a situation of diminished constraints, future research can take the next step to untangle the mechanisms involved. What we do need to know is how we can establish that constraints have diminished. In order to do so, we first need to know which constraints will diminish.

Authors advocating the crisis-reform thesis do not always explicitly tell us which constraints might diminish. The authors either name no constraints, as does Keeler (1993) when he writes that constraints are the factors that 'normally frustrate a government' (p. 436). Others sum up a limited number of constraints, as do Cortell and Peterson (1999) who essentially talk about organizational constraints (p. 190). Or they list a large number of constraints without defining them all, as does Kingdon when he lists his constraints. In Kingdon's view, the following constraints play a role: budgets, public acceptance, the distribution of resources (Kingdon, 1995: 189–90), national mood, political cultures and the fact that the amount of available political resources differs per group (Kingdon, 1995: 222) and between institutions (Kingdon, 1995: 230). Moreover, the more general literature on policy making provides a large number of constraints – most of them not mentioned in the crisis-reform literature. Nevertheless, when one compares the two bodies of literature one sees a certain overlap between the constraints the various authors sum up. It is therefore possible to create a list of constraints mentioned in both fields (see Table 2.2).

Table 2.2 The constraints taken into account

Type of constraints	Examples of constraints	How these constraints could diminish
Individual constraints	Invested interests	Membership of status quo coalitions declines
	Benefits	Atmosphere of urgency and fear results in (reluctant) support
Organizational constraints	Rules and decision-making procedures	Concentration of power
	Policy sector's paradigm	Fierce attack on current practices to deal with the prison service's features (that is, security and control, treatment, or conditions)
Political constraints	Budget	New money from the Treasury
	Policy inheritance	Fierce attack on existing policy

Individual constraints Those who have invested interests in the status quo can form status quo coalitions (also known as anti-reform coalitions). An indicator of a diminished invested interests constraint is when the membership of such a coalition diminishes and the former members become in favour of reform. The benefit constraint could diminish when there is an atmosphere of urgency or fear on the side of the policy makers, the public in general and the political and social (opposition) parties that inaction would exacerbate the situation. The feelings of urgency and fear lead to a general feeling that something needs to be done. This results in people who benefit from the status quo feeling compelled to (reluctantly) support changes aimed at ending the crisis but that negatively affect their benefits position (Keeler, 1993: 441–2).

Organizational constraints An indication that the rules and decision-making procedures constraint diminishes is a reduction of the number of veto points in decision-making procedures as a result of a concentration of power in the upper echelons of the policy sector (McConnell, 2003: 395; cf. Dinan et al., 2006: 314–15).[19]

The policy sector's paradigm constraint diminishes when the policy sector's paradigm is fiercely attacked by the media, MPs and interest groups as insufficient and outdated. Questions are asked whether the paradigm should be adapted since the policy sector is not functioning as it should. A policy sector's paradigm is 'the set of ideas about what constitute the main features and problems of the sector, and how these can be governed the best possible way' (Boin and 't Hart, 2000: 13). As the support for the paradigm dwindles, this constraint will diminish. Policy makers will be able to suggest, for instance, a new prioritization of goals for the policy sector that was hitherto impossible to suggest as these suggestions were not in line with the paradigm.

The prison service's main features and problems are how to keep prisoners contained (security and control), how to treat them (locking up and rehabilitation) and the conditions in which prisoners live (one person to a cell, doubling, trebling and toilet facilities). Hence the policy sector's paradigm is under attack if current practices to deal with these features are deemed unsatisfactory and in urgent need of replacement with new practices.

Political constraints The budget constraint diminishes when new money becomes available from the Treasury to implement policy; reshuffling money within the existing budget does not constitute a diminished budget constraint. An often expressed view in parliament and the media that a new path has to be taken if the policy sector is to function properly again indicates that holding on to existing policy is, for the moment, less important. It is no longer imperative that existing policies are continued. Instead, it is more important for the policy sector's policy makers to respond to the public outcry, even if that means that current policies are changed or withdrawn altogether.

The very nature of an institutional crisis should automatically lead to a diminished paradigm and policy inheritance constraint because the policies, values, goals and functioning of the policy sector are questioned during an institutional crisis. This brings us to the question of when a so-called macro-window will open. The literature on windows of opportunity distinguishes two types of window: micro-windows (which allow small changes) and macro-windows (which allow reforms to happen). The opening of a macro-window will make it more likely that reform is the outcome of the crisis as policy makers and entrepreneurs will have more room to manoeuvre compared to a situation where only a micro-window opens.

The diminishing of the paradigm and policy inheritance constraints is inherent to an institutional crisis (and the crisis-reform thesis' first benchmark will always be supported by empirical research when investigating institutional crises). In order to be able to maintain the distinction between micro- and macro-windows, a macro-window will not open when only the paradigm and policy inheritance constraints diminish (otherwise every institutional crisis will result in macro-windows). Instead, a macro-window will only open if either an additional constraint diminishes significantly or if more than one additional constraint diminishes at the same time.

Policy Makers

Policy makers are the ones in charge of a policy sector. Policy makers consist of the political masters of the policy sector (the minister and junior minister) and the administrative heads of the policy sector. As this book focuses on prisons, the following people make up the policy makers. The political masters consist of the Minister of State and the junior Minister of State. In England, these are the Home Secretary and the Prisons Minister. In the Netherlands, these are the Minister of Justice and the junior Minister of Justice. The administrative leaders of the prison service are the director of the prison service and (if applicable) his or her deputy director. Chapter 3 provides a list of the policy makers in the two prison services during the crises.

Entrepreneurs

One can roughly discern two different views on who can be an entrepreneur. In both views, the entrepreneur is someone willing to invest their resources and take chances in order to push for their pet solutions. In one view, however, only insiders can be entrepreneurs. Cortell and Peterson's state officials (1999: 183), Keeler's (members of) reform government (1993: 434), Teske and Schneider's entrepreneurial city manager, that is, the highest level bureaucrats in local communities (1994) and Richard and Smith's ministers of departments (1997) all pertain to insiders. The alternative view sees outsiders as well as insiders as possible entrepreneurs. Kingdon (1995) writes that entrepreneurs can be 'in or out of government, in elected or appointed positions, in interest groups or research organizations' (p. 122; cf. Roberts and King, 1996: 15).

As we are interested in reform, an entrepreneur is defined in this study as someone inside or outside of government who uses his or her resources to exploit the crisis and push for reform (Kingdon, 1995: 165). Entrepreneurs' resources include, for instance, their position within the policy sector and their network with other (influential) people, money and information.

Two restrictions to this definition are in order. First, it is necessary to make a distinction between policy makers who are entrepreneurs and non-policy makers who are entrepreneurs. As has been previously described, policy makers can be forced to adhere to a more reformist approach to ending the crisis if the crisis continues and even worsens. Their change in approach, however, does not indicate that they are entrepreneurs because they have been forced into accepting this approach instead of embracing it wholeheartedly. Consequently, the first restriction to the definition is that policy makers can only be labelled as entrepreneurs if they advocated reform measures before the crisis and if they use the crisis from the start to push for these reform measures.

Second, entrepreneurs can push for reform in three ways: they can change the way a problem is defined and thereby open up the possibility for reform (Zahariadis, 1999: 84; cf. Baumgartner and Jones, 1993: 29, 48); they can let their reform measure ride along with other measures introduced to end the crisis; and they can try to get their reform measure accepted independently from any other measure introduced to end the crisis.

When a problem comes to the fore, the way it is defined not only determines who is interested in it (Baumgartner and Jones, 1993: 42, 239; Teske and Schneider, 1994: 337), but also who has the solution to the problem and what the solution has to entail (Rochefort and Cobb, 1994). A prison disturbance, for instance, can be defined as a problem of control or as a problem caused by bad conditions (Adams, 1994: 104–69). A prison disturbance defined as a problem of control will result in solutions to increase control such as improving security. If a prison disturbance is defined as a problem of bad conditions, solutions such as ending trebling (that is, three people to a cell meant for one) and improving prisoners' rights will be needed to avoid disturbances in the future. Once a problem has been defined in a certain manner, an entrepreneur will be able to push their solution if it corresponds to the way the problem is defined. It is therefore important for an entrepreneur to be present when the problem is defined, otherwise they will not be able to sell their ideas as solutions to end the problem.

Having established who can be an entrepreneur (insiders as well as outsiders), when an entrepreneur becomes active (policy makers at the start of a crisis, non-policy makers at any point in time during the crisis) and the paths entrepreneurs can take to push for reform (adjusting problem definition, riding along, or riding alone), it is time to determine how one can establish the presence of an entrepreneur.

There are limits to what a researcher can do. It is, for instance, not possible to identify entrepreneurs who tried and failed because a researcher will (normally) only see the measures that policy makers were willing to suggest to parliament. Nor is it possible for researchers to identify entrepreneurs who pushed for reforms at closed meetings and hallway negotiations because there is no data available on these meetings.

Nevertheless, establishing that an entrepreneur was present is possible in two ways. The first way is to consider the actions taken by people participating in the crisis events. Was there someone who significantly affected the way the problem that caused the crisis was defined? If so, then these persons can be labelled an entrepreneur because they were able to redefine the problem and thereby opened up the possibility for reform. Moreover, if someone promoted a specific reform solution from the start and was able to get this reform proposal accepted, than this person can be labelled an entrepreneur as well. The second way is to rely on the observations of people present during the crisis. When several respondents link a certain person with a certain solution that was successfully planted in the set of measures created to end the crisis, that person can be labelled an entrepreneur.

Reform

In the crisis-reform literature, definitions of reform differ widely. Reform is defined as 'a policy innovation manifesting an unusually substantial redirection or reinforcement of previous public policy' (Keeler, 1993: 434). Or it is defined as radical change of the domestic structure (Cortell and Peterson, 1999: 179) and episodic change, which 'reinvents institutional patterns so as to break with prevailing customs and procedures' (Cortell and Peterson, 1999: 182). Reform is thus defined as policy innovation, changes in the domestic structure, or changes in institutions.

No matter how reform is defined, two components are nearly always part of the definition. First, reform is a drastic deviation from the existing structure – be it policy or administration (Keeler, 1993: 434, cf. Hall, 1993, Sabatier, 1998: 118). Second, reform is fundamental; it touches the core of a policy sector, its paradigm (Hall, 1993; Sabatier, 1998: 118; cf. Bannink and Resodihardjo, 2006). Both components will be incorporated into the definition of reform used in this study. Reform is the intended fundamental change of the policy and/or administration of a policy sector.

Intended fundamental change of the policy sector's policy means that the policy sector's paradigm has been changed. For instance, new goals have been added or the policy sector's priorities have been changed. Policy change in itself thus does not constitute reform. Only when a change in policy is accompanied by a change in the policy sector's paradigm can one speak of reform. Following Hall (1993), the three orders of change as described in Table 2.3 will be taken into account when investigating whether crisis resulted in reform.

This table shows how change that is either incremental or instrumental – that is, new policy instruments – does not constitute reform. Only if the change is fundamental and involves a radical change in the hierarchy of priorities (Hall calls this policy ends) can one speak of policy reform.

Table 2.3 Policy change according to Hall (1993)

	First order change	Second order change	Third order change (reform)
Kind of policy change	Incremental	Instrumental	Fundamental
What is changed	Incremental adjustments of current policy	Adjustment of policy New policy instruments	Setting of policy and instruments Policy instruments change radically (the new paradigm needs a different kind of instrumentation)
Hierarchy of policy ends	Hierarchy stays the same	Hierarchy will not change radically, only minimally	Hierarchy changes radically

Considering the information needed to determine whether all these phenomena and patterns occurred, extensive data is needed. For this study, newspaper articles from various newspapers (*The Times*, *The Sunday Times*, *The Guardian* (broadsheets) and the *Daily Mirror* and *Sunday Mirror* (tabloids)[20] for the British cases; and a variety of newspaper articles included in the news clipping service of the Dutch Ministry of Justice[21] were selected, using key words relevant for each crisis. The year prior to a crisis and the year after it had ended were included in the search to allow for comparison and thus establish whether media attention had doubled or not. All existing parliamentary documents were searched using the same key words. Taken together, the media and parliamentary data can be used to show the intensity of interest graphically while quotes can be used to show the tone of the debate. In addition, semi-structured interviews were held with various respondents, including prison governors, civil servants working in headquarters, prison directors, junior ministers, ministers, MPs, academics and members of inquiries, unions and other interest groups. When interviewing practitioners, the word crisis was not mentioned; instead the word event(s) was used, thereby avoiding influencing the respondents. Citations which include the word crisis are only used in this book when respondents labelled the events as such of their own accord. Even when not using the word crisis, all respondents described the various situations as pressing, with a lot of media attention, and stressed the need to do something to deal with the incidents. Interview data used in this study are cited anonymously; only a respondent's position

Table 2.4 An overview of the concepts, their definition, and their indicators (for constraints see Table 2.2)

Concept	Definition	Operationalization
Policy sector	'An institutional field of actors, rules and practices associated with state efforts to address a particular category of social issues and problems' (Alink et al., 2001: 289)	The prison service including the responsible ministers, unions, and interest groups, but excluding the parent ministry and female and youth prisoners.
Institutional crisis	An institutional crisis occurs when the policy sector's institutional structure 'experiences a relatively strong decline in (followed by unusually low levels of) legitimacy' (Boin and 't Hart, 2000: 13)	Increase in negative attention by the public and MPs: • media attention increases when it doubles, MPs attention increases when three out of four things happen: (1) long debates are held on the topic; (2) the topic is addressed on occasions where time is short; (3) emergency or *interpellatie* debates are held; and (4) the number of written questions increase; • negative attention occurs when journalists and MPs question the functioning of the prison service by stating one or more of the following: – the events are embarrassing and undermine the law and order in this country; – measures need to be taken as the current situation obviously cannot continue; – the prison service is not up to its task; – ministers and/or the prison service are malfunctioning; – something needs to be done.
Entrepreneur	Someone inside or outside of government who uses their resources to exploit the crisis and push for reform	• Policy makers can only be labelled entrepreneurs if they advocated reform measures before the crisis and if they used the crisis from the start to push for these reform measures; • non-policy makers can become active as entrepreneurs at any point during the crisis; • entrepreneurs can take three paths to push for reform (adjusting problem definition, riding along, or riding alone) Actors will be labelled entrepreneurs if: • they changed the way a problem was defined and thereby opened the possibility for reform; • they promoted a specific reform solution and were able to get their reform proposal accepted; • they acted behind the scenes and several respondents link them to a certain solution that was successfully planted in the set of measures created to end the crisis. As a consequence of this operationalization, unsuccessful entrepreneurs cannot be recognized.
Reform	Intended fundamental change of the policy and/or administration of a policy sector	Policy or administrative change has to be accompanied by a change in the prison service's priorities

is given. Thus the title 'prison governor' will be used but without mentioning whether the respondent is a Governor Grade 5 or 1. In addition to newspaper articles, parliamentary documents and interviews, data were gathered from the following sources: governmental documents and reports (including White Papers) and research published by academics and practitioners. Taken together, all these sources provided ample data to establish whether the crisis-reform thesis provides a plausible understanding of the crisis-reform process, while this thesis can be adjusted and extended with new insights if needed.

Notes

1. Parts of this chapter have been adapted from Bannink and Resodihardjo (2006) and Resodihardjo (2006b).
2. Reform can also be the unintended result of incremental policy making (Lindblom, 1959, 1979; Rose and Davies, 1994: 37) as well as the result of leaders who push for reform ('t Hart, 2000; Terry, 2003).
3. Reform can either refer to policy reform, for instance, deciding to opt for double bunking instead of one person to a cell, or to administrative reform, for example, agencification. Both types of reform have consequences for the organizational structure of a policy sector (such as building new cells or adjusting the organization in order to deal with agencification) and both can be hampered by organizational, political, and individual constraints. In this study, policy reform is the most common type of reform to occur. The term reform will therefore be used when describing policy reform.
4. The categorization is not always that clear-cut. A policy maker, for example, has vested interests in the status quo. Vested interests can be labelled as an individual constraint, but these interests are partly the result of standing policy. Hence, vested interests can also be categorized as political constraints because they are the result of actions in the political realm. Moreover, a person's perception of what may be endangered by reform proposals also depends on his position within the organization. When Leemans (1976b: 88–9) writes that reform proposals may affect policy makers' position and resources, then this is determined within the organization. As such, the constraint is also partly organizational in nature. The same goes for goals. On the one hand, goals are determined largely outside the organization by other actors (cf. Wilson, 1989: 115) and are categorized as a political constraint. On the other hand, goals can also become established over time as an organization becomes institutionalized and as previous policy becomes embedded in the organization. As such, it is an organizational constraint.
5. The most famous example of the Dutch culture of tolerance is its soft-drugs policy. Although soft drugs are formally illegal, the Dutch government does tolerate the possession and retail sale of soft drugs in certain circumstances.
6. For a summary and testing of Baumgartner and Jones' punctuated equilibrium model, see Howlett (1997).

7. It would thus be actually more appropriate to speak of an institutional crisis-reform thesis that is being investigated instead of the more general crisis-reform thesis (which includes all types of crises).
8. There is also the danger of goal displacement, in which case people working in an organization are more focused on abiding to the rules of the organization than on achieving the original aim of the organization. Instruments, for instance, have been created to reach a certain goal. When using the instrument gets more important than reaching the goal, there has been a goal displacement (Merton, 1949: 153–5).
9. Legitimacy is defined in this study as 'a generalized perception or assumption that the actions of an entity are desirable, proper, or appropriate within some socially constructed system of norms, values, beliefs, and definitions' (Suchman, 1995: 574).
10. Instead of a crisis-driven window and a mandate-driven window, Kingdon (1995) uses the terms problem window and politics window.
11. *Washington Post*, 24 September 2001, Patriotic Partisanship. Cf. S.J. Res. 23; submitted in Senate and agreed by Yea-Nay Vote 98–0, passed without objection in the House; S.J. Res. 22 submitted in Senate and agreed by Yea-Nay Vote 100–0, passed without objection in the House.
12. This study focused on the decisions of administrators concerning R&D funding. As such, the authors are ambivalent about the generalization of their experiment to real world events, especially political vulnerability. On the one hand, they believe in the strength of their experiment. On the other hand, they state that more field research is necessary to corroborate their findings (Fox and Staw, 1979: 469). Staw and Ross (1987) present an overview of current research on commitment during escalation situations in order to create a multi-variable model to predict whether decision makers will demonstrate commitment in times of crisis. Considering the variables typically present in decision making in policy sectors (such as long term investments, no readily available alternative, earlier reinforcement, and face saving), it seems plausible that decision makers are more likely to commit themselves rather than to withdraw at times of institutional crisis.
13. It should be noted, however, that the proposed reform measures could be nothing more than just symbolic gestures in order to assure the public that something is going to be done to end the crisis (Rose and Davies, 1994: 41–2; 't Hart, 2001: 79; Patashnik, 2003: 210).
14. For ideas on how, when and why policy makers change their conservative inclination into a reformist stance, see Boin et al., 2008.
15. They can also use the opportunity to get a certain problem that they want to see solved onto the political agenda (Kingdon, 1995: 20, 176, 202, 205).
16. Please note that not everyone considers the media to act as a translator of public interest. Instead, they see the media as instigators of public interest (cf. Hall et al., 1982: 62–3; McCombs, 1997).

17. Prime Minister's Questions (PMQs) is held four times a week. Prime Ministers Thatcher and Major used two of these meetings to answer MPs' questions for 15 minutes. MPs are allowed to ask any question, but not to express their opinions, on any subject that the Prime Minister is responsible for. Since time is short, only the most pressing topics are addressed. Questions on subjects that are not so high on the political agenda can be tabled for a written answer (Norton, 2001a: 358–9).
18. MPs have the right of interpellation (*interpellatie*), also known as an emergency debate (*spoeddebat*). MPs can ask for a debate on a topic currently not listed on the official agenda. Minister and junior minister have to answer written and/or oral questions during this debate and defend their policy and actions. A majority of MPs have to approve the MP's request for such a debate (Van den Berg et al., 1984; Postma, 1985).
19. For a contrasting view, see 't Hart et al. 1993.
20. The selection of broadsheets and tabloids is based on the fact that broadsheets are read by middle-class and well-educated people and the tabloids are read by predominantly working-class people (Jones, 2001a: 178).
21. As it turned out, the *Daily Mirror* and *Sunday Mirror* were not available in the British Newspaper Library's full-text, word-searchable computer system for the time period of the riots. The British Newspaper Library did contain the newspaper articles of the tabloids for the time period of 1 July 1992 until 31 December 1996. At the time of investigation, Lexis Nexis did not contain any information on the *Daily Mirror* and *Sunday Mirror* for the period of 1 January 1989 until 30 June 1992. As a result, information on the tabloids where the 1990 prison riots is concerned is missing. Lexis Nexis, however, did provide information on the selected broadsheets for both British cases.

    Regarding the Dutch newspaper articles, it is important to note here that at the final stage of this study, Lexis Nexis became available. Lexis Nexis has not been used to update the data on media attention because at that time it did not include *De Telegraaf* (a popular national broadsheet). Moreover, Lexis Nexis did not contain all articles as presented in the news clipping service, most notably opinion pieces and background articles. One should be aware, though, that Lexis Nexis did produce some articles that were not mentioned in the news clipping service. Research of media attention in the Dutch Lexis Nexis and news clipping service may therefore produce different results. However, because Lexis Nexis contained articles that were not included in the news clipping service and vice versa, these results will probably not vary that much.

Chapter 3
Two Prison Systems: Pre-Crisis Descriptions

Introduction

This study investigates three cases in two prison services to determine under which conditions crises lead to reform. The prison services to be investigated are the Dutch Prison Service and the Prison Service of England and Wales. In the Netherlands, one institutional crisis will be studied. In 1992–1993, escapes and cell shortages resulted in an institutional crisis. Two institutional crises in the British Prison Service will be investigated. The first one is the occurrence of riots in 1990, most notably the one at Strangeways Prison. The second case revolves around the institutional crisis caused by the escapes from Whitemoor and Parkhurst Prisons in 1994–1995.

This chapter describes both prison services at the start of their institutional crises. The chapter will neither give an encompassing historical account of these services[1] nor an up-to-date description of these services. Rather, it sketches the status quo of the two prison services before the crises broke out, paying special attention to the aspects that were of importance during the crises.

For each prison service, the organizational and political layouts and the prison service's priorities will be described, as well as the way in which each service dealt with escape-prone prisoners and cell shortage before the institutional crises broke out. In the 1980s, a number of violent escapes occurred resulting in a project team investigating how to deal with escape-prone prisoners. The way the Dutch Prison Service dealt with escape-prone prisoners in 1992 is based on this report and this report will therefore be addressed in this chapter. The Prison Service of England and Wales will be described for the 1990 situation as well as the 1994 situation – including the measures taken after the 1990 institutional crisis because they determined the priorities of the Prison Service in 1994. A reorganization plan called Fresh Start was implemented in 1987. As this reorganization plan was seen as one of the causes of the riots in 1990, it will be described in this chapter as well.

The Dutch Prison Service in 1992

The Organizational Map

The Dutch Prison Service (Directie Delinquentenzorg en Jeugdinrichtingen) is part of the Ministry of Justice.[2] The Minister of Justice and the Junior Minister of Justice[3] are responsible and accountable to parliament concerning the functioning of the Dutch Prison Service (see also the next subsection on the political map). The Ministry of Justice consists of a number of directorates, each headed by a Director-General. Mr Greven headed the Director-General of the Directorate Youth Protection and Prison Care in 1993. One of its subdivisions is the prison service. The Dutch Prison Service consists of two layers: the organizational layer of prisons and the strategic layer connecting the prisons and the Ministry of Justice: the Prison Board. Director Elting headed the Prison Board (Breur and Brekelmans, 1993: K–9).[4]

There are various types of prisons. Besides remand prisons and some specialized prisons, for instance for young offenders, drug abusers, and mentally ill prisoners, there are open, semi-open, and closed prisons. A so-called open prison has very limited security measures, prisoners work either inside or outside the prison and go on leave every weekend. A semi-closed prison has limited security and prisoners can go on leave one weekend per month. A closed prison has regular security and prisoners have to stay within the prison 24 hours a day (DJI, 1998: 13–14). In 1992, the Dutch Prison Service had a capacity of 7,773 cells and a total of 35,490 persons were imprisoned in that year.[5]

The Political Map

During the institutional crisis in 1992–1993, there was a coalition government (Lubbers III) consisting of the Christian Democratic Party (CDA) and the Social Democratic Party (PvdA). Prime Minister Lubbers (CDA) headed the government, assisted by vice-president Kok (PvdA). Minister Hirsch Ballin (CDA) and Junior Minister Kosto (PvdA) were responsible and accountable to Parliament for all matters concerning the Ministry of Justice. Junior Minister Kosto was responsible for all prison matters, private law, immigration, granting pardon, international legal aid, special laws, and laws concerning notary's practice and bailiffs. Minister Hirsch Ballin was responsible for all other matters (Breur and Brekelmans, 1993: K–3) (see Table 3.1).[6]

As explained in Chapter 2, policy makers are constrained by interest groups, because they have vested interests in the status quo and deals have been made with these interests groups that policy makers have to take into account when making new policy. In the Netherlands, one interest group is very prominent in the policy-making process of the prison service, namely the Union of Prison Governors (VDPI).

Table 3.1 The major actors in the Dutch Prison Service in 1992

Minister of Justice	Junior Minister of Justice	Director Prison Service
Hirsch Ballin (CDA)	Kosto (PvdA)	Elting

Priorities and Goals

In 1992, the people within the Dutch Prison Service were still working on the basis of a White Paper from 1982: *Task and Future of the Dutch Prison Service*. In this White Paper, rehabilitation had received a blow as scientific research had suggested that rehabilitation was not possible. The White Paper contained three aims and rehabilitation was only the third priority instead of the first priority (Franke, 1996: 281–3, 292; Van Swaaningen and Uit Beijerse, 1993: 136–9). The three aims were:

1. To try to carry out sentencing as humanely as possible,
2. To prevent or at least reduce the negative effects of imprisonment,
3. To prepare the prisoner for his return into society by creating opportunities for prisoners to work on their personal development and to solve their psychosocial problems. (Ministry of Justice, 1982: 22)

According to Boin (2001b: 64–7), there was no dominant, coherent correctional philosophy underpinning the prison service in the early 1990s. Even though there was the White Paper to fall back on, governors had created their own philosophy on incarceration. They either adhered to a liberal philosophy, that is, humane detention, a strict philosophy, where crime is seen as a career choice, or a mixed-bag philosophy.

Governors were not only free to determine their own correctional philosophy; they were also free to determine the regime within their prisons. Officially, the Ministry of Justice determined the regimes. Reality, however, was quite different (Boin, 2001b: 75). The result was a mixture of regimes and philosophies that could differ greatly per prison.

Dealing with Large Numbers of Prisoners: Waiting Lists and Sending People Home

In 1992, imprisonment in the Dutch Prison Service still consisted of a system of communal confinement during the day and solitary confinement at night. The Pennsylvania model had governed Dutch Prisons up until the end of World War II. In the Pennsylvania model, prisoners were locked up in solitary confinement for 24 hours a day and had to work in their cells. Talking was not allowed (Rothman, 1995: 106). Solitary imprisonment was seen as the best way to achieve rehabilitation. During the Second World War, however, political prisoners and members of the resistance experienced solitary confinement and considered it to be inhumane. As a result, the Fick Committee was installed in 1946 to investigate ways to achieve a more humane and effective imprisonment. The outcome of the Fick Report (1947) was a change of the solitary system into a communal system.[7] This system of communal confinement during the day and solitary confinement during the night was still in use in 1992.

As a natural outcome of the way the prison system in the Netherlands was formed, double-bunking was never really considered.[8] However, the effect of this one person to a cell rule was a cell shortage every time the prison population increased. Cell shortages were dealt with by either not admitting the prisoners (putting them on a waiting list instead) or by releasing prisoners before the end of their sentence in order to make room for the next prisoner.

The few times that these practices resulted in incidents that commanded the attention of the media and MPs, the Minister and Junior Minister of Justice would suggest double-bunking. But most MPs, academics and the VDPI (the Union of Prison Governors) opposed this practice. Instead of opting for double-bunking, those in charge of budgeting made money available to build more cells to deal with the cell shortage (Franke, 1996: 312–16; cf. Boin, 1999: 25–6).

In the 1980s, for instance, there was commotion about rising crime rates and decreasing public faith in the government to fulfil its role of protector.[9] In response to these feelings, the Justice White Paper *Society and Criminality*[10] was published (1985). This White Paper promised to expand cell capacity by 4,000 cells increasing cell capacity to approximately 7,600 cells by June 1992.[11] The estimate on which the expansion was based turned out to be incorrect. More cells were needed.[12] A new policy plan, JR-120, was written in 1990.[13] Cell capacity was to be increased to 12,000 cells. In the meantime, people working in the Dutch Prison Service had to deal with a cell shortage (see Figure 3.1).

Cell shortage was not the only problem. The way in which cell capacity was used was severely criticized. The National Court of Audit concluded in its report *Fighting Crime*[14] (1991) that the Ministry of Justice did not use its cell capacity efficiently. In response to the report, the Minister of Justice emphasized that the National Court of Audit had not taken into account the many legitimate reasons why a cell could not be used (National Court of Audit, 1991: 38–9). Junior Minister Kosto defended current practices by referring to the use of differentiation, a long-established practice in the Dutch Prison Service. Differentiation means that every cell has a designation, that is, some cells will be designated as cells for remand prisoners, while other cells in a prison will be designated for convicted prisoners. In this system of differentiation, cells designated for one category of prisoners could not be used for other categories.[15] During a budgetary debate, the problem of cell shortage and the National Court of Audit report were discussed. During the discussion, Junior Minister Kosto responded to MPs' questions regarding the possibility of double-bunking that 'We've had this discussion before in Parliament. We do not want that'.[16] In short, at the time of the institutional crisis, policy makers

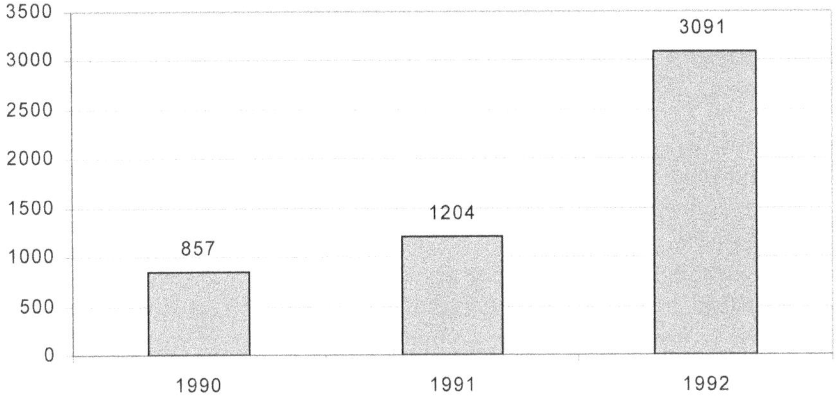

Figure 3.1 Number of adults sent away 1990–1992

Source: DJI (1999: 17).

were still reluctant to consider double-bunking as an option to deal with cell shortage.

Dealing with escape-risks: the creation of Special Security Units The institutional crisis in the Netherlands revolved around two topics: cell shortage and escapes. The escapes caught the attention of the Dutch public not only because they were violent, but also because some of these escapes occurred from Special Security Units. These units were supposed to be escape-proof. In this section, the way in which escape-prone prisoners and prisoners whose escape formed a great risk to society were dealt with before the institutional crisis broke out will be addressed.

In 1992, the Dutch Prison Service had a system of Special Security Units (SSUs). This system was the result of a series of violent escapes in the 1980s. Escaping by using violence and/or taking people hostage was a new phenomenon within the prison service. In 1985, seven prisoners escaped in this way, in 1986 one prisoner used violence and in 1987 ten prisoners used violence. In reaction to these violent escapes, 'prison officers felt unsafe while doing their job and there was a feeling of anxiety in Dutch society' (Ministry of Justice, 1987: 1).

Then Junior Minister Korte-van Hemel installed a project team to investigate the best way to deal with this relatively small group of dangerous prisoners. The project team was asked to come up with proposals regarding the secure imprisonment of three categories of prisoners: those with a high flight risk, those who were considered to be dangerous[17] and those who were escape-prone and dangerous at the same time. The project team had to consider the means for secure imprisonment, such as selection, regime, personnel, buildings and technical material (Ministry of Justice, 1987: 1).

The project team considered two alternatives: concentration of risk prisoners in one prison or de-concentration of these prisoners over several special units (but without mixing them with the more general prison population). The discussion whether prisoners should be concentrated in a single prison or concentrated in several units became a hot topic again during the institutional crisis.

What is interesting for this study is that the outcome of the project team's discussion had been set from the beginning. Several new prisons were being built at that time and Junior Minister of Justice Korte-van Hemel was very clear when she told the project team that their proposals had to focus on these prisons by using the so-called entry-units[18] for these categories of prisoners (Ministry of Justice, 1987: annex 1).[19] The project team followed the junior minister's line and concluded that the entry-units in the newly built prisons would have to be refurbished into Special Security Units.[20]

The project team did request extra security measures. The SSUs would have to have their own facilities and be built in such a way that the units would form a prison within a prison. In so doing, SSU-prisoners would not have to visit the parent prison to use central facilities such as sporting or visiting rooms. Moreover, the project team decided that SSU-prisoners would have to transfer to another SSU-unit every six months. This would limit the opportunities for SSU-prisoners to plot their escape (Ministry of Justice, 1987: 37).

In 1990, the SSUs became operational. There were SSUs at four locations: Hoogeveen, Leeuwarden, Rotterdam, and Amsterdam.[21] Each location had the following SSU-units (see Table 3.2).

Table 3.2 SSU units

Location (name)	SSU-units
Hoogeveen (De Grittenborgh)	1 SSU-remand unit 1 SSU-prison
Leeuwarden (De Marwei)	2 SSU-prisons
Rotterdam (De Schie)	1 SSU-remand unit 1 SSU-prison
Sittard (De Geerhorst)	1 SSU-remand unit

Source: Hoekstra Committee (1992: 31–2).

Within a few months, it became clear that combining the three categories of risk prisoners in one unit did not work. Escape-prone prisoners were able to live within a regular regime with communal activities, but dangerous prisoners needed more individual attention and a more structured environment. Combining these categories made it difficult for the prison officers to run the SSUs.[22] Six months after the SSUs became operational the decision was made to place only the following prisoners in the SSUs:[23]

escape-prone prisoners; or
escape-prone prisoners who were likely to use violence in an escape attempt.[24]

In Short

The situation in the Dutch Prison Service before the institutional crisis broke out in 1992 is a situation of fragmentation. Each governor had his own philosophy and determined his own regime instead of adhering to official guidelines from headquarters. This resulted in strained relations between governors and headquarters (Boin, 2001b).[25] It was also a situation where pressure was mounting as the prison population increased and there were not enough cells to accommodate all prisoners and suspects.

The Prison Service of England and Wales in 1990 and 1994

Two institutional crises in the Prison Service of England and Wales will be investigated in this study: the riots in 1990 and the escapes from Whitemoor and Parkhurst in 1994–1995. This section will therefore describe the prison service's status quo in 1990 and 1994.

The Organizational Map in 1990

The Prison Service of England and Wales is part of the Home Office.[26] The Home Secretary is ultimately responsible and accountable to Parliament for the functioning of the service. One of the junior ministers of the Home Office is responsible for the prison service. The Home Secretary and the junior minister constitute the political layer of the Prison Service (see also the subsection on the political map).

Within the Prison Service of England and Wales, two other layers can be discerned. First, there is the organizational layer of the prisons. Second, there is the strategical layer that connects the political layer and the prisons: the Prison Board at headquarters. In 1990, the Prison Board consisted of the Director General, the Deputy Director General, the four Regional Directors, the four Headquarters Directors and two non-executive Directors.

The composition of the Prison Board was to change in 1990, following a review of the way the service was organized. These changes occurred after the 1990 riots.[27] Furthermore, instead of four Regional Directors, there would be 14 (later 15) Area Managers. The reason why this reorganization is mentioned here is that the Prison Governors' Association (PGA) was opposed to the reorganization of the regional directors' positions. During the institutional crisis, the PGA tried to convince the Home Secretary to delay the implementation of the regional directors' reorganization (see Chapter 5).

Home Secretary Waddington decided to continue the reorganization. He also announced that the prison service would become a next steps agency (Woolf, 1991: 286–7), that is, an organization standing at arm's length from its parent ministry.

The Organizational Map in 1994

On 1 April 1993, the Prison Service of England and Wales became an executive agency (or a next steps agency) while continuing to be part of the Home Office. The prison service was responsible for operational matters and the Home Office was responsible for policy matters. The Home Secretary remained accountable to Parliament and continued to determine the strategic direction of the prison service and assign a junior minister to it. The Director General would answer MPs (written) questions and ministerial queries (Learmont, 1995: 93). The agency structure was set out in a Framework Document. Goals were set and specified with the help of Key Performance Indicators (KPIs) and targets. In 1994, the Prison Board consisted of the Director General, four non-executive board members, the Director of Services, the Director of Health Care, the Director of Programmes, the Director of Custody, the Director of Personnel and the Director of Finance (Learmont, 1995: appendix K).

The Political Map 1990–1994

During the 1990 disturbances and the escapes from Whitemoor and Parkhurst in 1994–1995, the same political party was in power. The political map for both institutional crises will therefore be described in one section instead of two.

The Conservative Party was the governing party in the United Kingdom and filled all the political positions in the Cabinet. There are a number of Secretaries of State in the Cabinet. Each Secretary of State[28] heads a department and is supported by a number of junior ministers. The senior minister determines the responsibilities of the junior ministers and how powerful a junior minister will be (Norton, 2001b: 438–9).[29]

The department of interest in this study is the Home Office, which is headed by a Secretary of State who is known as the Home Secretary. As with any other senior minister, the Home Secretary is supported by a number of junior ministers. Early 1994, for example, Home Secretary Howard was assisted by three junior ministers: Earl Ferrers, Lloyd and McLean. Lloyd was, amongst many things, responsible for prisons. Those junior ministers responsible for prisons are commonly referred to as the Prisons Minister.

Senior ministers are members of the cabinet; junior ministers are not. The composition of a cabinet can change at any time, even if no elections have been held. Such a change in composition is also known as a government reshuffle. Table 3.4 shows the major actors in the Prison Service of England and Wales between 1990 and 1996. An important change in political context occurred in November 1990 when Prime Minister Thatcher lost the Conservative Party leadership contest and was replaced by John Major.

In England, the opposition party forms a shadow cabinet. This means that frontbenchers of the opposition party shadow cabinet ministers. Shadowing cabinet ministers helps opposition MPs to prepare for office because they have detailed knowledge on what their predecessors have done (Kavanagh, 2001c: 430–31). In the years 1990–1996, Labour had three different shadow Home Secretaries. During the prison riots, Hattersley was shadow Home Secretary. Blair replaced him in mid 1992. When Blair became party leader and shadow Prime Minister in July 1994, Straw succeeded Blair as the new shadow Home Secretary.

Various interest groups influence the decision-making processes. On the one hand, you have the unions: the Prison Officers' Association (POA) and the Prison Governors' Association (PGA). Civil servants frequently consult with both unions when making new policy. One important POA weapon worth mentioning here is industrial action. Industrial action ranges from striking to not admitting any new prisoners because a prison is already above its CNA (Certified Normal Accommodation). The POA has used industrial action on a number of occasions to back up its demands.[30]

On the other hand, a large number of interest groups study prison conditions and try to improve these conditions. These interest groups are, to name just a few, the National Association for the Care and Resettlement of Offenders[31] (NACRO), the Prison Reform Trust[32] (PRT), the National Association of Probation Officers[33] (Napo), and the Howard League for Penal Reform.[34] These interest groups as well as the unions appeared frequently in the media during the institutional crises.

Priorities and Goals 1990–1994

In 1990, the Prison Service of England and Wales was working with a statement of purpose that had been adopted in 1988 (Cavadino and Dignan, 1997: 114). A statement of purpose contains its goals and the ways in which these goals should be achieved. The statement read: 'Her Majesty's Prison Service serves the public by keeping in custody those committed by the courts. Our duty is to look after them with humanity and to help them lead law-abiding and useful lives in custody and after release' (Home Office, 1991c: 9; Woolf, 1991: 240). The main task is to fulfil the statement of purpose and to 'build a safe, just, and tolerant society in which the rights and responsibilities of individuals, families, and communities are properly balanced, and the protection and security of the public are maintained' (HM Prison Service, 2000: 3). The prison service has to 'protect the public by holding those committed by the courts in a safe, decent, and healthy environment' and 'reduce crime by providing constructive regimes which address offending behaviour, improve educational and work

Table 3.3 The major actors in the Prison Service of England and Wales 1990–1996[a]

Change in situation in:	Home Secretary	Prisons Minister	Director General
February 1990 (start situation)	David Waddington	David Mellor	Chris Train
July 1990	David Waddington	Angela Rumbold[b]	Chris Train
November 1990	Kenneth Baker[c]	Angela Rumbold	Chris Train
August 1991	Kenneth Baker	Angela Rumbold	Joe Pilling[d]
April 1992	Kenneth Clarke[e]	Peter Lloyd[f]	Joe Pilling
January 1993	Kenneth Clarke	Peter Lloyd	Derek Lewis[g]
May 1993	Michael Howard[h]	Peter Lloyd	Derek Lewis
July 1994	Michael Howard	Michael Forsyth[i]	Derek Lewis
August 1995	Michael Howard	Ann Widdecombe[j]	Derek Lewis
October 1995	Michael Howard	Ann Widdecombe	Acting DG Richard Tilt[k]
March 1996	Michael Howard	Ann Widdecombe	Richard Tilt[l]

Notes:

a Based on the information in *Vacher's Parliamentary Companion* (1990–1996), the prison service's annual reports and several newspapers articles. The first four rows were previously published in Resodihardjo (2006a: 201).

b *The Sunday Times*, 29 July 1990, 'Born Winner Living in Suburbia's Fast Lane'.

c Following the fall of Prime Minister Thatcher and the installation of John Major as Prime Minister, a new cabinet was formed (cf. *The Guardian*, 29 November 1990, 'The New Cabinet').

d Home Office (1992), *Report on the Work of the Prison Service April 1991–March 1992*, London: HMSO: 61.

e *The Times*, 13 April 1992, 'Curious Shuffling'; *The Times*, 13 April 1992, 'Challenges and Change Await New Ministers'.

f *The Sunday Times*, 26 April 1992, Atticus (comment column); *The Guardian*, 15 April 1992, 'Profiles of New Government Appointments'.

g *The Times*, 22 December 1992, 'Clarke Chooses TV Chief to Lead Prison Service Reform'; cf. Home Affairs Committee (1997a: lxxxii).

h Lewis (1997: 102).

i *The Guardian*, 21 July 1994, 'Major's Reshuffle: Citizen John picks Lordly Cecil to Add Class to Cabinet'; Michael White on Lord Cranborne's rise to the top job in the upper house.

j *The Times*, 24 August 1995, 'Howard Wants to Jail Young Thugs in Army Glasshouse'.

k Richard Tilt took over as acting Director General of the prison service after Michael Howard sacked Lewis in October 1995 (*The Guardian*, 17 October 1995, '"Disloyal" Howard Under Fire; Sacked Jails Chief Unleashes Wrath').

l *The Times*, 7 March 1996, 'Ex-governor Picked to Run Prison Service'.

skills and promote law-abiding behaviour in custody and after release' (HM Prison Service, 2000: 3; cf. Home Office, 1990b; HM Prison Service, 1993).

The prison service needs to fulfil its tasks in an effective and efficient way. Since the 1980s, attention has shifted towards 'achieving greater economy, efficiency, and effectiveness in the use of resources' (King and McDermott, 1989: 109; cf. McDermott and King, 1989: 163; Bottoms and Stevenson, 1992: 37; King and McDermott, 1992: 100; Garland, 2001: 116), resulting in the Fresh Start programme in 1987 (see section on Fresh Start; King and McDermott, 1989; Adams, 1994: 118–34; Ryan and Sim, 1998: 177–8). The emphasis on effectiveness and efficiency gained greater strength as the prison service turned into an agency with KPIs that could be used to evaluate its functioning.

The prison service in 1994 was still affected by the Woolf Report that followed from the institutional crisis in 1990. The Woolf Report (1991) had recommended a balancing of three values: justice, control, and security. The Home Secretary had accepted these recommendations and a White Paper (*Custody, Care, and Justice*) containing the need for balance was published.[35] This White Paper formed the service's foundation in 1994.

Dealing with large numbers of prisoners: doubling and trebling Prison conditions before the riots broke out – and even after – in England can be roughly summarized as small one-person cells in old (Victorian era) facilities which prisoners had to share with one (doubling) or even two (trebling) other prisoners without access to integrated sanitation. Prisoners had a chamber pot at their disposal and every morning they had to slop out, that is, empty their chamber pots. Building programmes could not keep up with the increasing prison population, which resulted in overcrowding (cf. Mountbatten, 1966: 53–5). This situation was exacerbated by the fact that, unlike the Dutch Prison Service, the Prison Service of England and Wales generally cannot turn away suspects and convicted prisoners.[36] It has to accommodate them.

Officially, the number of prisoners a prison can hold is based on its CNA (certified normal accommodation), that is, the number of prisoners a prison can hold without overcrowding (Casale, 1994: 69; see Table 3.4 for data on accommodation). However, as Casale (1994) points out, the people within the prison service started to use the concept normal occupancy (or operational capacity) instead of CNA because CNA levels did not reflect every day practice. 'Normal occupancy is a euphemism: it stands for a prison establishment's customary level of overcrowding' (Casale, 1994: 70).

Overcrowding has at least five effects on prison conditions. First, overcrowding results in lack of resources, facilities, and space, which, in turn, results in restricted activities. Second, overcrowding hampers the much-needed refurbishment programmes because it often results in their postponement. Third, overcrowding results in the search for cell space for prisoners. As a result, prisoners are transported from one prison to another. This is very disruptive

Table 3.4 Average population in custody and certified normal accommodation 1990–1999

	1990[a]	1991	1992	1993	1994	1995	1996	1997	1998	1999
Population in custody	44,975	44,809	44,719	44,552	48,621	50,962	55,281	61,114	65,298	64,771
CNA on 30 June										
All establishments	42,804	43,875	46,239	46,646	48,291	50,239	53,152	56,329	61,253	62,369
Excess of average population over CNA										
Population in custody	2,832	2,022	(422)[b]	(2,080)[c]	503	808	2,129	4,785	4,045	2,402
All establishments	2,171	934	(1,520)[d]	(2,095)[e]	330	723	2,129	4,785	4,045	2,402

Notes:

a CNA was redefined in September 1992 to exclude accommodation in new establishments which is not yet operational.
b Excess of CNA over average population.
c Excess of CNA over average population.
d Excess of CNA over average population.
e Excess of CNA over average population.

Source: Home Office (2001: 35) (Crown copyright material is reproduced with the permission of the Controller of HMSO and the Queen's Printer for Scotland).

for prisoners and their families. Fourth, overcrowding results in increased tension and frustration. And fifth, because of these effects, overcrowding has a negative effect on living conditions within prisons (Cavadino and Dignan, 1997: 120).

As a result of the occurrence of bad conditions and overcrowding in prisons, some academics spoke of a prison service in crisis (Smith, 1983; King and McDermott, 1989; Adams, 1994: 124–9; Cavadino and Dignan, 1997: 8–31; 115–47). The bad prison conditions are seen by some as the cause of riots in the prison service in the late 1980s and 1990s (Adams, 1994: 161–9; Ryan and Sim, 1998: 182). The Woolf Report on the 1990 disturbances added two other items to the list of possible causes of disturbances: grievance and injustice (Woolf, 1991: 226; Sparks et al., 1996: 303; cf. Adams, 1994: 161).

Following the Woolf Report, a number of measures were implemented to improve conditions within prisons. Trebling ended by March 1994, use of police cells ended by June 1995, and slopping out ended in April 1996 (Home Affairs Committee, 1997a: xi; see Tables 3.5 and 3.6). In other words, by the time the institutional crisis broke out in 1994, cell conditions were already improving.

Table 3.5 KPI overcrowding: monthly average number of prisoners held in overcrowded conditions 1992–1996

Year	Prisoners held three to a cell for one	Prisoners held two to a cell for one	Prisoners held in police cells	Percentage of prisoners overcrowded
1992–93	468	7,251	715	21
1993–94	82	7,771	67	17
1994–95	0	8,426	163	17
1995–96	0	8,513	30	16

Source: Home Affairs Committee (1997c: 175) (Crown copyright material is reproduced with the permission of the Controller of HMSO and the Queen's Printer for Scotland).

Dealing with Escape Risks: Special Security Units and Dispersal Prisons

There is a system of Special Security Units (SSUs) (for Category A prisoners) and dispersal prisons (for Category A and B prisoners) to deal with escape-prone prisoners. The use of these two systems at the same time is the result of historical events.

On 12 April 1964, Wilson, one of the Great Train Robbers, escaped from Birmingham Prison. In response to this escape, then Home Secretary Brooke decided to improve security in parts of a small number of prisons in order to avoid escapes by prisoners who posed serious escape risks. On 16 August 1965,

Table 3.6 Access to sanitation

Year	Number of places provided	Percentage of population with 24 hour access
1992–93	4,246	82%
1993–94	4,724	91%
1994–95	4,191	95%
1995–96	2,424[a]	99.5%[b]

Notes:
a Provisional figure.
b '100% access was achieved on 12 April 1996' (Home Affairs Committee, 1997c: 176).

Source: Home Affairs Committee (1997c: 176) (Crown copyright material is reproduced with the permission of the Controller of HMSO and the Queen's Printer for Scotland).

the Special Security Wings (or units) at Durham[37] and Leicester were opened. The Special Security Unit at Parkhurst became operational on 31 January 1966 (Walmsley, 1989: 3–4).

Shortly after, on 22 October 1966, the spy Blake escaped from Wormwood Scrubs. A committee headed by Lord Mountbatten was installed. One of the effects of Blake's escape was a search within the prison population to determine whether other prisoners posed a serious security risk. If identified, these prisoners were placed in SSUs. As the number of inmates in these units increased, there was a need for an additional unit (Walmsley, 1989: 7).

Lord Mountbatten was very critical of the SSUs in his report and favoured a single purpose-built prison to house so-called Category A prisoners. Mountbatten's negative comments on the conditions within the units were supported by a later report published in 1968 on *The Regimes for Long Term Prisoners in Conditions of Maximum Security* – also known as the Radzinowicz Report. There was one major point where the two reports differed: the single purpose-built prison. The Radzinowicz Report favoured dispersal prisons as a solution to deal with Category A prisoners (see below for a definition) (Sparks et al,, 1996: 4–6).

The Home Office had made clear from the start that the SSUs were meant for temporary imprisonment because of the constrictive conditions. The Home Office accepted the Radzinowicz Report and with it the idea of using dispersal prisons for Category A prisoners (Walmsley, 1989: 17).[38] The Home Office planned to replace the SSUs with dispersal prisons.[39] However, IRA bombings in March 1973 showed that a new type of prisoner could be imprisoned in the SSUs: IRA terrorists (Walmsley, 1989: 21).

As the number of IRA prisoners – as well as the number of prisoners with financial means to escape – increased, the Home Office decided that keeping the SSUs was necessary because it was too expensive to increase security measures of the dispersal prisons to the level of the SSUs. Thus, a combination of dispersal prisons and SSUs still exists even though at one point the plan had been to replace the SSUs with dispersal prisons.

Whether prisoners end up in a SSU or dispersal prison depends on how they are categorized. Mountbatten introduced four categories for prisoners: A, B, C, and D (Mountbatten, 1966: 58). The categories are defined as follows (Prison Service, 2000: 6):

> Category A
> Prisoners whose escape would be highly dangerous to the public or the police or the security of the state, no matter how unlikely that escape might be, and for whom the aim must be to make escape impossible.
>
> Category B
> Prisoners for whom the very highest conditions of security are not necessary, but for whom escape must be made very difficult.
>
> Category C
> Prisoners who cannot be trusted in open conditions, but who do not have the resources and will to make a determined escape attempt.
>
> Category D
> Prisoners who can be reasonably trusted in open conditions.

Category A prisoners can be further categorized as follows (Learmont, 1995: 129; cf. Prison Service, 2001: 3):

> Exceptional risk, containing highly resourceful prisoners, valuable to criminal organisations outside and highly likely to escape; High risk, containing prisoners who may be marginally less likely to obtain help to escape; and Standard risk for those who have fewer resources.

Exceptional escape risk prisoners go to the SSUs. High escape risk, standard escape risk, and dangerous Category B prisoners go to dispersal prisons.[40] In 1997, the list of dispersal prisons and special security units was as follows:

> Dispersal prisons: Frankland, Full Sutton, Long Lartin, Wakefield, Whitemoor (Parkhurst no longer functioned as a dispersal prison after the 1995 escape).
> Special Security Units: Full Sutton, Whitemoor, and Belmarsh (Home Affairs Committee, 1997a: xxiii).

Fresh Start

A factor that played a role in the 1990 disturbances was the Fresh Start programme, which was implemented in 1987. One of the effects of the Fresh Start programme was a decrease in staffing levels at some prisons. Various actors wondered whether the low staffing levels had contributed to the outbreak of the Strangeways disturbance (see Chapter 5). In this subsection, the origins of the Fresh Start programme and its effects will be briefly discussed.

A report of the *Study of Prison Officers' Compensation and Shift Systems* had identified a number of problems within the prison service, most importantly overtime (Home Office, 1986: 3). The then existing manpower systems were 'overtime dependent and overtime driven' (Home Office, 1986: 3). The effects of overtime were threefold. First, prison officers' performance deteriorated. Second, prison officers began to rely on the additional income they could generate by working overtime. As a result, the POA did not really push for the ending of overtime. And third, the POA used overtime as a bargaining weapon. If the POA did not favour a proposal for change, it could threaten to reduce the number of overtime hours worked by its members (Thomas, 1994: 114; cf. Woolf, 1991: 338–48).

The Fresh Start programme was supposed to deal with overtime and other problems by, for instance, cutting back overtime and abolishing the role of Chief Officer in order to get to a unified single management structure instead of a separate officer and governor structure. According to Lord Justice Woolf, the programme 'involved a fundamental reorganisation of prison officers' working arrangements and of management within establishments. It was intended to increase the job satisfaction of prison officers and to improve their relations with management' (Woolf, 1991: 338). The Fresh Start programme also included incentives for the prison officers. These incentives were an increase in pay for every prison officer – with the additional benefit of an increase in pension benefits – and staff could buy their houses (Thomas, 1994: 115).

Regarding overtime, the idea was to gradually cut back the amount of overtime over a period of five years. In the first year, one hour was to be phased out and in the following years, two hours had to be phased out. The aim was for prison officers to work 39 hours a week by 1992. However, phasing out hours did not mean that the workload was reduced. The solution to handling the work that prison officers could not do because they were working fewer hours was to recruit additional staff and to improve efficiency (Woolf, 1991: 341).

Unfortunately, what was not taken into account in the phasing out process was a difference in experience of manning levels and difference in needs of the various prisons. 'It soon became clear that the setting of staff levels was going to be uneven, with a consequent allegation that there was now, in some places, understaffing' (Thomas, 1994: 115). Moreover, this feeling of anxiety with governors and officers was exacerbated by the feeling they had been cheated. In order to push the programme through, people at headquarters had not drawn adequate attention to the expected efficiency improvement. As a result,

> staff and governors were generally under the impression that the reduction in contracted hours worked at each establishment would be compensated for by the provision of new staff to be deployed at that establishment to make up for 50% of the reduction. In fact this was not the intention of the Prison Service. The intention was that the reduced hours would be replaced in the way that senior management (at that time Regions) considered would be appropriate. The Inquiry was constantly being told when visiting establishments that the Prison Service had not kept to its promise to provide them with more staff. Nationally, however, the Service could show the necessary increase had been provided. The general impression which staff and governors had was that staff resources were reduced to a much greater extent than they had envisaged. This produced a considerable degree of cynicism of the Prison Service's motive in introducing the package. (Woolf, 1991: 345)

In Short

The situation in 1990 consisted of bad prison conditions combined with turmoil among both the prison officers and the governors. The governors were not happy about reorganization at regional director level. At the same time, prison officers felt frustrated and betrayed by the Fresh Start operation. This unease came to the fore during the institutional crisis in 1990.

In 1994, there was no major dissatisfaction among governors and officers and prison conditions were improving. As advocated by Lord Justice Woolf, more emphasis was put on justice. However, the prison service was pressed to function as effectively and efficiently as possible. At the same time, it had to adjust to being a next steps agency headed by an outsider, a businessman from Granada Television and a Conservative Home Secretary who declared that prisons work – leading to an increase in the prison population. Moreover, it became clear during the institutional crisis that the division of operation and policy making as envisioned by advocates of next step agencies was not so clear cut.

Notes

1. For such an account on prison and punishment in Western society see Morris and Rothman (1998), for an account of the Prison Service of England and Wales see Cavadino and Dignan (1997), for an account of the Dutch Prison Service see Franke (1996) and for both see Downes (1988) and Weiss and South (1998).
2. The Dutch Prison Service became an agency on 1 January 1995.

3. *Staatssecretaris* is translated here as junior minister.
4. It is important to note here that in contrast to the Prison Service of England and Wales the bureaucratic leader of the Dutch Prison Service is called a Director, while the head of the Prison Service of England and Wales is called Director General.
5. In 1999, however, the Dutch Prison Service's capacity had almost doubled to 13,207 cells and 46,871 people had been imprisoned in that year (DJI, 2001: 13–15).
6. Due to an institutional crisis in the police sector (the IRT affair), the Minister of Justice Hirsch Ballin (CDA) and Minister of Interior Affairs Van Thijn (PvdA) resigned in May 1994 (cf. Dekker et al., 2000: 84). However, this happened when the institutional crisis in the Dutch Prison Service had ended.
7. Parliament abolished the cellular system officially in 1951 (Franke, 1996: 279).
8. For an article on the recent changes in double-bunking in the Netherlands, see Dekker et al. (2003).
9. Tweede Kamer (hereafter: TK), 1984–1985, 18995 nos 1–2: 7.
10. Samenleving en Criminaliteit. TK, 1984–1985, 18995, nos 1–2.
11. TK, 1991–1992, 22649, no. 1: 1.
12. TK, 1984–1985, 18995 nos 1–2: 96.
13. The *planning JR-120* was an annex to the White Paper *Accommodation Judicial Services* which was presented to parliament on October 16 1990 (TK, 1990–1991, 21840, no. 1). JR-120 was based on the report *Facilities for Prisoners and Youth Prisons 1990–1994* [*Voorzieningenbeleid delinquentenzorg en jeugdinrichtingen 1990–1994*] which included an inventory regarding the problems of the prisons (TK, 1990–1991, 21840, no. 2: 7). Besides building new courtrooms and other buildings, cell capacity had to be expanded (TK, 1990–1991, 21840, no. 11: 2) with approximately 2,000 cells (TK, 1990–1991, 26385, no. 2: 9).
14. Criminaliteitsbestrijding. TK, 1991–1992, 22355, no. 2.
15. TK, Handelingen, Justitie, 31 October 1991, TK 18, 18–968 – 18–984: 18–979. See also the answer of Kosto to a question of MP Van den Berg during the interpellation of 10 June 1992 (TK, Handelingen, Cellentekort, 10 June 1992, TK 87, 87–5256 – 87–5272: 87–5271).
16. TK, Handelingen, Justitie, 31 October 1991, TK 18, 18–968 – 18–984: 18–980.
17. Prisoners are considered dangerous when their antisocial or mentally disturbed behaviour influences the prison community in a negative way.
18. These entry-units are units where newly arrived prisoners are held for a short time. Prison officers observe prisoners during their stay in these units. Based on these observations, prison officers decide which unit the prisoner will go to.
19. The project team claims in the report's introduction that the necessity to use these entry-units had no effect on their deliberations.
20. Extra Beveiligde Inrichting (EBI or EBIs).
21. There was also an SSU in Arnhem. But it was unsuitable for the job and soon used for other purposes (Hoekstra Committee, 1992, Part I: 32).

22. The reports (for example, *Vluchten kan niet meer?*) mention that there were problems. They do, however, not specify the nature of these problems (cf. Borst, 1991: 27).
23. Those prisoners who were both dangerous and escape-prone remained in the SSU as well.
24. Hoekstra Committee, 1992, Part I: 31.
25. For the effects of the institutional crisis on the relation between governors and headquarters, see Boin (2001b).
26. The Home Office is responsible for the prisons, the police and the probation service.
27. The Prison Board would consist of the Director General, two non-executive members, the Director of Buildings and Services, the Director of Prison Medical Services, the Director of Personnel and Finance, the Director of Inmate Administration, the Director of Custody and the Director of Inmate Programmes, while the position of Deputy Director General was to be abolished (Woolf, 1991: 287).
28. A Secretary of State is also known as a Minister of the Crown or a senior minister.
29. Both senior and junior ministers can be assisted by Parliamentary Private Secretaries (PPS) and special advisers (Norton, 2001b: 438–9).
30. The POA's abilities for industrial action were curbed in the 1990s. In 1994, a court decision ruled that prison officers must carry out the Home Secretary's orders (Cavadino and Dignan, 1997: 15). The ban on industrial action was lifted in 2003 (BBC News, 21 May 2003, 'Prison Officers Regain Strike Rights', http://news.bbc.co.uk/go/pr/fr/-/1/hi/uk_politics/3047151.stm, accessed 21 May 2003).
31. NACRO aims to help offenders to reintegrate within society without a stigma. The crime reduction charity also helps deprived communities and disadvantaged people to build a better future (http://www.nacro.org.uk/about/index.htm, accessed 29 September 2004).
32. The PRT is a charity in favour of a more humane and effective penal system. It tries to achieve this aim by disseminating information (to offenders, government, and the public), conducting research, and campaigning (http://www.prisonreformtrust.org.uk, accessed 15 August 2008).
33. Napo is the trade union, professional organization and campaigning group for those people working in the national probation service and child and family service (http://www.napo.org.uk/about.shtml, accessed 15 August 2008).
34. The Howard League was established in 1866. The organization aims to reform the penal system in order to create a more humane penal system (http://www.howardleague.org, accessed 15 August 2008).
35. The White Paper was titled *Custody, Care and Justice: The Way Ahead for the Prison Service in England and Wales* (Home Office, 1991c).
36. In some instances it is possible for convicted persons to get on a waiting list to get into prison. Moreover, early release can be used to ease overcrowding (Cavadino and Dignan, 1997: 181–201).

37. The security at the Durham unit was not seen as adequate and the unit was changed into a unit for control as well as security risk prisoners. Leicester and Parkhurst continued to handle prisoners who posed 'really serious escape risks' (Walmsley, 1989: 6).
38. Prisons that would become dispersal prisons were 'Parkhurst, Wakefield or Wormwood Scrubs, and as they became available Gartree, Hull, Albany, Long Lartin, and a new prison to be built in the North' (Walmsley, 1989: 17).
39. In 1971, Durham special security unit closed and the unit at Chelmsford followed in 1972. Early 1973, the Home Office considered closing the Parkhurst unit and let Leicester take all the prisoners 'who presented security risks greater than the dispersal prisons could handle' (Walmsley, 1989: 21).
40. Interview with civil servant.

Chapter 4
The Dutch Prison Service: Cell Shortages and Escapes (1992–1993)

Introduction[1]

In the early 1990s, policy makers of the Dutch Prison Service faced two critical problems.[2] First, there were too many prisoners for the available number of cells. Cell shortage had in past decades not been unusual (see Chapter 3), but the number of people sent away as a result reached record highs in these years. Second, a number of high profile escapes occurred. The overall number of escapes was actually declining, but the escapes that did occur were spectacular – using, for example, helicopters to escape – and violence was used, especially during escapes from Special Security Units (SSUs).

Media and MPs came to consider prison security as lax and labelled the prison service as malfunctioning and pampering prisoners. The intense media and parliamentary scrutiny of the prison service, an uncommon topic in these forums, indicated that the Dutch Prison Service was losing legitimacy.

At the start of the crisis (spring 1992), policy makers installed an inquiry to investigate the SSU escapes. As the inquiry proceeded to study the SSU escapes, problems concerning cell shortage and security continued. From the spring of 1992 until June 1993, these incidents put the prison service firmly in the media spotlight and on the parliamentary agenda. The incidents took turns: escape incidents were followed by cell shortage incidents, which, in turn, were followed by escape incidents until the two problems became linked in the eye of the media and MPs. When that happened in the spring of 1993, the crisis reached its zenith. The Minister and Junior Minister of Justice not only faced the wrath of opposition parties in Parliament, but also of their own government parties (CDA (Christian Democrats) and PvdA (Social Democrats)).

In the end, the supermax solution (that is, building SSUs: prisons within prisons with extreme high security measures) was embraced and double-bunking was allowed in special circumstances. Both changes can be qualified in terms of reform as they drastically deviated from existing policy and were accompanied by a change in the prison service's priorities.

Escapes and Cell Shortages

Increasing Cell Shortage

Cell shortage had already caught the eye of MPs following the publication of the report by the National Court of Audit titled *Fighting Crime*[3] (October 1991) which showed that the prison service was not able to deal with cell shortage. MPs asked questions and discussed this report in Parliament (see Chapter 3). At the same time, prisoners escaped from SSUs and other prisons. In 1990, the SSUs had become operational. SSUs were supposed to be escape-proof, but prisoners did escape. By spring 1992, seven out of 55 SSU prisoners had managed to escape (Hoekstra, 1992: 18). In response to these SSU escapes, Junior Minister of Justice Kosto installed an inquiry headed by Secretary-General Hoekstra from the Ministry of General Affairs to investigate the functioning of the SSUs on 2 April 1992.[4]

While the Hoekstra Inquiry was under way, a problem occurred: severe cell shortage. Sending people home when there were no cells available was standard practice in the Dutch Prison Service at that time. In May 1992, media and MPs started to pay attention to the lack of cells as more and more incidents occurred. In the second week of May 1992, suspects in a million-guilders[5] public transport ticket fraud were sent home because no cells were available for them. This incident was just one of many cases where people were sent home because of cell shortage. In the same week, only three out of 98 suspected drug dealers could be incarcerated in Amsterdam-Southeast. Amsterdam police commissioner Nordholt demanded that Minister of Justice Hirsch Ballin would take steps to end this 'insane situation'.[6] Nordholt suggested the use of containers, empty army barracks or double-bunking to detain criminals. 'The current situation is dangerous, unsocial, and ridicules government in general and justice in particular.'[7]

In response to Nordholt's charges, Minister of Justice Hirsch Ballin (CDA) said that Nordholt's options to deal with cell shortage should be investigated. Moreover, he announced that he did not exclude double-bunking as a way of dealing with the current cell shortage. Hirsch Ballin agreed with Nordholt that sending people home 'discredits police and justice'.[8] The Minister of Justice announced that a package of measures dealing with cell shortage would be presented to Parliament on the third Thursday of September (Prinsjesdag, that is, the day that the Dutch government presents its budget to parliament).[9]

Responses to Hirsch Ballin's suggestion to allow double-bunking varied. His own Junior Minister of Justice Kosto (PvdA) was against double-bunking. Kosto would only allow it for a very small group of prisoners, which, in turn, would only alleviate cell shortage slightly.[10] CDA leader in Parliament Brinkman said in a radio interview that the CDA 'did not have any fundamental objections' to double-bunking.[11] VVD MP Wiebenga (Liberals) was in favour of double-bunking; a measure that the VVD had already proposed a year before.[12] At that time, the VVD was the only one in favour of double-bunking. Now, the CDA was in favour as well. PvdA-spokesperson Swildes, however, considered double-bunking 'horrendous' and preferred alternative sanctions.[13] The PvdA made it clear that double-bunking was out of the question and that the subject was non-negotiable.[14]

The VDPI (Union of Prison Governors) opposed double-bunking as well. It was a topic that, as far as the VDPI was concerned, was non-negotiable. President of the VDPI Boeij thought it 'unfair' that double-bunking was suggested again as a means of dealing with cell shortage.[15] He told the media: 'I thought that we had already discussed this issue on principles. I am sure that as soon as the Minister is properly informed about this topic, he will back off immediately.'[16] Boeij's main concerns were the deterioration of the quality of incarceration and the controllability of the prison.[17] Prison officers supported the VDPI, because prison officers were afraid that double-bunking would lead to more violence.[18]

The Select Committee on Justice met to discuss the problems surrounding the Dutch Prison Service on 27 May 1992. During that meeting, MPs expressed their fear that the current plan to build new prisons (JR-120)[19] would be insufficient to deal with the ever increasing number of prisoners. VVD MP Korthals, for instance, said that it was 'of the utmost importance for our legal system to actually implement prison sentences. … For that reason, cell capacity has been doubled in the 1980s. Why have the MPs not been warned that cell shortage has reached such a level that [people] are sent home again?'[20] VVD MP Korthals also 'had the impression that the government is solely focussed on implementing the budget cuts of 12 million guilders'.[21]

On 2 June 1992, Minister of Justice Hirsch Ballin and Junior Minister of Justice Kosto wrote a letter to Parliament. In this letter, they announced a set of emergency measures (total cost about 10 million guilders) creating 175 to 200 extra cells in order to deal with cell shortage in Amsterdam and Rotterdam. These measures included using containers in the Bijlmerprison (Amsterdam), using a border prison to hold illegal aliens in order to free up space in remand centres, and expediting prison cells' refurbishment to create additional cell capacity.[22] Talks with the Minister of Defence to use army prisons were under way.

At a press conference, Kosto told the media that the Minister and Junior Minister would not opt for double-bunking. In a letter to Parliament, Kosto and Hirsch Ballin explained that double-bunking 'would not present a short term solution to the problem at hand, because the law has to be changed to allow multiple use of a cell'[23] and cells would have to be refurbished to accommodate double-bunking.[24] Moreover, double-bunking would completely turn 'the fundament of our prison system on its head'.[25] The Minister and Junior Minister also announced that they wanted to present Parliament with a list of more structured measures on Prinsjesdag (third Tuesday in September when the cabinet presents next year's budgeting)[26] at which time they would also present their final view on double-bunking.[27]

VVD MP Korthals was not pleased about the letter sent by Hirsch Ballin and Kosto. Korthals requested – and was granted – an emergency (*interpellatie*) debate, that is, a debate that was previously not on the official agenda. This debate was held in Parliament on 10 June 1992.[28]

During this debate, it became clear that MPs saw the plans as presented in the letter by Hirsch Ballin and Kosto as just a beginning of dealing with the problems. MPs were very critical of the Dutch Prison Service and demanded more action by the policy makers. SGP MP Van den Berg (Christian Party), for instance, told Minister Hirsch Ballin:

> Every time I have to conclude that we are running after the facts. I find that lamentable. However painful it is to say, the truth is that consecutive governments have failed. … We have ended up in a very serious situation. … [I]f I read that 90% [of the suspects] had to be sent away in Amsterdam in the beginning of April, then that is a very tragic situation, which undermines law and order, discourages everyone involved in fighting crime, and frustrates our policy. Something has to be done.[29]

CDA MP Soutendijk-van Appeldoorn concurred:

> If criminals, whether they are robbers or drug dealers, cannot be locked up, then this frustrates intensive police work, endangers the safety of the public, and insults our feelings of justice. That is unacceptable for a legal state such as the Netherlands. That is why policy must aim at delivering sufficient cells in order to be able to fight crime. … The CDA party wants extra cells as soon as possible. In order to achieve this, we find it acceptable that other principles of prison policy, such as quality of imprisonment, rehabilitation … are somewhat violated. When we have to weigh these principles against the security of society, then the balance will tip in favour of security.[30]

Double-bunking was a hot topic during this debate. CDA MP Soutendijk-van Appeldoorn endorsed double-bunking. 'Why is it not possible to place two persons in one cell in the current situation where hundreds get sent home? Does the privacy of a prisoner mean more than the privacy of the sick and elderly who share a room with five other people?'[31] CDA was also in favour of using police cells to deal with cell shortage. Not everyone, however, was in favour of double-bunking. Groen Links (Green Left) and D66 (Democrats) were against it. Groen Links MP Brouwer, for instance, was surprised that government was considering double-bunking. After all, 'in England they have finally decided to end double-bunking because of aggression and inhumane circumstances'.[32]

During the debate, the PvdA changed its mind. PvdA MP Zijlstra announced that the PvdA accepted double-bunking under special circumstances, such as for people who had defaulted on their fines. As a result of the PvdA's altered position, a majority of MPs was now in favour of double-bunking.[33]

MPs submitted two motions during this debate. VVD MP Korthals submitted the first motion in which he asked for more money in order for the Ministry of Justice to function properly.[34] He wanted a budget increase of at least 100 million guilders.[35] Parliament rejected this motion. CDA MP Soutendijk-van Appeldoorn and PvdA MP Zijlstra submitted the second motion. In this motion, they requested government to take emergency measures on short notice to create additional cell capacity for Amsterdam and Rotterdam and to adjust JR-120 (the prison-building programme) as soon as possible in order to end cell shortage in a more structured way.[36] This motion was accepted.

Hirsch Ballin and Kosto defended themselves during the debate. They mostly agreed with what was said in Parliament about 'the importance of sufficient cell capacity as the end station ... of the judicial-penal line',[37] but they had shown to be on top of things by continuously monitoring cell capacity and by proposing measures on 2 June 1992.[38] Kosto added that JR-120 could not be brought forward. It seemed to him that creating over-capacity was the only way to avoid such debates in the future, but creating over-capacity was impossible budgetary wise. Options such as prison boats and army barracks were unrealistic because security was insufficient and it would take a lot of money to install security. In response to the allegations that hotel chains were able to allocate rooms for guests but prisons were not, Kosto answered that remand prisons had an occupancy rate of 98.2 per cent – which was far higher than any hotel. An occupancy rate of 100 per cent was impossible because cells had designations either as remand cells (for suspects) or as prison cells (see Chapter 3). As a result, one could not just put anyone in any cell. Kosto also repeated that Hirsch Ballin and he would present their view on double-bunking in September 1992.[39]

In the following months, a public debate ensued on whether or not double-bunking should be permitted. Professor Kelk considered it 'inhumane and dangerous'.[40] Newspapers printed numerous articles on the pros and cons of double-bunking.[41] Prisoners played their part as well as some of them, for instance in prison De Marwei (Leeuwarden), went on strike because of the proposed double-bunking. The Dutch union of prisoners wanted to use the strikes to force the Ministry of Justice to allow the union to participate in the negotiations on changes in the Dutch Prison Service.[42] Boeij, president of the VDPI, wrote:

> The last couple of months, the media have given ample attention to the problem that too many suspects are sent away because there are not enough cells available. Chiefs of police and mayors complain. Public opinion is mobilized with a reference to the unacceptability of sending away yet another

> heavy criminal and some advocate double-bunking. … It is striking how the prison service twists itself around in order to find solutions for the problem. Suddenly, old buildings have to be used again, emergency capacity has to be created, and security services' personnel are hired and trained in a week to work as prison officers. Panic is therefore substantial, interests are ignored, and the burden is shifted to prison officers. This would be even worse if one decided to opt for double-bunking. This would mean that the already heavily burdened prison officers would be burdened even more. It would also mean a considerable drop in quality of detention … Even though double-bunking may seem societally appealing, it creates more problems than it solves. Nonetheless, suspects should not be just sent away. That has a negative effect on police and society and on suspects as well. After a solid investigation of the structural need for cells, money should become available to build more cells if necessary and to hire and train the needed extra prison officers. If that happens, all parties involved will have found a good solution. (Boeij, 1992)

In September 1992, Junior Minister of Justice Kosto announced that he wanted to build two new prisons in order to create 400 additional cells.[43] At the same time, Kosto and Hirsch Ballin decided to speed up the building of prisons already planned. As promised, Hirsch Ballin and Kosto gave their opinion about double-bunking in their explanatory memorandum to the Ministry of Justice's budget. They announced that they would not opt for placing two prisoners in one cell to end cell shortage. 'The atmosphere in prisons is already tense as a result of a changing prison population. The situation would become even more tense if we were to opt for double-bunking, thereby endangering the safety of personnel and prisoners alike.'[44] They would, however, consider placing together several people who were not likely to escape and who would only be in prison for a short time in one large room.[45]

The Hoekstra Report on the SSU Escapes

While the Hoekstra Inquiry was investigating the SSUs, escapes continued to occur (see table 4.1 for the number of escapes).

Table 4.1 Number of successful escapes from closed prisons with or without taking people hostage 1991–1995

	1991	1992	1993	1994	1995
Without taking people hostage	50	31	33	18	22
With taking people hostage	0	13	26	3	0
Total	50	44	59	21	22

Source: CBS (1997: 27).

On 2 August 1992, for example, a prisoner managed to escape from a remand centre (Hoorn) by helicopter. An accomplice of the prisoner had hijacked a helicopter and forced the pilot to land in the courtyard.[46] In an interview, the newly appointed director of the Dutch Prison Service Elting said

> He was aware that the prison service had been in the news this summer following escapes and cell shortage. 'In my previous job as Director of Aliens at the Ministry of Welfare, Public Health, and Culture, I often faced crisis situations. This is not any different for the prison service. On the contrary.' Elting understands the public's outrage when yet another heavy criminal managed to escape. 'But people should understand that these escapes are just incidents. In 1984, there were 118 escapes. This year, only 16 escapes have occurred so far. At the same time we have twice as many prisoners as eight years ago', according to the top level official. 'Granted, every escape is one too many. We aim at a 100% security, but even if we just manage 99.9% then that is anything but bad.'[47]

In the same interview, Elting said that he thought double-bunking would not be necessary as new cells were already being built. 'In five years, we hope to have 9,000 cells, but I do not dare to say that capacity will be sufficient by then.'[48]

Two other spectacular escapes occurred before the Hoekstra Report was published in September 1992. On 24 August 1992, a prisoner got on a forklift and another prisoner lifted him over the prison walls of Esserheem Prison. On 3 September 1992, four prisoners armed with knives escaped from SSU De Schie (Rotterdam) (De Jong and Van Vliet, 1993: 93).[49]

In September 1992, the Hoekstra Inquiry published its report. The inquiry was disappointed that 13 per cent of escape-prone prisoners locked up in SSUs had managed to escape. This high percentage was particularly damning for the prison service because these prisoners had been specifically imprisoned in SSUs to prevent their escape (Hoekstra, 1992: 8). The inquiry concluded that incorrect implementation of the philosophy behind SSUs had caused the escapes. Because of money constraints, it was decided to refurbish entry-units of prisons which were being built at that time into SSUs instead of building completely new SSU prisons (see Chapter 3). As a result, the SSUs had to depend on their parent prison to provide certain facilities such as sports and recreation to its prisoners. Escapes occurred during transfer to these facilities or in these facilities because there were fewer security measures in these areas (Hoekstra, 1992: 9, 31; cf. De Borst, 1991).

The Hoekstra Inquiry recommended the building of two completely new SSUs[50] that did comply with the SSU security philosophy. In addition, the selection criteria for people to get into SSUs should be twofold, pertaining (1) to prisoners who are likely to escape – with or without help from outside –

and (2) to prisoners whose escape would be socially unacceptable (Hoekstra, 1992: 9).

Kosto decided that he needed some time to consider the inquiry's recommendations, but he did change the security regime in SSUs in response to the SSU escapes and based on a report by the study group *Re-Assessing Security Regime Concerning Escape-Prone Prisoners*.[51] Changes included airing prisoners only once a day for a maximum of 45 minutes and allowing prisoners to receive one visit once a week for a maximum of two hours under strict security measures.[52] A study group on security was installed following the Hoekstra Report to help improve security in closed prisons.[53]

In the two months following the Hoekstra Report, there was a public debate in the press on whether the SSUs – basically super maximum security prisons – would be humane or not. VDPI president Boeij emphasized that 'the Hoekstra Report did not suggest any hardening of the climate in prisons. Providing security for society is one side of the story, treatment of prisoners is the other side. These prisoners will be released one day. We have to guard ourselves that we do not let ruined people loose on society. Desperados are dangerous to society'.[54] Professor Beyaert, former head of the Pieter Baan Centre, known as doubting the use of prison sentences longer than five years, and a member of the Hoekstra Inquiry, supported the inquiry's recommendation for a stricter regime for SSU prisoners. He told *NRC Handelsblad* that some of the recommendations were 'cruel and horrible ... yet if you want to build prisons for extreme escape-prone prisoners than you are obliged to do so as decently as possible. The whole inquiry supported that idea. ... An answer was needed to the occurrence of the escapes. This was the only possible answer'.[55]

Governor Kranendonk of De Grittenborgh Prison (Hoogeveen) avidly supported the idea of two supermax prisons.[56] Governor and president of the VDPI Boeij did support the idea to concentrate escape-prone prisoners, but he also voiced three points of criticism. First, the recommendation to put escape-prone prisoners as well as prisoners whose escape would be socially unacceptable in the supermax prisons 'set aside an important premise that people's behaviour determines where they will be incarcerated.[57] Moreover, this will result in a strange mixture in prison population in SSUs with all the corresponding consequences'. Second, building the two new SSUs would cost 24 million guilders. The Hoekstra Inquiry had said 'money should be derived from the current budget', but Kranendonk stated that the prison service was already thinly stretched in order to deal with cell shortage. Additional money to deal with this cell problem had just become available a few months earlier. An extra commitment of 24 million guilders would result in cell shortage. Kranendonk: 'One can predict that this will result in another cry for extra cells.' And third, the Hoekstra Inquiry still tried to balance treatment and security, but the prisoners who ended up in SSUs 'want to escape instead of engaging in meaningful relations. As a result, prison officers focussing on security should work in SSUs rather than regular prison officers'. Boeij ended his plea with

'One thing must be clear by now. Whatever the prison service comes up with, stopping every escape is impossible and will always be impossible.'[58]

Governor Suspended after Another Escape

While the discussion whether security and humane treatment were mutually exclusive[59] continued, another SSU escape occurred. On 23 October 1992, four prisoners managed to escape from SSU De Grittenborgh (Hoogeveen). The escape started in the gym, which was part of the parent prison and thus less secured. One prisoner pressed a sharp object to the throat of a gym instructor, while two other prisoners overpowered the three prison officers present. On their way out, they held two more prison officers hostage. A fourth prisoner was picked up from another ward. One prison officer was knocked out and another received lacerations to his face. When the prisoners got outside, three of them hijacked a car from a prison officer who just happened to arrive, while the fourth escaped on foot.[60]

A spokesman from the Ministry of Justice told the press he was 'shocked and unpleasantly surprised by this new escape', especially because the SSU security had just been increased.[61] This increase in security measures was perceived by the president of the De Grittenborgh's prison officers' committee as the cause of the escape. He was seriously concerned with the safety of the prison officers and he thought the change in regime should be reversed. The mayor of Hoogeveen, the city where the prison was located, had had enough. He demanded that Kosto guaranteed that no more escapes would occur.[62]

Junior Minister of Justice Kosto's response to the escape was twofold. First, he told the press he was concerned about the violent way prisoners tried to escape. Yet at the same time he tried to put everything into perspective by stressing that the number of escapes had decreased. 'In 1990, 75 escapes from closed prisons occurred, last year only 50, this year 29. From those 29, sixteen prisoners have already been recaptured. But the [violence used by] escaping prisoners does increase.'[63]

Second, Kosto accepted the Hoekstra Inquiry's recommendation to build two new extra special secured units, that is, supermax prisons, but he did not accept Hoekstra's recommendation to create an additional SSU category of prisoners, that is, the ones whose escape would create societal unrest.[64] He asked for extra money to build these new prisons.[65] Building these new SSUs would take time, of course and, in the meantime, better ways to improve security in the courtyard would be investigated, a study group would continuously monitor security in all prisons[66] and security in the SSUs was increased.[67] The latter measure did not go down well with SSU prisoners, who filed a complaint in court about how increased security had negatively affected their treatment.

Media attention, which was already high following the De Grittenborgh-outbreak, increased even further when prison officers made allegations that Governor Kranendonk of De Grittenborgh had known about the impending escape and that he had knowingly and wilfully done nothing to prevent the escape in order to publicly criticize Kosto's prison policy.[68] On 19 November 1992, Governor Kranendonk was suspended and a police investigation commenced to determine what had happened.[69] The VDPI was not too pleased about the governor's suspension. The relationship between governors and headquarters, already in a fragile state (Boin, 2001b),[70] deteriorated rapidly. The VDPI sent a letter[71] with an ultimatum: governor Kranendonk should be reinstated as governor of De Grittenborgh (Hoogeveen) by Monday 30 November noon the latest. In the letter, governors expressed their surprise at the suspension. 'Non-verified information forms the basis for a publicly expressed measure. The decision to suspend is based on rumours. Carefulness and legal protection, as the fundament of decent administration, have not been taken into account.'[72] As the letter did not produce any results, the governors decided to boycott regional meetings with headquarters.[73] In the end, the investigation showed that the governor had indeed received a translation of a phone conversation in which the impending escape was mentioned, but that the governor had not purposefully ignored the information to put Kosto's policy in a bad light. The governor's suspension was ended on 8 December 1992.[74]

The next day, the Ministry of Justice's budget was discussed in Parliament. MPs severely criticized the Ministry of Justice. VVD MP Korthals, for instance, thought:

> … government is not doing its job properly. … The trouble with that [people sent away] is that the cabinet does not warn us that this is going to happen. Instead, we have to read in the newspapers that category A [suspects] are sent home. This creates a huge shock. Moreover, when an 'interpellatie' debate on this topic is requested, then within a matter of days or a couple of weeks an additional capacity of 600 cells is possible. Escapes also occur. … Time after time, [you told us] that one should not imprison people in such a way that they can no longer harbour any hope of escape. What happens next? The Hoekstra Inquiry is installed, headed not by a civil servant of the Ministry of Justice but of the Ministry of General Affairs. The report states that extra SSUs are needed. Chairman! This is running after the facts, which is caused by a lack of leadership from the Ministry of Justice.[75]

CDA MP Soutendijk-van Appeldoorn agreed with Korthals. 'As I have said before, the chain is as strong as its weakest link. Fighting crime is not credible when suspects are sent home because of cell shortage or when helicopters pick up prisoners. That is why the CDA has advocated the need for sufficient capacity for years now. … [I]t is therefore unbelievable that the JR-120 budget has been cut by 16 million guilders.'[76] She also found it incredible that Kosto and Hirsch Ballin were still defending their decision not to opt for double-bunking with the argument of privacy. She thought that the policy makers were still valuing privacy higher than the safety of citizens.[77] PvdA MP Van der Berg pointed out that the Ministry of Justice not only faced budget cuts, on the contrary. She was pleased 'that the cabinet has decided this summer to reallocate money from Defence to Justice and Internal Affairs for external and internal safety. It was right for the Ministry of Justice to be spared the rounds of budget cuts and receive additional money to fight organized crime and social security fraud'.[78]

A New Year, a New Beginning?

Following the parliamentary debate, the media's attention decreased slowly (see also Figure 4.1 in the next section), while giving ample attention to any (attempt to) escape. The new year, however, held some nasty surprises for the Dutch Prison Service. On 6 January 1993, three prisoners escaped from the youth ward of De Grittenborgh (Hoogeveen). One prison officer was seriously injured; two prison officers received only minor injuries. This escape was particularly painful after the recent SSU escape from the same prison. The mayor of Hoogeveen told the press: 'De Grittenborgh is not suitable to hold long-term prisoners. If the prison is not refurbished soon, then these prisoners should be incarcerated somewhere else. … The line of what is acceptable and what is not has been crossed.'[79] Prison officers' unions were shocked by the violent nature of the escape and said that tension between prisoners and officers in prisons had risen.[80] One prison officers' union wanted Kosto to install an especially tough regime – somewhat like SSU security regimes – for people suspected of seriously violent crimes in remand centres.[81]

In response to the latest escape from De Grittenborgh, police security outside prisons was increased[82] and prisoners' freedom of movement was limited.[83] Kosto said, 'If I have to choose between my prison officers, society, and prisoners, then I will choose in favour of the first two'.[84]

D66 MP Wolffensperger did not take the increase in police security outside prisons very serious. 'Kosto's remark is not very realistic considering the current discussions about a shortage in police men. Kosto probably said it just to reassure the public.'[85] PvdA MP Zijlstra also doubted whether the measure could be implemented. CDA MP Van den Burg was the only one enthusiastic about the measure. At the same time, however, the CDA party was bewildered that headquarters had ignored an emergency letter by the Board of Visitors of De Grittenborgh about recent incidents.[86] A discussion about whether increased security resulted in more violence and aggression ensued. PvdA MP Zijlstra did not see any connection between heightened security and aggression, though he did say that further isolating prisoners would be a bad idea because that would result in more tension in prisons.[87] A governor working at the Bijlmerprison (Amsterdam) and a lawyer disagreed. In their view, better security meant that prisoners could no longer escape the old-fashioned way and instead opted to use violence to escape.[88] President of the

VDPI Boeij opposed increasing security measures for all prisoners, because that would look as if all prisoners had to be punished for the fact that some prisoners had managed to escape. He acknowledged that increased security was needed for a certain type of prisoner. At the same time, he was aware that increased security led to hostage taking and violence towards prison officers. Boeij recommended putting armed guards in prison towers to create additional security in SSUs and youth prisons containing long-term prisoners.[89]

To top things off, on 8 January two prisoners managed to escape from the Bijlmerprison (Amsterdam) in a very classical way: they tied sheets together to climb out of their cell. The media had a field day and pictures of the sheets hanging from the window were on the front pages of the newspapers.

On 15 January 1993, the court came back with its verdict on SSU regimes. The stricter SSU regime was not considered unjust, but the Ministry of Justice should look for less intrusive security measures (Sancties, 1993: 195–200). The judge recommended allowing unsupervised family visits and easing up on phone privileges where lawyers and probation service was concerned.[90]

In a letter to Parliament, Kosto announced plans to punish prisoners who used violence during their escape by not automatically granting them early release. Moreover, Hirsch Ballin and Kosto wanted to increase the punishment for accomplices from a maximum sentence of two years to a maximum sentence of four years. Besides these plans, Kosto also decided to implement a number of building, technical, and organizational changes to limit the chances of hostage taking, that is, a so-called closed doors policy whereby doors would automatically close and remain closed during hostage takings. A study group that had investigated how to improve security in closed prisons and how to prevent hostage takings provided the basis for these changes.[91] In his letter, Kosto also referred to security measures already taken: all prison governors had been asked to diagnose their own prison in terms of escape risk and security measures in closed prisons had been increased. Regarding the latter security measure, money to increase security would have to come from the prison service's own budget. Kosto believed that these measures would improve security and safety within prisons. Nevertheless, escapes could not be ruled out completely.[92]

Plans to punish prisoners who tried to escape by not granting them early release did not sit well with the Union of Offenders and the Coornhert Liga (the organization for penal law reform). The largest union for prison officers, on the other hand, was very glad about this decision.[93] Prison officers, however, were not too keen to have closed doors.[94]

Escapes continued to occur. On 21 January 1993, a man escaped from a remand centre by helicopter.[95] On 23 January 1993, another four prisoners managed to escape from the Bijlmerprison (Amsterdam) with the help of sheets. Kosto was very irritated that such an escape could happen so soon after the previous one. A security expert was sent to investigate how security could be improved in the Bijlmerprison.[96] The media were not too impressed with the prison service's record of keeping prisoners inside. The *Algemeen Dagblad*, for instance, wrote: 'Stricter measures are needed immediately. … It is very annoying that after the similar escape on 8 January 1993 no harsh internal measures have been taken. It is a disgrace that this prison has not learnt anything from the previous incidents.'[97] According to *De Volkskrant*, the second escape from the Bijlmerprison had severely embarrassed the Dutch Prison Service, but Kosto did not consider it an option to station armed guards outside the prison as suggested by VDPI president Boeij.[98] Despite Kosto's aversion to armed guards outside the prison, these additional forces were added. Kosto was not amused and as soon as he heard about the armed guards, he had them removed.[99]

On 30 January 1993, Kosto announced during a radio interview that the Ministry of Justice was to write a new White Paper.[100] Kosto explained in response to a remark made by a journalist that governors thought that the current regime was too humane and prisoners had too much legal protection: 'I think it is indeed time to consider a number of developments within the prison service. That is why I want to write a new White Paper. The last White Paper, *Task and Future*, dates back from 1982. Times have changed.'[101]

On 18 February 1993, two prisoners escaped from a remand centre in Den Bosch. They threatened a female prison officer and took her hostage.[102] On 19 February 1993, a man escaped from the remand SSU De Schie (Rotterdam). He was returning to his cell from the gym when he took out a gun and escaped while trying to shoot a prison officer.[103] On the same day, a man used sheets to escape from a remand centre in Zwaag.[104] According to a spokesperson of the Ministry of Justice, Kosto 'was really looking forward to the two new SSUs'.[105]

As a result of the escapes, a debate started about the regimes in prisons. On 2 March 1993, the issue was discussed in the Select Committee on Justice. CDA MP Soutendijk-van Appeldoorn started the meeting by saying that the CDA party was in favour of a more sober regime, that is, less communal and educational activities, for certain types of prisoners. In her opinion, there was too much emphasis on proper treatment of prisoners and not enough attention for keeping them behind bars. She was pleased that Kosto seemed to be heading in the same direction as he was writing a new White Paper. She ended her speech by stating that it was shocking that 3,000 people had been sent home because of cell shortages in 1992.[106] VVD MP Korthals did not want to pay any attention to cell shortage in this meeting, though it was a very important topic especially now that almost all political parties agreed to fight crime more intensively. Like Soutendijk-van Appeldoorn, Korthals paid attention to the possibility that the 1982 White Paper *Task and Future* was outdated. 'No one is against humane imprisonment and rehabilitation, but the prison population has changed dramatically. The question then rises whether this philosophy is still valid.'[107] PvdA MP Zijlstra was glad that the number of escapes had decreased in 1992, but he was distraught that escapes had become more and more violent. He was, however, not in favour of ever more security and harsher regimes in prisons because that would endanger the people working in prisons. A balance should be struck between a safe society and a safe working place for prison officers. He was afraid that more security would lead to more violence in prisons. Regarding cell shortage, Zijlstra told Kosto 'the large number of people who are being sent away negatively affect the credibility of government as the upholder of law and order'.[108]

In his reply to the MPs' statements, Kosto stressed that 'every escape is one too many. Yet, there were only 44 escapes in 1992 compared to 118 in 1984, when we had 50% less cells'.[109] Kosto hoped to have the new White Paper finished by the end of the year. Round table conferences with governors were conducted to discuss the matter and a large meeting, which would include MPs, was planned for May 1993.[110] He explained to the MPs that only regimes in SSUs had been restricted, but that regimes would be less restricted in the new SSUs because they would have maximum security.[111] However, because the current SSUs were improvised prisons, escapes could still occur in the less secure areas of the parent prison. Moreover, a budgetary balance had to be struck: 'Should one invest so much money in order to make escapes completely impossible or should one use the resources to increase cell capacity and stop sending away people?'[112] Kosto also agreed with the MPs' remarks on cell shortage. 'Cell capacity has been increased ... yet the number of people sent away has increased. This is completely unacceptable. During the spring cabinet negotiations about the Ministry of Justice's budget, a request for additional funding to pay for 1,000 extra cells will be submitted.'[113]

Interest groups were quick to respond to the select committee's meeting. VDPI President Boeij made it clear to the press that he thought MPs should not interfere with prison regimes.[114] The Coornhert Liga considered the call for 1,000 extra cells 'hysterical' because 'we do not have a cell shortage ... there are just too many people in prison'. Moreover, 'a stricter regime would lead ... to a deterioration of the relationship between prisoners and prison officers ... and result in more and more violent incidents in prison'.[115] The Union of Offenders and the Dutch Federation of Probation Organizations rejected a stricter regime as 'asocial and inhumane'.[116]

Another Escape Debacle

On 30 March 1993, two armed prisoners attempted to escape from SSU De Schie (Rotterdam), but were captured right outside the prison complex. They had a gun in their possession.[117] On 3 April 1993, six out of seven prisoners out of cell escaped from SSU De Geerhorst (Sittard) at the same time.[118] On 4 April 1993, a prisoner managed to escape from De Grittenborgh (Hoogeveen) by changing clothes with his brother.[119]

Every newspaper paid generous attention to the escapes. Interest groups expressed their views in the media as well. According to an AbvaKabo (one of the prison officers' unions) spokesperson, security of prison officers had to become the first priority of the prison service. 'Prisoners know that the new SSUs are being built … and they think they ought to try to escape while they still can. … An interim measure is needed. Those 30 [SSU prisoners] should no longer be allowed to interact with other [SSU] prisoners.' And prison officers should deal with only one SSU prisoner at a time.[120] The Christian Federation of Civil Servants (another union) thought that the SSU regime had become too limited. The Coornhert Liga agreed. De Jonge, spokesperson of the Coornhert Liga: 'The current regime has turned SSU cells into tombs. Last year, a dangerous dynamic has been established … When there is a spectacular escape, the media screams blue murder, and regime is restricted. As a result, more people are taken hostage, which, in turn, leads to even more stricter regimes. It's just panic policy.'[121] Prison officers of the SSU De Grittenborgh (Hoogeveen) wrote a letter to the Select Committee on Justice claiming 'the current adjustments in the SSU regime has not resulted in an increase in security, but in more pressure on prison officers. As a result, choosing to take someone hostage becomes more desirable instead of less'.[122]

Moreover, and as a result of the escape from the SSU in Sittard, coalition parties CDA and PvdA were divided on how to respond. The CDA wanted to increase security, but the PvdA thought that increased security had led to violent escapes and proposed decreasing security.[123] The VVD announced that the recent escapes indicated that an independent non-parliamentary inquiry should be held. The inquiry should investigate the relationship between prison officers and prisoners, the presence of weapons and drugs in prisons, and the rumours of corruption.[124] VVD MP Korthals said about the recent series of escapes 'I am really fed up. The Ministry of Justice's measures – increasing security – did not have the intended effects'.[125] A couple of days after the escape, Justice spokespersons of the coalition-parties PvdA and CDA announced that they were in favour of a closed door policy – similar to the British one – where doors close automatically to prevent prisoners from taking people hostage.[126]

Minister of Justice Hirsch Ballin did not intend to ease the SSU regime. 'Do not expect to keep [Category A] prisoners inside when using a more friendly way to detain them.'[127] Junior Minister of Justice Kosto 'regretted' the SSU escape, 'but we just have to make do'.[128] He thought that problems would diminish once the new SSUs were operational.[129] He also was of the opinion that the abundant media attention was partly to blame for the violent escapes; prisoners showed copycat behaviour.[130]

In response to the commotion, Kosto asked civil servants to investigate the possibility of implementing a system of earned privileges, that is, a system where prisoners would have to earn privileges. Kosto hoped to be able to publish the results of this investigation in his White Paper.[131] Kosto also planned to go to England to study the prison service over there.[132] Another reaction by Kosto was not to await the new SSUs, but to place prisoners in a temporary SSU (TEBI) in Nieuw Vosseveld (Vught) to await their transfer to the real SSUs. Following the SSU escape from De Geerhorst (Sittard), there were a number of telephone conferences between 'the top of the Ministry of Justice', Koehorst, governor of Nieuw Vosseveld (Vught) and governors of SSUs.[133] Governor Koehorst and headquarters agreed pretty quickly to host SSU prisoners at Nieuw Vosseveld till the new SSUs were operational.[134] Kosto announced the decision on 23 April 1993.[135]

In a letter to Parliament dated 19 May 1993, Kosto informed Parliament about the internal investigation into the SSU escape from De Geerhorst (Sittard) and the measures taken following the escape. The investigation had shown that seven prisoners had been out of cell instead of the maximum of four prisoners as indicated by the restricted SSU regime. The investigators concluded that it did not matter that seven prisoners were out of cell, the escape could also have occurred with only four persons present because of the bad building structure. Measures following the escape included the decision to construct a temporary SSU at Nieuw Vosseveld (Vught) to place prisoners there while awaiting the construction of the real new SSUs. Kosto argued that five reasons had convinced him to take this measure. First, Vught was one of the places where the new SSUs were to be built. Second, experienced prison officers worked at Nieuw Vosseveld prison. Third, Nieuw Vosseveld prison complex had a good level of security. Fourth, the building to be used as a temporary SSU had structural building qualities needed to create a properly functioning SSU. And fifth, a suitable anti-hostage policy could be used in this prison. The downsides of this decision – temporary loss of SSU cells and additional funding – were considered to be negligible.[136] Until the temporary SSU would become operational, regimes in SSUs would be restricted even further. The most important measures were allowing a maximum of two people to participate in communal activities, removing objects that could be used to threaten personnel, searching prisoners whenever they leave their cells, and increasing police control outside of SSU prisons.[137]

Though escapes did not suddenly stop after 23 April, the number of escapes declined – and once the temporary SSU (2 August 1993) and the official SSU (7 August 1997)[138] were operational, no SSU prisoner has ever escaped – and media attention started to dwindle. However, the Dutch Prison Service did not get any rest as another unfortunate incident concerning cell shortage occurred.

The Final Straw: Sending a Murder Suspect Home

In April 1993, cell shortage was put back onto the media agenda. The cause of this attention was a record high number of people who were sent home (see Figure 4.1). *NRC Handelsblad*, for example, wrote that Amsterdam's public prosecution needed additional cells to handle the large number of street crime suspects. In order to provide these cells, public prosecutions in other cities such as The Hague and Rotterdam had to give up a number of their cells to imprison Amsterdam prisoners. As a result, 16 Category A prisoners were sent home on 13 April 1993 in The Hague because no cells were available for them. Other people were sent away as well such as 'eleven burglars, a man who had thrown boiling water on his wife's head, a man who had threatened with arson, a fraud, and a car thief who was running a large-scale operation'.[139] The same problem occurred in Rotterdam, where all burglars had been sent away from remand prisons to make room for violent offenders. Yet, there were still not enough cells available in Rotterdam and the local District Attorney had to decide which violent offender to send home.[140]

In a response to the accusation that cell shortage was now plaguing other cities because they had to give up cells for Amsterdam, Minister of Justice Hirsch Ballin said that these cells had been promised to Amsterdam, but they had not yet become available to Amsterdam. Instead, Hirsch Ballin saw the cell shortage in The Hague and Rotterdam as something of a 'more structural nature'.[141]

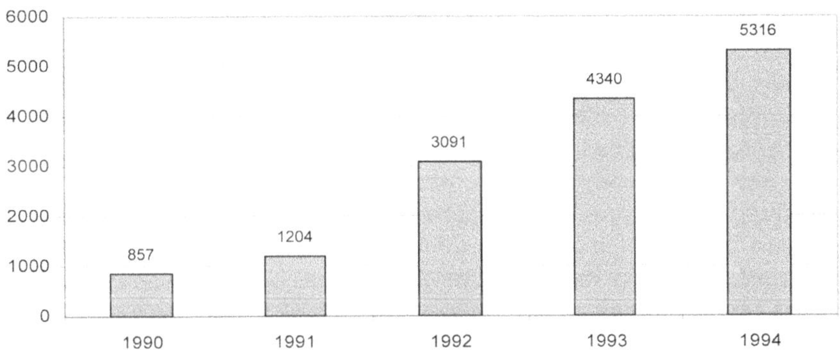

Figure 4.1 Number of adults sent away 1990–1994

Source: DJI (1999: 17).

Attention on cell shortage received an additional push when a 19-year-old who had confessed to a murder was sent home in May 1993. Almost a week later, he was arrested again, this time for fighting. During his interrogation, he confessed to having committed more than 20 violent street robberies in the previous week.[142]

The VVD made it clear that 'enough is enough'.[143] VVD MP Korthals wanted the minister to resign.[144] PvdA MP Zijlstra declared, 'this cannot continue to occur'.[145] Such mistakes 'violate the citizens' sense of justice'.[146] Even the Minister of Justice's own party, CDA, turned against him. CDA MP Soutendijk-van Appeldoorn gave Hirsch Ballin a last warning: 'If another serious criminal is released because no cells are available, then Hirsch Ballin must resign.'[147] Moreover, the CDA party thought it to be 'unacceptable that Hirsch Ballin, despite repeated warnings, had not taken any measures to stop sending away suspects of serious crimes'.[148] If Hirsch Ballin did not come up with proper measures to deal with cell shortage, he should leave.[149] CDA MP Soutendijk-van Appeldoorn said: 'This diminishes your credibility. The situation demands unorthodox measures. We have suggested them again and again: double-bunking, extending the use of police cells, and house arrest. This can be realized on a short-term notice. A bunk bed is easily made.'[150] Kosto was still set against double-bunking, because it would make prison officers' jobs more difficult which, in turn, would lead to more aggression and more attempts to escape. Moreover, the law had to be changed to allow double-bunking. Kosto's reply that double-bunking would also result in an increase in financial costs was deemed 'unbelievable' by CDA MP Soutendijk-van Appeldoorn. She also thought that double-bunking small-time offenders would not create any additional problems.[151]

Amsterdam Chief of Police Nordholt supported Soutendijk-van Appeldoorn's idea to change the law concerning the use of police cells. This would allow the Ministry to extend a person's stay in a police cell, which at the time was legally restricted to three days at the most.[152]

The media's coverage of cell shortages was negative in tone. *Trouw* wrote, for example, 'The Public Prosecution Office has to watch bad guys. But it also has to watch out a little for its own credibility'.[153] The *Algemeen Dagblad* completely understood the MPs' outrage. 'It is just simply unbelievable that something like this could have happened.'[154] The extra cells planned for 1996 were just insufficient and too late to deal with the existing problems. 'In the meantime, emergency measures have to be taken. Unconventional solutions should not be shunned. ... Formal rules can be broken when necessary.'[155]

MPs demanded an emergency debate. Minister of Justice Hirsch Ballin had to cut short an EU-summit for Ministers of Justice in Kopenhagen, Denmark, in order to attend this emergency debate.

The emergency debate was held on the night of Wednesday 2 June 1993. MPs criticized Hirsch Ballin and Kosto for not having been able to end the cell shortage, but the tone of their comments was not so harsh as it had been in the newspapers. The main reason for CDA MP Soutendijk-van Appeldoorn to be more mild in her criticisms – she only said that she was shocked by the sending home of a suspect of such a serious offence[156] – was that Hirsch Ballin and Kosto had presented measures to deal with cell shortage. PvdA MP Zijlstra criticized the release of the murder suspect. It 'violates the feelings of justice of the public and frustrates police'.[157] Zijlstra could not understand why every hotel chain in the world was able to work with a system that told you where rooms were available and the prison service could not.[158]

Hirsch Ballin agreed: 'All our feelings of justice have been hurt because of these incidents. ... [W]hat happened in Amsterdam is incomprehensible.'[159] He explained that the larger number of sentences and that the increased length and severity of sentences caused cell shortage.[160] He also defended himself by summing up the measures taken in the previous 12 months: building an additional 600 cells, creating an emergency plan, building another 100 cells following the motion by Van der Heijden/Stoffelen which released money to build these cells and government approval for the building of 1,000 more cells in the spring of 1993 during the budget negotiations – the Ministry of Justice was one of the few ministries to receive additional funding instead of facing budget cuts.

Nonetheless, cells remained scarce and Hirsch Ballin agreed that extra measures were needed to deal with cell shortage. Hirsch Ballin and Kosto therefore presented a set of emergency measures. These measures consisted of moving forward the building of these 1,000 cells, building approximately 2,000 cells extra within the next two years and a set of temporary measures to deal with cell shortage at short notice. This package of emergency measures included an increase in the use of police cells, freeing up space in remand prisons that were currently still reserved for illegal aliens who had to be deported, the use of penalty cells and recreational spaces for normal suspects and prisoners and placing two prisoners in one cell by putting a camp bed in the cell.[161]

Hirsch Ballin emphasized that double-bunking would only be possible if extra personnel became available. Additional prison officers were needed because double-bunking created extra stress at night and weekends and it also created stress because prison officers had to deal with a difficult prison population. Thus, double-bunking as well as the other proposed emergency measures cost money. That money 'is not yet available. We will discuss this with the cabinet'.[162]

Junior Minister Kosto was still not in favour of double-bunking, even though he and the Minister had agreed to allow it in case of emergency. Kosto told Parliament that double-bunking was expensive (the measure would cost approximately 50 million guilders a year) and that there were risks of rape, HIV infection and of placing mentally disturbed people with others who were not mentally disturbed (cf. Fiselier, 1992).[163]

The Cabinet discussed what had been said during the debate and approved the measures as presented by Hirsch Ballin and Kosto, but considered that a further investigation of the extra 2,000 cells was needed.[164] On 17 July 1993, the Cabinet approved Hirsch Ballin's request for 2,000 additional cells.[165] Moreover, another temporary measure to deal with cell shortage was implemented in August 1993: the 103 per cent rule. This rule meant that prisons would have to accept more prisoners than there were cells for – hence '103 per cent'. Double-bunking could be used to reach this norm or every available space, including broom cupboards, could be converted into cells.[166] Another measure implemented to control cell shortage was the creation of an additional category: Category A+ prisoners were prisoners who could not be sent home in any circumstance.[167] From 8 July 1994, double-bunking was allowed to avoid sending these Category A+ prisoners away.[168]

Following the debate in June 1993, attention on the Prison Service in the media and Parliament continued for a short while before it started to dwindle. This does not mean that the attention of MPs and media ended completely. There was some attention, but it was neither as intensive nor as negative as during the previous months. The Select Committee on Justice, for instance, discussed SSUs after the summer break on 25 November 1993.[169] It also discussed the White Paper *Effective Detention* on 17 March[170] and 11 April 1994.[171] The White Paper will be discussed in the remainder of this section.

The White Paper, Effective Detention

The White Paper *Effective Detention* (*Werkzame Detentie*) was published on 4 February 1994. The officially cited reasons for publishing a new White Paper were fourfold: the changing demands on the prison service as a result of an integrated crime policy; the changing prison population because criminals were more hardened (cf. WODC, 1997; Helgers, 1993); the violence of escapes; and the increase in cell capacity (Ministry of Justice, 1994: 4). The title of the new White Paper, *Effective Detention*, refers to two dominant ideas in this paper, that is, that detention should be effective and that prisoners should effectively use their time by working. In this section, the most important notions incorporated in the White Paper will be described.

The White Paper focused on security: 'Escapes have to be prevented. Optimal security is therefore one of the key aims of prison policy' (Ministry of Justice, 1994: 26). Measures to improve security included the building of two new SSUs and a closed doors policy.

In addition, a new prison regime was introduced: the standard regime. This regime implies that prisoners have to work instead of receiving rehabilitation programmes. Only approximately 20 per cent of the prisoners who were really motivated and suitable could follow rehabilitation programmes (Ministry of Justice, 1994: 16–18; cf. Franke, 1996: 311; Boin, 1998: 101).

In terms of cell capacity, the White Paper summed up the measures taken to increase cell capacity, including building extra cells, the 103 per cent rule, a new software programme to make optimal use of prison cells and double-bunking. Regarding the double-bunking, the White Paper noted that it was already used for about 400 spaces and that this number would increase in the future. Moreover, as it was so important to avoid sending people away, double-bunking would be allowed when possible. People who could double bunk were illegal aliens and people who were sent to prison as an alternative punishment, for example, they had defaulted on their fines or community service. Prisoners in preventive detention were considered eligible for double-bunking as well. 'From the view of control, double-bunking will mainly be used for alternative prisoners and illegal aliens' (Ministry of Justice, 1994: 33).

The White Paper ended by noting that changes in personnel and organization were necessary. Headquarters would be solely responsible for the main lines of policy while executive responsibilities were delegated to the field. The Dutch Prison Service would become an agency on 1 January 1995 (Ministry of Justice, 1994: 39).

Crisis and Reform in the Dutch Prison Service

Before discussing how the institutional crisis led to reform (see Chapter 7), it is important to show that there was a crisis and that reform was the outcome of this crisis process. An institutional crisis occurs when the institutional structure of a policy sector 'experiences a relatively strong decline in (followed by unusually low levels of) legitimacy' (Boin and 't Hart, 2000: 13). This section will show that an increase in negative attention towards the way the prison service was performing its duties did indeed occur. This indicates that the prison service's legitimacy declined in 1992–1993. The section ends by describing whether the measures taken in this case constitute reform or not.

From Incidents to Institutional Crisis

The various incidents, from a helicopter escape to hostage taking and sending a murder suspect home, resulted in increasingly negative public attention. The media portrayed the prison service as lax in security. Especially the violent escapes, often combined with hostage taking, commanded the attention of the media because violent escapes were a rare event in the Dutch Prison Service (see Table 4.1).

Normally, the prison service does not get much coverage in the newspapers (De Jong and Van Vliet, 1993). An occasional incident may receive a small column in the newspapers, but that is usually all. As Figure 4.2 shows, the media's attention on the Dutch Prison Service increased immensely in 1992–1993 (cf. De Jong and Van Vliet, 1993). Every incident resulted in another peak in the media's attention. The media's attention towards escapes increased dramatically after the classical escapes from Bijlmerprison (Amsterdam) in January 1993 and the SSU escapes from De Schie (Rotterdam) and De Geerhorst (Sittard) in March and April 1993. Similarly, the media's attention towards cell shortage rose after the incidents in May 1992 and the release of a murder suspect in May 1993.

At first, the newspaper articles were neutral in tone and only described the events. The tone of reporting the events, however, became more and more negative. On 2 June 1993, *Trouw*, for example, wrote:

> Parliament acts now ... because a suspect is involved who is clearly a dangerous person for society. Parliament normally responds sporadically to

> the dozens of people who are sent home (last year over 3,000) because of lack of cells. But this incident is seen as a deplorable excess. The freed man was suspected of manslaughter, was part of a gang of illegal aliens who tried to survive by robbing and selling drugs, and he had already confessed to stabbing a boy to death on 7 May [1993].[172]

An article in *De Telegraaf* provides an example of what was being said and written about the Dutch Prison Service:

> [T]his year, more than 1,300 suspects of serious offences have been sent home. Even people who have committed life-threatening crimes and rapists could not all be held behind bars. That constitutes a serious and intolerable corrosion of our legal order. Minister Hirsch Ballin and junior Minister Kosto are responsible for this corrosion.[173]

A year before these articles appeared in the newspapers, the *Algemeen Dagblad* had already written:

> CDA and PvdA have submitted a motion in which they insist that [the Ministry of Justice should come up with] an emergency plan, but the disconcerting truth is that we will have to wait till Prinsjesdag before we get any clarity on the matter. MPs from governing parties were too easily appeased by Minister Hirsch Ballin's promise that by the time of Prinsjesdag, he will be able to suggest definite plans. The number of people sent home because of cell shortage has risen to over 50% in Amsterdam and Rotterdam. This high percentage is unacceptable.[174]

As can be seen in Figure 4.2, the two problems were linked in the media in February 1993. Before February 1993, media attention was either focused on escapes or on cell shortages. From February 1993 onwards, the press started to address both problems in one article. After the Sittard escapes, for example, articles appeared referring to cell shortages when describing the functioning of the prison service. References were also made to escapes in articles focusing on the release of a murder suspect.[175] At the same time, the media's attention on the Dutch Prison Service started to intensify. The *Algemeen Dagblad*, for example, wrote:

> The Ministry of Justice finally seems to do something about the acute shortage of cells and the easy way in which prisoners can escape. Thursday, the cabinet decided to build a couple of hundred new cells. Yesterday, Junior Minister of Justice Kosto announced special measures for escape-prone prisoners. Both measures have to be implemented as quickly as possible. It must be very frustrating for the Public Prosecution, the judiciary, and police to see criminals walking around again because there is no cell available or

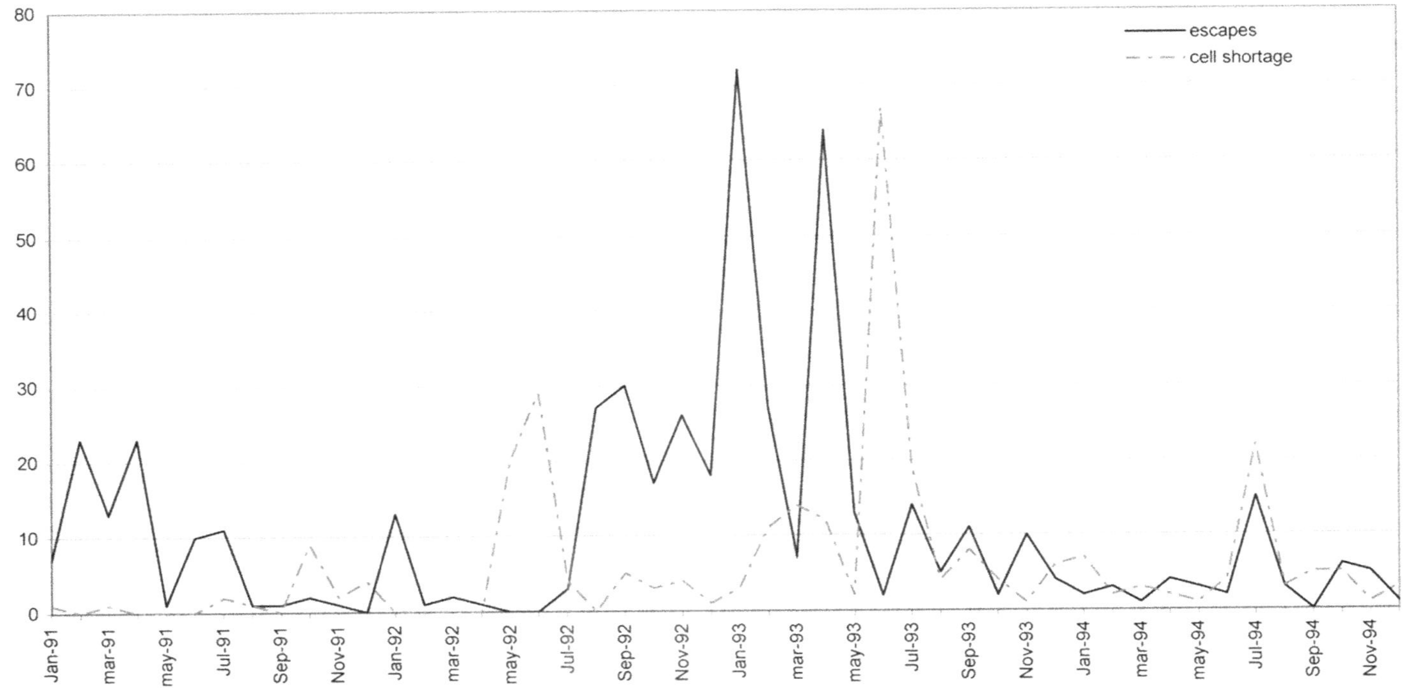

Figure 4.2 Media attention: number of articles published in the media on cell shortages and escapes between 1991–1994

Note: Based on the Dutch Prison Service's newspaper clipping service.

Source: Boin and Resodihardjo (2000: 71).

> there is insufficient security. The public's criticism is enormous and must have had a very negative effect on the motivation of police, judges, and DAs. It also negatively affected the credibility of politics in general.[176]

MPs' attention followed along the same lines as the media attention. The Dutch Prison Service normally does not command a great deal of attention in parliament. As Figure 4.3 shows, this changed in 1992–1993 (cf. Kelk, 2001: 492). Figure 4.3 shows the number of times attention was paid to the prison service in parliament. This attention ranged from meetings in select committees to debates and to questions asked about the number of people sent home, the number of escapes, and the measures taken to tackle both problems. Figure 4.3 serves as a very rough indicator of parliamentary attention because any event in which the prison service featured has been counted as one event, regardless of the weight of the event, for example, parliamentary debate or just a letter from a minister.

As Figure 4.3 shows, the MPs' attention first increased following the publication of the National Court of Audit's report on the ineffective use of cells in October 1991. In June 1992, attention was focused on the measures taken by Hirsch Ballin and Kosto to deal with cell shortage. In December 1992, MPs discussed building new SSUs and the suspension of governor Kranendonk. The SSU escapes and the release of a murder suspect in April-May 1993 generated further attention. Finally, in December 1993 amendments to the penal code concerning escapes were considered in Parliament.

The budgetary debate was another indicator of the priority Dutch MPs were giving the prison service. Each year during the budgetary debates, MPs can discuss any topic they want in their allocated time slot as long as it relates to the ministry whose budget is being discussed. As time is limited, MPs have to decide what to focus on. In the parliamentary debates on the 1992 Ministry of Justice's budget, MPs asked a number of questions focusing on the report of the National Court of Audit. The debate on the 1993 budget almost solely focused on the failing prison service. Though MPs did pay attention to the prison service when debating the 1994 budget, attention had already waned and was no longer negative in tone (cf. Singer-Dekker, 1992: 72).

From December 1992 onwards, cell shortage and escapes got linked in the Parliamentary arena. VVD MP Korthals, for instance, said during the emergency debate on cell shortage on 2 June 1993:

> We face a range of problems. The number of escapes is seriously increasing. First, the junior minister said that that was just part and parcel of a prison service and that we have to learn to live with escapes. Otherwise aggression in prisons will only increase. Measures were limited to responding to those incidents. Structural solutions were only presented after the heli-escape, when MPs were demanding action. Nevertheless, escapes continue to occur.[177]

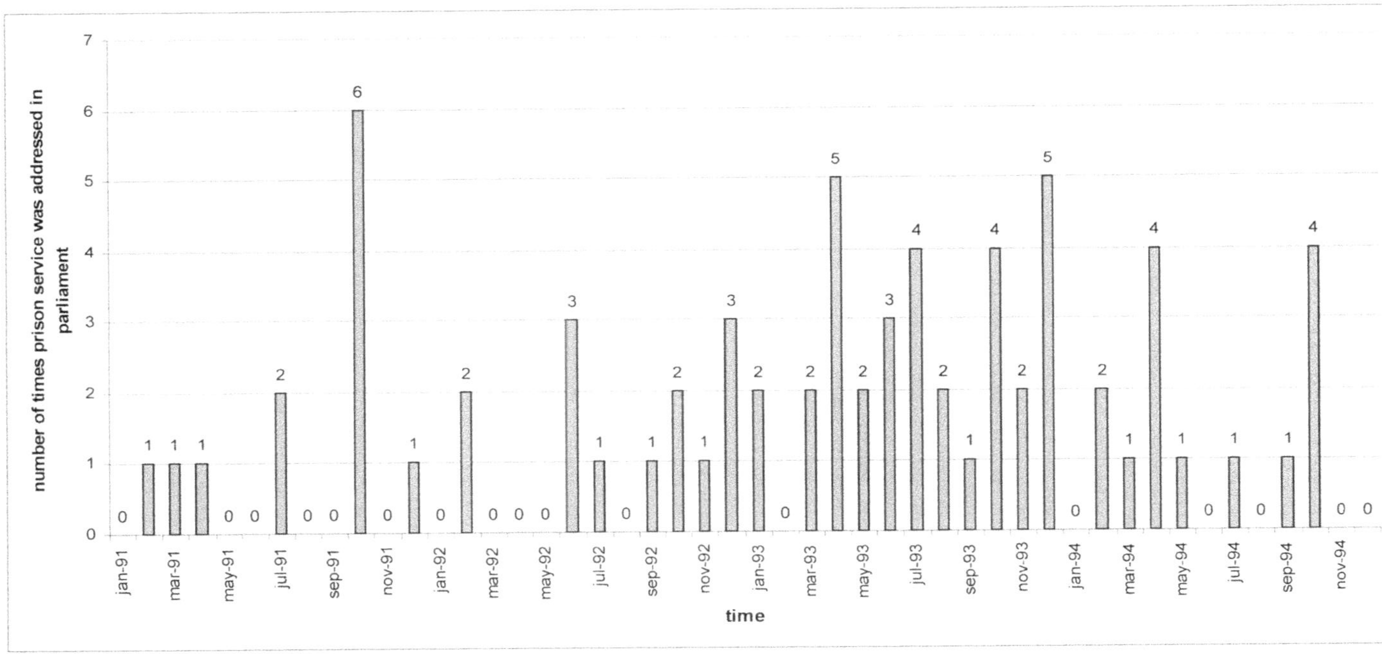

Figure 4.3 **Number of times parliament addressed cell shortage and escapes in debates, meetings, or letters in 1991-1994**

Note: Motions are excluded as they are submitted during debates.

Another distinct feature of MPs' attention towards the prison service was that the CDA was attacking its own Minister of Justice. It is surprising that calls for resignation not only originated from the VVD and PvdA, but also from the CDA. Although CDA MP Soutendijk-van Appeldoorn did not demand Hirsch Ballin's resignation in Parliament, she did threaten him when she said to journalists: 'If another serious criminal is released because no cells are available, then Hirsch Ballin must resign.'[178] This is surprising because Hirsch Ballin was believed to be able to achieve great things together with future party leader Brinkman[179] and Hirsch Ballin was seen as the person who formulated the CDA's ideology (cf. Downes, 1998: 156).[180] Possibly the upcoming national elections played a role in the CDA's stance towards its own minister– elections were to be held in less than a year on 3 May 1994.

As explained by the *Rotterdams Dagblad*: 'A party that lets a minister stay after murderers are freed does not score very well with the public. That is why the CDA wants to show its teeth under the banner of enough is enough.'[181]

Furthermore, the CDA was trying to depict itself as a party that valued norms and that was tough on crime.[182] When defending the Ministry of Justice's budget for 1994, Hirsch Ballin said:

> What we need to do in the next cabinet-reign is to use new tools and use a judicial organization that has been strengthened to fight organized crime and the dangers of violence. The word "fight" may seem too harsh, but it is exactly what I mean. That is, as far as I am concerned, the essential part. Police, Public Prosecution, and judiciary must fight a battle that is basically a battle for who has the power in our society. ... Protecting civilians from violence is one of the most fundamental tasks of a state.[183]

Meanwhile, the penal climate was changing. 'Crime became a national obsession. Public opinion polls pushed crime to the top of the political agenda. Police chiefs of the big cities made national headlines with their battle cries against the rising crime tide' (Boin, 2001a: 337; cf. Van de Bunt, 2004). The penal climate had become tougher since the 1980s. 'Economic depression and unemployment, a sharp increase in crime, an increase of drug-related trouble, and politics sliding to the right, resulted in a quickly toughening of the Dutch penal climate in the 1980s' (Franke, 1996: 308; cf. van Swaaningen and De Jonge, 1995: 42–3; Moerings, 1994). The CDA party was sliding to the right as well, with its emphasis on norms and values and its toughness towards crime. Failing on this topic proved detrimental to Hirsch Ballin's position during the institutional crisis as even his own party started to frown upon his actions – or lack thereof.

In short, there was a substantive increase in negative attention from the media and MPs towards the Dutch Prison Service regarding the way escapes and cell shortages were handled. Values and policies on double-bunking and concentrating SSU prisoners were questioned. Policy makers in this policy sector faced an institutional crisis.

According to Boin (2001a: 340),

> Escape rates had shown a downward trend since 1990, but the dramatic dimensions of these escapes created a common opinion that 'Dutch prisons were leaking.' The damage to the prison system was enormous. The public perception of the prison system as an expensive hotel chain, with great service and no vacancies was confirmed. The escapes signalled incompetence, bad security and a lack of discipline. With 1993 being a pre-election year, the opposition was all too willing to put political pressure on the responsible Minister of Justice and, indirectly, on the prison system itself. (Cf. Boin, 1995)

The weekly journal *HP/De Tijd* described the crisis as a period of time when PvdA and CDA were trying to show which party was more concerned about society's safety (cf. Singer-Dekker, 1994).[184] Moreover,

> a stampede of people sent away and newspapers' covers showing sheets where yet again another extra secured hardened criminal has slid down to freedom, has mobilized public opinion. Announcing a state of emergency has brought a complete army of law enforcers and security restorers into the spotlight. Anyone who has anything to do with investigation, trials or incarceration of criminals, and who has wanted to toughen things up for some time now, has used the opportunity. The label 'serious increasing crime' sticks on every form of crime and the public looks afraid but hopeful how fighters of evil join up.[185]

Dhondt writes (1993: 143–4):

> The ever continuing cell shortage, but especially the series of violent escapes from most notably the Special Security Units (SSUs) has resulted through the media in a broad public debate on the policy of the prison service. This debate is not limited to dealing with the very small group of prisoners who pose extreme security risks, but pertains to dealing with all (youth) prisoners. The tenor of this debate is that (young) prisoners are too well off. They should receive a tougher treatment (some even argue in favour of corporal punishment), which will result in better security as well as having a rehabilitative effect.

A civil servant close to the study group security installed following the Hoekstra Report said that the taking of hostages had 'reached such a scale that the situation became critical'. A senior civil servant described the sense of urgency when the escapes escalated.

> When it really went out of control, we took the following steps in a few weeks time. First, there was a meeting in The Hague with Paul Koehorst [governor Vught], other prison governors, and civil servants. This meeting lasted for one or two days. At the meeting, we concluded that we needed to do something about the wave of escapes. The realization had sunk in that within the main task of the prison service – imprisonment – there was a category of prisoners that really should not be able to escape ... but that we could not hold. This was unacceptable. Prison personnel's lives were at stake. ... Second, all governors of SSUs met to conduct the same discussion in Vught. This group realized the same things. A plenary conclusion was drawn that this could not be.

A governor added:

> Cell shortage, pressure mounted as the number of nasty incidents increased. This resulted in publicity, which in turn increased pressure even more. The Minister felt that he was under pressure. He came up with the 103 per cent rule, the A+ policy, CAP'96, and other capacity increases .... [Regarding the escapes]. The attention was really annoying. First, the newspapers started out neutral, but became increasingly critical. MPs became more critical as well: 'the prison service costs more and more money and more and more prisoners walk away. What are you guys doing?' Elting warned: 'watch out, or we will have to face a Parliamentary inquiry.' At some point, that became the biggest threat. At the same time, the escapes and hostage takings continued to occur. It was a really bad period, when the fear hit you.

Policy makers perceived the situation in terms of a crisis as well. One described the situation as follows. 'The dominant idea "government has no cells so suspects have to be sent away and if they do have a cell, then it is very easy to escape" was an undermining idea. You had to maintain the authority of government and uphold the order of law. That idea had to be stopped.' A PvdA MP said about the release of a murder suspect, 'That was the limit. [We] then asked for an emergency (*interpellatie*) debate. ... The signal was clear: something had to be done. ... MPs are sensitive about what is being said in the media because it reflects what people are thinking. We were swamped with the number of people we had to send away; we were confronted with various people being sent away'. To the question whether the minister, junior minister and policy sector were functioning properly, he responded: 'The policy sector was failing. Government has to keep these people inside prison, thus you have to address government when escapes occur. Cell shortage is also a task that government should be taking care of.' Regarding the crisis and how parliament perceived it, a senior civil servant said: 'It is very clumsy if your prisoners escape from extra secured prisons.' A member of the Hoekstra Inquiry agreed that there was a sense of urgency and pressure. 'At the same time, you had sending people away, cell shortage, and to top things off, the escapes. The whole country was laughing about it and was annoyed with it. ... It was as if the devil was playing with it.'

The Outcome of the Events: Reform

The institutional crisis ultimately resulted in five reforms in three different but linked dimensions in the prison service. These dimensions were cell shortage (allowing for double-bunking), security (concentration in a supermax prison, closed doors policy, focussing primarily on security in the new White Paper), and prison regimes (the standard regime). Each reform will be elaborated upon in the remainder of this section.

The first dimension to be reformed was cell shortage. Before the crisis broke out, Kosto had assured parliament that double-bunking was not an option.[186] By the end of the crisis, however, double-bunking had become an option in certain circumstances. Some may not see this as reform, because double-bunking was only allowed in specific circumstances. Nonetheless, for a prison service with a tradition of one person to a cell, accepting double-bunking even in this minor way was a radical change in thinking about imprisonment.[187]

Van Hattum writes 'Imprisonment has to be implemented in a very careful manner so that the punishment will not be heavier than absolutely necessary and that the punishment is not more harmful than it already is. Placing two or more persons in a cell meant for one does not comply with this view. Cell shortage is insufficient reason [to do this]. When necessary, less dangerous persons ... should be sent home instead of A or A+ prisoners' (Van Hattum, 1995: 220). A prison governor observed:

> The release of people became an issue in 1992 and 1993, resulting in CAP'96. In the meantime, there was a feverish search for means to get cell shortage back under control. Of course, there was the double-bunking discussion again. The unions were against this. Fortunately, double-bunking did not go through, except if you got a category A+ prisoner on Friday night. Then you placed an extra bed in a cell or in a broom closet, but you didn't send him away. The Minister had promised that. This was the 103 per cent policy. Governors received bonuses if they could refurbish offices into cells. That money was interesting.

In terms of the second dimension, that is, security, prison policy was reformed in three ways. First, Kosto accepted Hoekstra's recommendation to build two new SSUs. Instead of a policy of deconcentration, that is, spreading SSU prisoners over the whole country in special units (see Chapter 3), Kosto now opted to concentrate SSU prisoners in two – ultimately only one – SSU prisons (Boin, 2001a). According to an interviewed MP, the temporary SSU 'was unDutch'.[188]

The second reform concerning security was the introduction of a closed doors policy. Before the crisis, it was practice to allow prisoners to escape when they were holding someone hostage. Once out, they would become the problem of the police who had to catch them again. During the crisis, there was a shift in thinking about outer wall security. Instead of letting prisoners walk, there was talk of armed guards in watchtowers and doors staying closed. The outer perimeter should become impenetrable. This shift from letting prisoners walk out to the realization that prisoners should not be able to escape by taking someone hostage resulted in a closed doors policy (Boin and Resodihardjo, 2000: 76–7).

The third security reform was the emphasis laid on security in the White Paper *Effective Detention*. Linked to this focus on security, was the introduction of the standard regime – where rehabilitation did not play such a big role as it used to play. The new White Paper focused mainly on security, almost ignoring humane treatment of prisoners and rehabilitation. The ideal of rehabilitation had already watered down in the previous White Paper *Task and Future* (Ministry of Justice, 1982; see Chapter 3). Nonetheless, rehabilitation continued to play a role as one of the core values of the prison service. On 4 July 1990, before the crisis broke out, Kosto had sent a letter to parliament in which he continued to abide with the double aim of the prison service to imprison prisoners and to help prisoners prepare for their return to society (Van Essen, 1990: 314). In the new White Paper, however, rehabilitation seemed to have dropped off the map almost altogether as little attention was paid to the topic.

Boin writes, 'The most important change concerns the emphasis on the aims of retribution and security compared to the aim of rehabilitation' (Boin, 1995: 148; cf. Wiewel, 1994: 9; Franke, 1996: 309). Wiewel (1994, 19–20) explains:

> The White Paper *Effective Detention* is a sad story. Time has been turned back ... Humanity of imprisonment has been cut back in this White Paper to the requirement that prisoners should not be damaged. This is obvious. But as a result, the prison service has lost some of its shine. Until recently, the priority was to support prisoners from imprisonment to returning to society. Prisons will no longer give this support to prisoners. ... Buildings are built in such a way that escaping is no longer easy. According to the information provided by the junior minister, 53% of the total prison population does not pose a control risk. Nowhere is there a justification for the limiting of freedom of movement for these prisoners. Nor can be explained why every possibility of rehabilitation for almost all prisoners has been abolished. The implementation of incarceration in the Netherlands – once famed for its humane character – has now become what it once was: doing time.

The new focus on security was not the only topic that was dominant in the new White Paper. The new standard regime was introduced in this White Paper – the third dimension where reform occurred. Before the introduction of the standard regime, rehabilitation had been a top priority. This changed with the new regime, as only 20 per cent of prisoners would be eligible for rehabilitation programmes. The president of the Coornhert Liga (the organization for penal law reform) observed that with the new White Paper, the ideal of rehabilitation had been lost. In his opinion, the need to increase security combined with the need to be efficient and effective had resulted in a reallocation of money from regimes to security. Hence, the standard regime was introduced as a way to reallocate money from the new regime – which required less money – to security (Wiewel, 1994: 11). The prison service's director Elting defended the new regime by referring to the changing prison population. People currently incarcerated were often re-offenders with an addiction, or mental or behavioural problems. They were unfit for the old regime. They needed a more structured regime (Elting, 1994). Kosto considered the White Paper 'a "U-turn and a change in direction" of Dutch prison policy'.[189]

All five changes are changes at the most fundamental level of the Dutch Prison Service, because they pertain to the core of how the prison service should deal with its main task: imprisonment. Moreover, these changes were linked to a new prioritization of the prison service's aims. Consequently, these changes can be labelled reform.

The reforms are the outcomes of the responses to the call for a toughening up of penal policy. Downes (1998: 156–7, 165) observed about the White Paper *Effective Detention* that it 'signals ... that prisons must be seen to be toughening up, along with the rest of the criminal justice system, as part of the process of public reassurance that all possible measures are being taken in the control of crime ... A harsher climate is explicitly wrought to appease public opinion'. Kelk (1994) writes that punishment and security dominate the White Paper. Moreover, 'the White Paper breathes a general image which is mainly focused on the importance of an efficient organization, in which a lean management and a hierarchical structure dominate and in which the prisoner is mostly seen as an incorrigible person who poses a danger to his fellow citizens' (Kelk, 1994: 111; cf. Heinrich, 1994: 36). According to Franke (1996: 315):

> Even though the Netherlands seem to accept, at least in principle, the one person to one cell idea, the enormous increase of cell capacity indicates a more repressive penal policy. The repeated calls from MPs (left-wing as well as right-wing MPs) to toughen prison regime, increase security, and weaken the legal status of prisoners, indicate this as well. *Effective Detention* obliged to these wishes to some extent, for example the sober standard regime and the experimental scheme for youth prisons (characterized by 'strict discipline').

A policy maker observed about their responses to the crisis:

> We built the temporary SSU and created extra cell capacity. The number of escapes dwindled. As a result, public unrest ended. ... It was also no longer an issue in the media. ... You do not follow the media, but you do respond to Parliament. MPs translated (media) unrest in political unrest. Parliament was extraordinarily focussed on what happened. We were very busy building prisons. There was agitation because of the escapes and the prisoners sent home. As a result, we needed extra cell capacity.

Notes

1. Parts of this chapter have been adapted from Boin and Resodihardjo (2000).
2. This happened at a time when media and MPs were paying more and more attention to organized crime in the Netherlands (Van de Bunt, 2004).
3. Criminaliteitsbestrijding (Kamerstukken, TK, 1991–1992, 22355 no. 2).
4. The terms of reference were as follows: (1) to evaluate SSU-policy; (2) to establish possible problems when implementing SSU policy; (3) to determine the balance between SSU detention and other detention goals such as preparing prisoners for release; and (4) to compare Dutch SSU policy with the policy of other countries (Hoekstra, 1992: 7).
5. €1 = 2.20371 guilders.
6. *De Telegraaf*, 22 May 1992, 'Nordholt: Criminelen in containers opsluiten'.
7. Ibid.
8. Ibid.
9. Ibid.
10. 10 *NRC Handelsblad*, 3 June 1992, 'Noodoplossing van cellentekort staat nu al onder druk'.
11. *NRC Handelsblad*, 25 May 1992, 'Mogelijk twee gedetineerden in één cel geplaatst'.
12. *De Volkskrant*, 26 May 1992, 'Justitie sluit samen vastzetten gevangenen niet op voorhand uit'.
13. *NRC Handelsblad*, 25 May 1992, 'Mogelijk twee gedetineerden in één cel geplaatst'.
14. *NRC Handelsblad*, 3 June 1992, 'Noodoplossing van cellentekort staat nu al onder druk'.
15. *NRC Handelsblad*, 25 May 1992, 'Directeuren gevangenissen tegen "twee in dezelfde cel"'.
16. Ibid.
17. Ibid.
18. *De Telegraaf*, 27 May 1992, 'Gevangenispersoneel kraakt plan meerdere gedetineerden in een cel "verdubbeling van agressie"'.

19. The JR-120 was a cooperation between the Ministry of Justice and the government buildings service to build extra cells and other judicial buildings such as courts. The 120 stands for 120 million guilders. JR-120 would result in an increase of cell capacity by 2,000 cells (TK, 1998–1999, 26 385, nos 1–2: 9).
20. TK, 1991–1992, 21 840, no. 15: 4.
21. Ibid.
22. TK, 1991–1992, 22 649, no. 1: 2.
23. *NRC Handelsblad*, 2 June 1992, 'Extra celruimte via noodmaatregel. Voorlopig geen 2 mensen in één cel'.
24. TK, 1991–1992, 22 649, no. 1: 2.
25. *NRC Handelsblad*, 2 June 1992, 'Extra celruimte via noodmaatregel. Voorlopig geen 2 mensen in één cel'.
26. Ibid.
27. *De Telegraaf*, 2 June 1992, 'Nog in juni 175 tot 200 cellen erbij. Plan Hirsch Ballin en Kosto'.
28. MPs have the right of interpellation (*interpellatie*), also known as an emergency debate (*spoeddebat*). MPs can ask for a debate on a topic currently not listed on the official agenda. Minister and junior minister have to answer written and/or oral questions during this debate and defend their policy and actions. A majority of MPs have to approve the MP's request for such a debate (Van den Berg et al., 1984; Postma, 1985).
29. TK, Handelingen, Cellentekort, 10 June 1992, TK 87, 87–5256–87–5272: 87–5260.
30. TK, Handelingen, Cellentekort, 10 June 1992, TK 87, 87–5256–87–5272: 87–5265.
31. *De Volkskrant*, 11 June 1992, 'Twee man in cel ook voor PvdA aanvaardbaar'.
32. TK, Handelingen, Cellentekort, 10 June 1992, TK 87, 87–5256–87–5272: 87–5262.
33. *De Volkskrant*, 11 June 1992, 'Twee man in cel ook voor PvdA aanvaardbaar'.
34. TK, 1991–1992, 22 649, no. 2.
35. TK, Handelingen, Cellentekort, 10 June 1992, TK 87, 87–5256–87–5272: 87–5259.
36. TK, 1991–1992, 22 649, no. 3.
37. TK, Handelingen, Cellentekort, 10 June 1992, TK 87, 87–5256–87–5272: 87–5267.
38. TK, Handelingen, Cellentekort, 10 June 1992, TK 87, 87–5256–87–5272: 87–5258–59.
39. Handelingen, Cellentekort, 10 June 1992, TK 87, 87–5256–87–5272: 87–5269–70.
40. *NRC Handelsblad*, 18 June 1992, 'Twee op één cel is inhumaan en levensgevaarlijk'.
41. Cf. *NRC Handelsblad*, 12 June 1992, 'Cellentekort is niet het echte probleem'; *NRC Handelsblad*, 17 June 1992, 'Als iedereen achter de tralies moet, krijg je altijd cellentekort'.

42. *Algemeen Dagblad*, 30 June 1992, 'Staking in gevangenis nauwelijks zichtbaar'; cf. *De Telegraaf*, 30 June 1992, 'Gedetineerden staken tegen noodmaatregel 2 in één cel'.
43. *NRC Handelsblad*, 12 September 1992, 'Kosto wil snel twee nieuwe gevangenissen'.
44. TK, 1992–1993, 22 800 VI, no. 2: 47.
45. Ibid.: 47–8; cf. Press release Ministry of Justice, 15 September 1992, 'Uitbreiding cellencapaciteit en scherpere beveiliging'.
46. *Algemeen Dagblad*, 3 August 1992, 'Ontsnapping per heli. Gevangene spoorloos na spektakel in Hoorn'.
47. *De Telegraaf*, 7 August 1992, 'Iedere ontsnapping is er één te veel'.
48. Ibid.
49. *Trouw*, 22 September 1992, 'Moderne versie van Duivelseiland is niet gewenst'.
50. The idea of the two new SSUs was based, among other things, on Whitemoor Prison (*NRC Handelsblad*, 24 September 1992, 'Je moet langgestraften fatsoenlijk behandelen'; Hoekstra, 1992).
51. Taakgroep Herijking beveiligingsregiem ten aanzien van gedetineerden met een hoog vluchtrisico. During a regular meeting between the junior Minster of Justice and the Board of Directors of the prison service, the idea for such a study group was mentioned on 5 November 1991. The study group was installed on 6 January 1992 (Study group re-assessing security regime concerning escape-prone prisoners, *The Chain is as Strong as Its Weakest Link*, 1992: 1–2 – confidential).
52. Press release Ministry of Justice, 28 September 1992, 'Nieuwe regiemsrichtlijnen voor extra beveiligde inrichtingen'; cf. *Trouw*, 29 September 1992, 'Strenger regime zware jongens. Extra beveiligde gevangenissen extra beveiligd'.
53. Projectgroep Beveiliging, *Rapport van de werkgroep meldpunt CRI*, April 1993: 3 – confidential; Projectgroep Beveiliging, *Rapport Ontvluchtingsonderzoek*, december 1993: 6 – confidential.
54. *Algemeen Dagblad*, 22 September 1992, 'Nieuw soort gevangenis moet vluchten inperken. Nog geen commentaar Kosto op plan commissie Hoekstra'.
55. *NRC Handelsblad*, 24 September 1992, 'Je moet langgestraften fatsoenlijk behandelen'.
56. *Nieuwsblad van het Noorden*, 22 September 1992, 'Grittenborgh juicht bouw ondoordringbare cellen toe'.
57. Cf. *Trouw*, 2 October 1992, 'Resocialisatie blijft mogelijk. Strenge beveiliging en humane behandeling geen tegenstelling'.
58. *Trouw*, 30 September 1992, 'Goed plan commissie-Hoekstra. Nieuwe extra veilige gevangenissen noodzakelijk'.
59. Cf. *Trouw*, 2 October 1992, 'Resocialisatie blijft mogelijk. Strenge beveiliging en humane behandeling geen tegenstelling'.
60. *De Volkskrant*, 24 October 1992, 'Boze Kosto wil snel geld voor cellen. Gedetineerden gijzelen zes bewaarders bij ontsnapping in Hoogeveen'.
61. Ibid.
62. Ibid.

63. Ibid.
64. Current practice was to include societal unrest as one of the indicators to decide whether or not a prisoner should be sent to a SSU. Kosto did not want to turn this indicator into an independent criterion for putting prisoners in SSUs. He doubted whether societal unrest could be used objectively (TK, 1992–1993, 22 800 VI, no. 11: 4).
65. *De Volkskrant*, 24 October 1992, 'Boze Kosto wil snel geld voor cellen. Gedetineerden gijzelen zes bewaarders bij ontsnapping in Hoogeveen'.
66. Press release Ministry of Justice, 3 November 1992, 'Kosto wil twee extra zwaar beveiligde inrichtingen bouwen'.
67. *De Telegraaf*, 4 November 1992, 'Toezicht vluchtgrage gevangene strenger. Ontsnapping uit De Schie en Grittenborgh te gortig'.
68. *Algemeen Dagblad*, 18 November 1992, 'Rel over ontsnapping. Directie zou uitbraakplan gevangenen hebben gekend'.
69. *Trouw*, 9 December 1992, 'Schorsing directeur van gevangenis opgeheven'.
70. The planned reorganization – without the proper means to accomplish the reorganization – and the way headquarters evaluated how governors were functioning did not sit well with the governors (*De Volkskrant*, 2 December 1992, 'Schorsing gevangenisdirecteur gaat collega's te ver. Voorzitter Boeij van vereniging directeuren wijst op al langer bestaande onvrede over optreden ministerie').
71. *Algemeen Dagblad*, 26 November 1992, 'Brandbrief aan justitie. Ver*Trouw*en opgezegd door directies strafinrichtingen'.
72. *Trouw*, 27 November 1992, 'Bajesdirecties dreigen overleg met justitie te boycotten'.
73. *De Volkskrant*, 2 December 1992, 'Schorsing gevangenisdirecteur gaat collega's te ver. Voorzitter Boeij van vereniging directeuren wijst op al langer bestaande onvrede over optreden ministerie'.
74. *Trouw*, 9 December 1992, 'Schorsing directeur van gevangenis opgeheven'.
75. TK, Handelingen, Justitie, 9 December 1992, TK 33, 33–2409–2433: 33–2410.
76. Ibid.: 33–2416–7.
77. Ibid.: 33–2416–7.
78. Ibid.: 33–2422.
79. *Het Parool*, 7 January 1993, 'Regime strenger na nieuwe ontsnapping'; cf. *De Volkskrant*, 8 January 1993, 'Kosto zal desnoods gevangenisregimes strenger maken'.
80. *NRC Handelsblad*, 8 January 1993, 'Ontsnappingen'.
81. *Het Parool*, 9 January 1993, 'Bewaarders vragen aparte opsluiting geweldplegers'.
82. *NRC Handelsblad*, 8 January 1993, 'Twee man via lakens weg uit "Bijlmerbajes"'.
83. *Het Parool*, 7 January 1993, 'Regime strenger na nieuwe ontsnapping'; cf. *De Volkskrant*, 8 January 1993, 'Kosto zal desnoods gevangenisregimes strenger maken'.

84. *NRC Handelsblad*, 8 January 1993, 'Kosto wil paraatheid politie verhogen rond gevangenissen'.
85. *NRC Handelsblad*, 8 January 1993, 'Kosto wil paraatheid politie verhogen rond gevangenissen'.
86. Ibid.
87. *Het Parool*, 9 January 1993, 'Kamer wil meer en beter opgeleide bewakers'.
88. *NRC Handelsblad*, 9 January 1993, 'Meer geweld bij betere beveiliging'
89. *HP/De Tijd op zondag*, 17 January 1993, 'Buitenbewaking bij gevangenissen nodig'.
90. *Algemeen Dagblad*, 16 January 1993, 'Rechter leest Kosto de les over regels in gevangenis. Gedetineerden vechten streng regime vergeefs aan'.
91. This study group had been installed in November 1992.
92. TK, 1992–1993, 22 999, no. 1; cf. *De Volkskrant*, 20 January 1993, 'Ontsnappen kost gevangene vervroegde invrijheidstelling. Bewindslieden willen strafmaat voor hulp bij vluchtpoging verdubbelen'.
93. *Algemeen Dagblad*, 21 January 1993, '"Aantal uitbraken zal niet afnemen". Organisaties zien weinig in wetswijziging invrijheidstelling'.
94. *Trouw*, 16 April 1993, 'De gevangenispoort'.
95. *De Volkskrant*, 22 January 1993, 'Gevangene ontsnapt per helikopter uit huis van bewaring'.
96. *Het Parool*, 25 January 1993, 'Expert naar de Bijlmerbajes'.
97. *Algemeen Dagblad*, 26 January 1993, 'Justitie hardleers'.
98. *De Volkskrant*, 25 January 1993, '"Irritante" ontsnapping brengt justitie in verlegenheid. Vier gevangenen ontvluchten Bijlmerbajes volgens beproefde route'.
99. *Elsevier*, 6 February 1993, 'Staatssecretaris Aad Kosto: "Bezinnen maar niet verstrakken"'.
100. *NRC Handelsblad*, 2 February 1993, 'Resocialisatie gedetineerden in het gedrang'.
101. *Elsevier*, 6 February 1993, 'Staatssecretaris Aad Kosto: "Bezinnen maar niet verstrakken"'.
102. *NRC Handelsblad*, 19 February 1993, 'Twee mannen met geweld ontsnapt'.
103. *NRC Handelsblad*, 19 February 1993, 'Gevangene ontsnapt gewapend uit De Schie'.
104. *De Volkskrant*, 20 February 1993, 'Gedetineerde schiet op bewaarders. Rotterdamse politie vlak voor ontsnapping Italiaanse gevangene getipt'.
105. Ibid.
106. Ibid.: 1–2.
107. Ibid.: 3.
108. Ibid.: 4.
109. Ibid.: 6–7.
110. Ibid.: 7; cf. TK, 1992–1993, 22 999, no. 3.
111. TK, 1992–1993, 22 999, no. 2: 10.
112. Ibid.: 8.

113. Ibid.: 7.
114. *De Volkskrant*, 3 March 1993, 'Justitie claimt honderd miljoen voor extra cellen'.
115. *NRC Handelsblad*, 4 March 1993, 'Coornhert Liga noemt roep om duizend cellen hysterisch'.
116. *De Gelderlander*, 4 March 1993, '"De touwtjes strakker aantrekken werkt averechts". Discussie over strenger regime in gevangenissen laait op na recente reeks ontsnappingen'.
117. *De Volkskrant*, 31 March 1993, 'Chauffeur justitie-auto maakt einde aan vlucht 2 gevangenen'.
118. TK, 1992–1993, 22 999, no. 4: 2.
119. *De Telegraaf*, 5 April 1993, 'Gevangene ontsnapt in kleding van zijn broer'.
120. *NRC Handelsblad*, 6 April 1993, 'Bewaarder en minister voor verscherpte bewaking. "Grote kerels zijn bang omdat ze zich niet meer veilig voelen"'.
121. *NRC Handelsblad*, 7 April 1993, 'Gaten blijven in extra bewaking'.
122. *De Volkskrant*, 19 April 1993, 'Bewakers Grittenborgh tegen strenger regime'.
123. *NRC Handelsblad*, 5 April 1993, 'Ontsnapping van gevangenen splijt coalitie'; *NRC Handelsblad*, 5 April 1993, 'CDA dringt aan op stringenter beleid gevaarlijke gevangenen'.
124. The VVD withdrew its request for an independent inquiry to await the new White Paper (TK, Handelingen, Justitie, 20 October 1993, TK 14, 14–891–914: 14–903.
125. *NRC Handelsblad*, 6 April 1993, 'Hirsch Ballin: geen versoepeling regime'.
126. *NRC Handelsblad*, 14 April 1993, 'Coalitie voelt voor extra beveiliging van gevangenissen'.
127. *NRC Handelsblad*, 6 April 1993, 'Hirsch Ballin: geen versoepeling regime'.
128. *NRC Handelsblad*, 5 April 1993, 'CDA dringt aan op stringenter beleid gevaarlijke gevangenen'.
129. Ibid.
130. *NRC Handelsblad*, 6 April 1993, 'Hirsch Ballin: geen versoepeling regime'.
131. *Het Parool*, 20 April 1993, 'Gevangenen beloond na goed gedrag'.
132. *NRC Handelsblad*, 14 April 1993, 'Coalitie voelt voor extra beveiliging van gevangenissen'.
133. *Trouw*, 27 April 1993, 'Ervaren personeel beste wapen. Gevangenis Nieuw Vosseveld profileert zich als "zware inrichting"'.
134. Ibid.
135. *De Volkskrant*, 24 April 1993, 'Gedetineerden ebi's samen in één inrichting'.
136. TK, 1992–1993, 22 999, no.4.
137. Ibid.: 3.
138. As it turned out, a second SSU was not necessary because the SSU population remained very limited (letter of Ministry to Justice to Parliament, 5002015/99/ DJI d.d. 29 February 1999).
139. *NRC Handelsblad*, 14 April 1993, 'Recordaantal verdachten weggestuurd. Cellentekort buiten Amsterdam'.
140. Ibid.

141. *NRC Handelsblad*, 15 April 1993, 'Meningsverschil binnen Justitie over cellentekort'.
142. *De Volkskrant*, 2 June 1993, 'Hirsch Ballin krijgt laatste kans van CDA'; *Trouw*, 2 June 1993, 'Kamer zet minister Hirsch Ballin in de beklaagdenbank'.
143. *De Volkskrant*, 2 June 1993, 'Hirsch Ballin krijgt laatste kans van CDA'.
144. *Trouw*, 2 June 1993, 'Kamer zet minister Hirsch Ballin in de beklaagdenbank'.
145. *De Volkskrant*, 2 June 1993, 'Hirsch Ballin krijgt laatste kans van CDA'.
146. *Trouw*, 2 June 1993, 'Kamer zet minister Hirsch Ballin in de beklaagdenbank'.
147. *De Volkskrant*, 2 June 1993, 'Hirsch Ballin krijgt laatste kans van CDA'; cf. *NRC Handelsblad*, 2 June 1993, 'Brinkman zegt Hirsch Ballin de wacht aan'.
148. *De Volkskrant*, 2 June 1993, 'Hirsch Ballin krijgt laatste kans van CDA'; cf. *NRC Handelsblad*, 2 June 1993, 'Brinkman zegt Hirsch Ballin de wacht aan'.
149. Het *Algemeen Dagblad* 2 June 1993, 'Fractie velt oordeel binnen een kwartier'.
150. *De Volkskrant*, 2 June 1993, 'Hirsch Ballin krijgt laatste kans van CDA'; cf. *NRC Handelsblad*, 2 June 1993, 'Brinkman zegt Hirsch Ballin de wacht aan'.
151. *NRC Handelsblad*, 2 June 1993, 'Brinkman zegt Hirsch Ballin de wacht aan'.
152. *De Volkskrant*, 2 June 1993, 'Hirsch Ballin onder druk'.
153. *Trouw*, 2 June 1993, 'Cellentekort?'.
154. Het *Algemeen Dagblad*, 2 June 1993, 'Terecht kwaad'.
155. Ibid.
156. TK, Handelingen, Cellentekort, 2 June 1993, TK 74, 74–5380–74–5400: 74–5386.
157. Ibid.: 74–5380.
158. Ibid.: 74–5380.
159. Ibid.: 74–5381.
160. Ibid.: 74–5381–2.
161. Ibid.: 74–5382; *De Volkskrant*, 3 June 1993, 'Noodpakket Hirsch Ballin voor celtekort'.
162. TK, Handelingen, Cellentekort, 2 June 1993, TK 74, 74–5380–74–5400: 74–5383.
163. *De Volkskrant*, 3 June 1993, 'Noodpakket Hirsch Ballin voor celtekort'; cf. TK, Handelingen, 2 June 1993, TK 74, 74–5380–74–5400: 74–5385.
164. TK, 1992–1993, 23 175 no. 5.
165. TK, 1992–1993, 22 999, no. 6; cf. *NRC Handelsblad*, 19 July 1993, 'Kabinet besluit 2.000 cellen extra te bouwen'. 'In the beginning of the 1990s, the number [of suspects] sent home increased rapidly and Parliament demanded extra attention for this problem. As a result, Parliament approved expansion of cell capacity with a 100, 600, and 1,000 cells (mainly emergency cells and replacement of old cells). The Ministry of Justice's budget of 1994 included a plan to create an additional 2,000 cells. The 27 most important projects ended up in a project organization called CAP'96 (CAP stands for Capacity expansion justice buildings and 96 for the year 1996 when these projects should be finished). One of these projects was moved to CAP'98. CAP'96 resulted in an increase of prison cell capacity of 8,740 in 1990 to about 13,500 cells in 1996. … In 1991, the costs of the [JR-120] … was estimated to cost 420m-460m guilders (price level 1991). By mid-1997,

investment costs for the 26 CAP'96 projects were almost 1.4 billion guilders (price level 1996)' (TK, 1998–1999, 26 385, nos 1–2: 9).

166. TK, 1993–1994, 22 999, no. 9: 2; *NRC Handelsblad*, 13 August 1993, 'Kosto wil cellen twee jaar lang voor 103 pct bezetten'.
167. TK, 1993–1994, 22 999, no. 9: 2.
168. By decree of 8 July 1994 Stb. 527; cf. TK, 1994–1995, 22 999, no. 22. Double-bunking was already allowed in certain circumstances (cf. van Hattum, 1995: 207–8).
169. TK 1993–1994, 22 999, no. 8.
170. TK, 1993–1994, 22 999, no. 12
171. TK, 1993–1994, 11 April 1994, UCV 38.
172. *Trouw*, 2 June 1993, 'Kamer zet minister Hirsch Ballin in de beklaagdenbank'.
173. *De Telegraaf*, 3 June 1993, 'Cellentekort'.
174. *Algemeen Dagblad*, 11 June 1992, 'Onthutsende werkelijkheid'.
175. Cf. *De Volkskrant*, 1 February 1993, 'Bijlmerbajes wordt beter beveiligd tegen ontsnapping'; *NRC Handelsblad*, 2 February 1993, 'Resocialisatie gedetineerden in het gedrang'; *Elsevier*, 6 February 1993, 'Staatssecretaris Aad Kosto: "Bezinnen maar niet verstrakken"'.
176. Het *Algemeen Dagblad*, 24 April 1993, 'Veiligheid bevorderen'.
177. TK, Handelingen, Cellentekort, 2 June 1993, TK 74, 74–5380–5400: 74–5389.
178. *De Volkskrant*, 2 June 1993, 'Hirsch Ballin krijgt laatste kans van CDA'; cf. *NRC Handelsblad*, 2 June 1993, 'Brinkman zegt Hirsch Ballin de wacht aan'.
179. The Dutch party system distinguishes two types of leaders: the party leader – who is the general leader of the party – and the party leader of the members elected in an elective organization (*fractie leider*) – this is the person who is the head of, for example, the party's MPs in parliament or the party's elected members in the city council. At the time of the crisis, Brinkman was the party leader of the MPs and was supposed to become the general national party leader of the CDA.
180. *Haagsche Courant*, 2 June 1993, 'Zwaar geschut tegen minister'.
181. *Rotterdams Dagblad*, 2 June 1993, 'Minister in het nauw'.
182. *Algemeen Dagblad*, 2 June 1993, 'Fractie velt oordeel binnen een kwartier'; cf. *NRC Handelsblad*, 3 June 1993, 'Noodverbanden'.
183. *De Volkskrant*, 16 October 1993, 'Voor naïviteit is geen ruimte meer'.
184. *HP/De Tijd*, 16 April 1993, 'Misdaadpsychose'.
185. Ibid..
186. TK, Handelingen, Justitie, 31 October 1991, TK 18, 18–969–18–984: 18–980.
187. Moreover, allowing partial double-bunking probably paved the way for allowing double-bunking for other categories of prisoners in 2002. Following a crisis concerning drug runners at Schiphol airport, the newly elected Minister of Justice Donner announced that double-bunking would be possible for other offenders as well (see Chapter 2; Dekker et al., 2003).
188. The SSU population consisted of prisoners who were escape-prone and whose escape would pose unacceptable danger for society in terms of re-offending. In 1995, a second category of SSU prisoners was introduced. Prisoners whose

escape would create social unrest were to be placed in the SSU as well (circulaire van 1 maart 1995, no. 481138/95/DJ).

189. *De Volkskrant*, 8 February 1994, 'Justitie begint nog dit jaar proef met elektronische detentie'.

Chapter 5
Riots and Reform in England (1990–1991)

Introduction[1]

In 1990, the Prison Service of England and Wales was shaken to the core by the most serious series of riots ever experienced (James et al., 1997: 58). The riots started on 1 April 1990 in Strangeways Prison, Manchester and spread to prisons throughout the country. By the time the Strangeways riot ended on 25 April 1990, disturbances had broken out in more than 20 prisons. The most serious incidents occurred in Manchester, Long Lartin, Glen Parva, Dartmoor, Cardiff, Bristol, Stoke Heath and Pucklechurch.[2] When the quiet returned, three people had died, 133 inmates and 282 prison staff had been injured and there the cost of the damage ran into millions of pounds.[3] These costs and the subsequent cost of keeping prisoners in custody in police cells exceeded £100 million.[4]

The largest riot occurred at Strangeways Prison in Manchester. It was notable because of its length and the constant media attention. Prisoners on the roof of Strangeways Prison appeared frequently on television; newspapers published stories of the horrors supposedly committed by the rioters in Strangeways. These stories proved largely incorrect, but people were injured and property was damaged: one inmate and one prison officer[5] died, 75 inmates and 197 prison officers were injured[6] and it cost £60 million to repair the prison.

During the riot period, the media portrayed the entire prison service as malfunctioning. MPs questioned the functioning of the prison service and the measures taken to deal with the riots. They demanded explanations from the Home Secretary on how these disturbances could have broken out. Interest groups and unions linked the disturbances to bad prison conditions and a failing prison service. The public perceived the prison service as unable to remain in control and unable to regain control once it was lost. In short, the prison service suffered an institutional crisis.

The response by policy makers, prison governors and prison officers to the riots and the ensuing institutional crisis was threefold. First, prison officers and governors tried to end the disturbances in their prisons. Second, policy makers came up with measures to convince the public that these incidents would not occur in the future. Third, a well-known tactic was used to divert the attention of the media and MPs: the policy makers installed an inquiry headed by Lord Justice Woolf. By installing an inquiry, policy makers were able to deflect questions, at least for the time being, regarding the way they had dealt with the disturbances.

As it turned out, the inquiry had a decisive impact on the outcome of this crisis. Even though policy makers were not inclined to reform the prison service, the Woolf Inquiry contradicted them as it recommended that prison conditions should be improved and that the balance between security, control and justice be restored. In the end, the Woolf Report resulted in a reformed prison service. In this chapter, all these events will be described in detail followed by an analysis in which the occurrence of an institutional crisis and reform is determined.

The Riots and their Aftermath

The Strangeways Riot and Copycat Behaviour

At 10 o'clock on 1 April 1990, a religious service started in the chapel of Strangeways Prison. Seven prison officers supervised the 309 prisoners who attended the service (Woolf, 1991: 4). During the service, a prisoner grabbed the microphone and addressed the congregation. Soon after, the prisoners became disorderly. Prison officers were unable to control the disturbance, which then quickly spread to the rest of the prison.[7] Prisoners set fire to parts of the prison. At that time, there were 1,647 prisoners present, 677 above CNA (certified normal accommodation), which had been set at 970 for Strangeways as a whole (Woolf, 1991: 3). It would take the prison service 25 days to regain complete control of Strangeways.

The Strangeways disturbance posed a complex problem for the prison service because, while trying to subdue the riot and manage the intense media attention, the prison service also had to deal with the prisoners who had surrendered and who had to be transferred to other prisons. A large number of these were remand prisoners who – in contrast to convicted prisoners – were entitled to more frequent family visits and who had to attend their trials. Police cells were used to hold some of these prisoners while others were sent to prisons in the South of England. The Home Office considered various emergency plans, such as the use of empty cells in young offender institutions, to reduce the high levels of overcrowding in other prisons. The situation was exacerbated by fears that the Prison Officers' Association (POA) would start industrial action over staffing levels. According to the POA, the additional 3,000 officers who had been recruited since 1987, so that overtime could be abolished via the Fresh Start programme, were not sufficient to make up for the loss of staff hours when overtime was phased out (see Chapter 3).[8] The POA considered these low staffing levels to be one of the reasons that the Strangeways riot could happen.

Meanwhile, disturbances spread across the country. On 7 April 1990, a disturbance broke out in Dartmoor prison. The next day, nine other disturbances erupted in other prisons, including Bristol, Brixton, South London and Cardiff.[9] Some of these disturbances were peaceful, such as the one at Armley jail in Leeds, where prisoners held a sit down strike. Other disturbances were more violent; prisoners and prison officers were injured and property was damaged.

On 9 April 1990, prison officers trained in control and restraint stormed Bristol prison at dawn and restored control over the prison. It was the first time since the outbreak of the Strangeways riot that force was used to regain control of a prison. The way in which the Bristol disturbance was ended marked a shift in the way disturbances were traditionally dealt with in the prison service.[10] Before the storming of Bristol prison, the so-called softly softly approach had been used at other prisons to deal with the disturbances.

This approach consisted of laying siege of the prison to await the surrender of prisoners,[11] thus depending on negotiations and deteriorating conditions created by hosing the prison with water or playing loud music (cf. Woolf, 1991: 86-7). This approach had been shown not to work as the Strangeways riot entered its second week.

The media became impatient with the softly softly approach. *The Times*, for example, wrote: 'At Bristol it was proven beyond doubt that force was the answer to the sporadic disturbances that have erupted in British jails in the past few days. ... It is possible, but cannot be ascertained for certain until detailed reports of all the prison riots have been analysed, that the death at Dartmoor could have been avoided if control and restraint teams had been used to clear the occupiers within hours of the riot starting.'[12] A member of the Prison Officers' Association at Bristol observed: 'There has been a shift in attitude in the last couple of days. Our intelligence is that a decision has been made in the highest authority that we had to stop pussy-footing about and we had to get in there because prisoners were not going to give it back.'[13]

On 11 April 1990, Home Secretary Waddington (Conservative) met with representatives of the Prison Governors' Association (PGA) and POA to discuss the situation. Before the disturbances broke out, the POA had been unsatisfied with the effects of Fresh Start and the PGA was unhappy with a planned reorganization at the regional level (see Chapter 3). Following the discussion with the PGA and POA, Waddington announced that the Home Office would bring forward the recruitment of 200 prison officers, buy extra protective clothes and riot gear and make room for the 2,000 inmates who could no longer stay in Manchester, Dartmoor and Bristol due to the rioting that had taken place there. The POA had also hoped for an additional 600 officers to the 200 officers who had already been planned for 1990, an end to slopping out[14] and minimum standards of care for prisoners. The Home Secretary did not approve these additional requests, but said that he would think about it. He would also think about the PGA's request to delay a reorganization to replace the four prison regions with 15 areas until the results of the Woolf Inquiry were known.[15]

The Strangeways situation intensified, as details on the difference of opinion between the governor of Strangeways O'Friel and headquarters on how to deal with the Strangeways riot became public knowledge. The governor had wanted to storm the prison on the second day of the siege, but was ordered not to do so by Deputy Director General Emes (Woolf, 1991: 76–9).[16] Moreover, the Greater Manchester police announced that it would ask the Home Secretary to pay the bill of up to £2 million for assisting in dealing with the riot. The government had already consented to pay half of the bill, but the Greater Manchester police wanted the government to pay the whole bill.[17]

On 22 April 1990, Home Secretary Waddington visited the besieged prison in Manchester. On that same day, staff, police, and the army discussed possible tactics. On 23 and 24 April, C&R (control and restraint) units made incursions into the prison, thereby securing a number of wings. On 25 April, staff stormed Strangeways Prison and got the last nine prisoners out who had not yet surrendered. At 6. 20 p.m. the prison was back under the control of the Home Office.[18]

Media, MPs, and Interest Groups Respond to the Disturbances

Home Secretary Waddington (Conservative) officially notified the House of Commons of the events in Manchester on 2 April 1990. In his speech, the Home Secretary stressed the improvements to the prison system already under way, such as the new policy to keep those people out of prison who did not need to be there, a refurbishment programme and a building programme, that the prison population had declined with 2,100 prisoners and that expenditure had risen by 20 per cent in the previous 12 months. The Home Secretary added that he thought a thorough inquiry into the Strangeways disturbance was needed.[19]

Shadow Home Secretary Hattersley's (Labour) first response was that the Home Office had 'failed hopelessly in its management of the prison and neglected its duty to prepare for disturbances'.[20] The Home Office had also failed to 'improve conditions, increase staffing and take heed of warnings of trouble earlier last week'.[21] Moreover, Hattersley framed the crisis in terms of overcrowding and custodial sentencing practices: 'It is our long-standing belief that the recurring crisis in our prisons is the consequence of overcrowding, which results from too many custodial sentences and too little punishment within the community.'[22] Hattersley also referred to the Fresh Start programme and wondered whether the low staffing levels at Strangeways Prison in the pre-riot days were the result of this programme.[23]

The Shadow Home Secretary was not alone in framing the riot in terms of overcrowding, prison conditions and understaffing. Unions, pressure groups and the media followed his lead. Evans, the POA's general secretary, described the situation at Strangeways as a 'war zone' and 'had little doubt that poor conditions had sparked the disorder'.[24] Moreover, he was 'extremely disturbed, especially when we informed the prison department of the likelihood of this happening, with the poor conditions and insufficient number of staff to supervise prisoners. No one should be surprised'.[25] The POA rejected the claims made by prisons minister Mellor that conditions had improved at Strangeways following Governor O'Friel's work to treble the hours prisoners spend outside of prison and increase opportunities for free association (Woolf, 1991: 41).[26] 'If the minister thinks that five officers [during the service in the chapel][27] to supervise 300 prisoners is suitable then I suggest he puts on a uniform and faces the reality as our staff have to do.'[28] Labour Home Affairs spokesman Sheerman said that the riot was 'the worst prison disturbance this century' and that 'disturbances had been predicted as the result of overcrowding in the prison'.[29]

The spreading of the disturbances to other prisons increased the attention paid to the prison service by the media, MPs'and interest groups. They blamed three causes that, in their opinion, had created the copycat disturbances. First, the extensive and sometimes incorrect media coverage was seen as provoking new riots. Headlines included '12 dead in jail drug riot', '10 die in jail riot horror', '12 murdered in jail riot', 'Prison mob hanged cop', 'Prisoners die as rioters burn jail' and 'Bodies cut up and dumped in sewer' (cf. Press Council, 1991).[30] The president of the National Viewers' and Listeners' Association urged the BBC and Independent Television News chiefs to reduce the coverage.[31] Shadow Home Secretary Hattersley condemned the media for contributing to 'brutalism in society'.[32] Second, the non-violent approach adopted at Strangeways Prison was seen by governors and the POA as encouraging prisoners at other prisons to riot as well.[33] And third, the moving to other prisons of prisoners who had participated in riots had spread the riots to other prisons. The governor of Bristol prison, where a disturbance had broken out, thought 'some of the ringleaders could have come from Dartmoor after the disturbance there [had ended]'.[34] The POA concurred: 'the policy of moving prisoners involved in riots to other jails simply moved the trouble around.'[35]

On 25 April 1990, the Strangeways riot was brought to an end. The next day, Prime Minister Thatcher came under attack during Prime Minister's Questions.[36] MP Townend (Conservative) asked the Prime Minister if she was aware of the growing public anger at the costs of the riots and he asked why the riots had not been stopped more forcefully by, for example, using the SAS (Special Air Service), teargas, or arms. Thatcher replied that Home Secretary Waddington would deal with the matter of costs and that it was the people on the spot who should be allowed to make decisions without being second-guessed by MPs.[37]

Later that day, Home Secretary Waddington addressed the issue of the Strangeways riot in the House of Commons. During the debate, Shadow Home Secretary Hattersley and Home Secretary Waddington both attacked the extensive and sometimes irresponsible reporting of the events. Besides asking whether the allegations that the governor of Strangeways had been ordered to stand down and not attack the prison on the second day were true and repeating their questions on the effect of Fresh Start on the outbreak of the Strangeways riot, MPs also continued to frame the crisis in terms of overcrowding and bad prison conditions. Shadow Home Secretary Hattersley, for example, condemned the actions of the prisoners at Strangeway prison and other prisons, but he could understand that 'clearly some were caught up in the early days of the riot because of the despair that they felt at the conditions in the prison: three men in one cell; only 11 hours a week outside those cells, slopping out, one shower and one change of clothes a week if they were lucky'.[38]

The Policy Makers' Response to Events

The major policy makers were Home Secretary Waddington, prisons minister Mellor – succeeded by Rumbold in July 1990 – Director General of the prison service Train and Deputy Director General Emes.[39] The policy makers faced three problems: the riots' effects, the POA and the public's dissatisfaction with the way the prison service functioned.

The Strangeways riot by itself resulted in a prison that was completely out of commission. Prisoners were waiting in police cells for transfer to other prisons. At the beginning of May 1990, for example, there were over 500 prisoners in police cells in North England[40] (cf. Woolf, 1991: 41–2). This resulted in pressure on other prisons to cope with these prisoners. The Home Office pressed ahead with repairs to Strangeways' K-wing, the prison's least damaged wing, in order to make room for 200 prisoners so that pressure on police cells and other prisons would lessen.[41]

The POA had been unhappy with the effects of the Fresh Start programme to reduce overtime from the beginning. The Association had expected the prison service to hire extra personnel to fill the gap caused by abandoning overtime. The prison service, however, wanted to fill this gap by hiring extra personnel as well as by improving efficiency of current staff. The latter had not been communicated properly to the POA. Hence, the organization had expected more new personnel to be hired than the prison service was willing to hire. The POA felt that the shortage of staff following the Fresh Start programme was one of the causes of the disturbances. The need to deal with the prisoners who had to be relocated as their prisons were damaged during the disturbances resulted in additional pressure for prison officers in other prisons. As a result, industrial action was taken in a number of prisons. Prison officers at Walton Prison, Liverpool, for example, had voted 'not to accept any remand or convicted prisoners from outside their catchment area [that is, the area they serve]. They [would] also refuse to take any prisoners with disruptive records' for fear of spreading unrest to their prison.[42] On 6–8 July 1990, the POA held a three-day action. Inmates were barred from entering or re-entering prisons with populations above CNA (certified normal accommodation).[43] The POA demanded 600 extra officers. The Home Office ministers proposed a package, including hiring 400 extra prison officers, in response to POA's pressure.[44]

The policy makers also had to deal with the widespread feeling that the prison service was malfunctioning. Ironically, the prison service had been on its way to becoming a better organization before the disturbances started. In November 1989, Home Secretary Waddington had said in his first prisons speech that the sharp decrease in prison population would have advantageous side effects. The population pressure would diminish, allowing prison officers to do more than just warehousing. Overcrowding would be eliminated very soon – the prediction was for it to end in 1991 or 1992 – and money could be used to refurbish prisons to end slopping out instead of having to build new prisons.[45] The eruption of disturbances, however, abruptly changed this positive image of the prison service and its future.

The policy makers' response to these feelings of dissatisfaction was twofold. First, measures were taken to prevent the occurrence of such riots in the future. On 26 April 1990, Waddington told the House of Commons that MPs would 'accept that vigorous action is now necessary to try to prevent further disturbances'.[46] The Home Secretary had already announced two of these measures on 11 April 1990: the bringing forward of the recruitment of 200 more prison officers and the ordering of an extra £750,000 worth of protective equipment and clothing. The other measures presented to the House of Commons were new and included the training of staff, improving new and existing establishments, investigating access to roof tops and security around the prison and especially the kitchens, studying the physical protection of vulnerable prisoners and considering a prison mutiny offence.

Second, Waddington installed an inquiry to investigate the riots. In so doing, he showed the public that policy makers were in control of the crisis. Moreover, the inquiry allowed him to deflect questions – as happened in the case when Home Secretary Waddington responded to questions in the House of Commons: 'In any event, those matters are for Lord Justice Woolf's inquiry. I do not think that it helps when Hon. Members propagate various rumours. All those matters can be established in due course by the inquiry.'[47] *The Guardian* labelled Waddington's tactic as trying 'to contain the disturbances and delay any policy initiatives until Lord Justice Woolf's report on Strangeways'.[48] The tactic of installing an inquiry proved to be effective, as media and MP attention dwindled (cf. McConnell, 2003).

The Woolf Inquiry

On 5 April 1990, Home Secretary Waddington appointed Lord Justice Woolf to head the inquiry concerning the Strangeways disturbance. His terms of reference were to 'inquire into the events leading up to the serious disturbance in Her Majesty's Prison Manchester which began on 1 April 1990 and the action taken to bring it to a conclusion' (Woolf, 1991: 28). Lord Justice Woolf was allowed to interpret the terms of reference as he liked.[49] On 10 April 1990, Lord Justice Woolf's terms of reference were changed in light of the recent disturbances at other prisons to include the most serious disturbances (Woolf, 1991: 28). A month later, Lord Justice Woolf requested (and was granted) the appointment of Judge Tumim, HM Chief Inspector of Prisons, to assist in writing the second part of the Woolf Report on the prevention of disturbances.

The inquiry started right away. Information was received and gathered, prisons were visited, interest groups were contacted and a preliminary hearing was held on 14 May 1990. The public hearings into the disturbances, at which inmates were heard as well, lasted from 11 June to 1 August 1990. During the inquiry, 170 witnesses testified at the formal hearings, numerous meetings were held with staff, prisoners and organizations. Staff and prisoners sent 1,730 letters, organizations and individuals sent 150 submissions for the public seminars and members of the public sent 180 letters for the public seminars (Woolf, 1991: 2, 36). The Woolf Inquiry used a new procedure for judicial inquiries: the public seminar. Five public seminars, each with its own topic, were held in public so that interested parties could submit evidence and offer their points of view (Woolf, 1991: 28–38).

Nuances and emphasis differed, but the participants in the public seminars painted a picture of a prison service in need of change. According to many witnesses, the prison service's central problems consisted of the unsanitary and overcrowded conditions, the ineffective regime, the difficulty for prisoners to maintain contact with family and friends, staff feeling undervalued, the bad relations between governors and headquarters and the lack of respect with which prisoners were treated, lack of procedures to redress grievances, lack of staff, lack of training for staff, lack of leadership within the prison service and lack of coordination between the different organizations in the criminal justice system (Woolf, 1991: 16–17). Woolf combined all these causes and put them under the banner of the need to balance security, control and justice.

Interested parties not only subscribed to these causes of the riots, they also suggested improvements. The National Association for the Care and Resettlement of Offenders (NACRO), the Prison Reform Trust (PRT), the National Association of Probation Officers (Napo) and the Prison Officers' Association (POA), for instance, submitted their own ideas on how to improve prison life. Their ideas ranged from minimum standards for prisoners (that is, minimum rights for prisoners regarding their life in prison, for example, ending slopping out, receiving education and the number of hours spend out of cell), to a prison ombudsman, no censorship of mail and improved judicial redress.[50] The POA also asked for an additional 3,463 prison officers because the Home Office had made a mistake when implementing Fresh Start.[51]

The Woolf Report

The Woolf Report, which was published in February 1991, is widely considered to be a seminal piece of work (cf. Resodihardjo, 2006a). Two reasons inform this status: Lord Justice Woolf did not limit his investigation to the (f)actual causes of the disturbances, as his terms of reference suggested, but decided to 'address the wider issues the disturbances raise', that is, to try to 'identify underlying problems and suggesting solutions' without becoming an inquiry investigating the whole prison system (Woolf, 1991: 31). Lord Justice Woolf conducted the inquiry in an unprecedented way by organizing public hearings and seminars at which interested parties, including prisoners, could voice their opinion. This was all in stark contrast to the usual closed way in which disturbances were investigated. Consequently, the report provided an in-depth view of the causes of the disturbances as well as the solutions to prevent such disturbances in the future, which was supported by nearly everyone (if not everyone) with an interest in the prison service (from prisoners, governors and civil servants to interest groups and academics).

The report contained 12 recommendations and proposals following from them. These 12 recommendations included better cooperation between the different parts of the criminal justice system, ending slopping out and improving the possibilities for prisoners to maintain links with their families and communities.

According to Lord Justice Woolf, all recommendations had to be implemented if a balance between security, control and justice was to be established. Security referred to the prevention of escapes, control referred to the prevention of disturbances and justice referred to humane and fair treatment of prisoners (Woolf, 1991: 17). In fact, the Woolf Inquiry made it clear that the three elements were connected. 'If there is an absence of justice, prisoners will be aggrieved. Control and security will be threatened' (Woolf, 1991: 17). If one wanted a well-run humane prison, then these three elements had to be in balance. Ending slopping out, for example, would result in better living conditions and prisoners would be less inclined to create disturbances. Ending slopping out would therefore lead to better control. The same would go for improving standards of justice. If means for prisoners to address their grievances were increased and improved, they would be less likely to revolt.

Policy Makers and Woolf

According to *The Guardian*, Home Office officials were afraid that the Woolf Inquiry would turn into 'a wide-ranging policy scrutiny, tantamount to a Royal Commission on the future of the prison service', because Lord Justice Woolf had requested the appointment of Judge Tumim to become joint chairman for the second part of the inquiry.[52] According to *The Guardian*, the appointment was

> viewed as an attempt to increase the clout of his final report which may form the basis for reform of the 1952 Prisons Act. Judge Tumim has used his inspector's reports to criticise the Home Office and maintains a sturdy independence from the Government. Mr Waddington's officials are understood to have been alarmed that the Woolf exercise may be getting out of control, but he [Waddington] was not able or willing to refuse the request.[53]

Home Secretary Waddington sometimes responded to what was being said during the inquiry's hearings and seminars. Regarding the request for minimum standards made by several interest groups, the Home Secretary agreed that 'there was a lot to be said for setting a target date for new standards on clean underwear, regular showers, a reasonable level of activity, and the ending of slopping out',[54] but he opposed statutory standards for two reasons. First, enormous costs were involved in improving prisons.[55] And second, minimum standards would either be set too low, thereby accommodating the existing situation and avoiding having to go to court (and as a result would not improve the situation), or they would be set too high and thus be unfeasible.[56]

The policy makers' resistance towards minimum standards had apparently changed when Director of Inmate Administration Dunbar, a member of the Prisons Board, told the Woolf Inquiry on 31 October that a minimum standard for prisoners was needed. He was speaking in a personal capacity, but 'his remarks suggest ministers may be ready to drop their long-term objection to enforceable standards which they feared could cause them frequent embarrassment in the courts. ... Although ministers are not committed by his statement, it increases the probability of a recommendation for minimum standards in Lord Justice Woolf's report.'[57]

In November 1990, the new Prime Minister Major and the new Home Secretary Baker came into office (see Chapter 3). They supported a new and more progressive direction where the running of the prison service was concerned.[58] Baker claimed to be more committed to radical reform than either Hurd or Waddington.[59] This redirection by the Home Office was further promoted by 'public disquiet about penal conditions'[60] and negative reports on prisons by the Prison Inspectorate.[61] This view in the media was corroborated by a policy maker who said that the Woolf Report attracted 'public attention, secured a little more money to improve prisons, and things were supposed to get better. It's not that the government at the time was hostile to Woolf's description, but was driven to it by public outcry and the opposition's claims'.

The policy makers' commitment to reform became clear when Home Secretary Baker presented the Woolf Report to the House of Commons on 25 February 1991. In his speech, Baker officially announced a number of measures to improve the prison service. These measures included the bringing forward of the sanitation deadline as proposed by Lord Justice Woolf, who had recommended to end slopping out by February 1996. Baker brought the deadline forward to the end of 1994, which would cost an extra £36m over the next four years. The extra cash needed would come from existing budgets (£18m) and the other £18m would be 'provided'. Other measures included ending the practice of juveniles having to wait in jail for their trial, increasing the number of prisoners receiving education and training in skills in prisons, retaining family ties by increasing the number of visits, financial assistance and home leaves, making card phones available and abolishing censorship of letters except for dispersal prisons.[62]

Baker emphasized that the Woolf Report contained many more recommendations and that it would take some time for the prison service to consider these recommendations. A new White Paper would be published later in 1991 to take these recommendations into account. The White Paper would provide 'a major opportunity to set out and chart the course of developments for the rest of this century and, indeed, beyond'.[63]

A New White Paper

In September 1991, the new White Paper written by the Home Office was published. Titled *Custody, Care and Justice: The Way Ahead for the Prison Service in England and Wales* (1991c), the White Paper set forth a new policy for the prison service. The White Paper not only took the Woolf Report into account, but also the Tumim Report on suicides (Home Office: 1990a),[64] the report on prison education by the House of Commons Committee (House of Commons Education, Science and Arts Committee, 1991) and the reports by HM Chief Inspector of Prisons (Home Office, 1991b) and Lakes/Hadfield (1991) following the Brixton escape on 7 July 1991.[65] The White Paper formulated 12 priorities. Besides improving necessary security measures, the newly formulated priorities included more drastic alterations in prison policy such as ending overcrowding and slopping out, and providing a code of standards for activities and conditions in prisons (Home Office, 1991c: 15–16).

The 12 recommendations were in line with the Woolf Report: 'The Government accepts the central propositions in the [Woolf] Report that security and control must be kept in balance with justice and humanity and that each must be set at the right level' (Home Office, 1991c: 5).

Security predominates the White Paper; after all '[t]he first priority of the Prison Service is to hold and manage prisoners in such a way as to prevent escapes and absconds' (Home Office, 1991c: 19). This did not mean that the prison service did not wish to acquire the balance as prescribed by Woolf. As Home Secretary Baker pointed out, 'In the White Paper I have emphasised the central importance of keeping those sent to prison securely in custody. But bolts, bars and barriers are not enough by themselves. Constructive regimes, respectful relationships and sound justice are all essential elements of a properly secure prison'. The White Paper spelled out 'a clear vision by government and a continuing commitment to reform'.[66]

The White Paper also alluded to a possible agencification of the prison service. The government, however, would await the review by Sir Raymond Lygo to determine the prison service's administrative future. Sir Raymond published his report in December 1991 and concluded that the prison service should become an agency, with a clear distinction between ministers, who set policy and who remained accountable, and the agency, which was responsible for operations (Lygo, 1991). This would give the prison service a 'greater independence ... from day-to-day ministerial oversight'.[67] Home Secretary Baker accepted this recommendation and announced that the prison service would become an agency from 1 April 1993.[68]

Penal reformers and opposition MPs criticized the contents of the White Paper. Their criticism focused on the emphasis laid in the White Paper on security, the fact that no extra resources would be available to implement the White Paper and the absence of a clear timetable.[69] Shadow Home Secretary Hattersley, for example, said that 'paragraph after paragraph ends with a statement which says this year, next year, sometime, never'.[70]

The White Paper deviated in three ways from the Woolf Report. First, the optimism of the Woolf Report was already being overtaken by a new incident: the escape of two IRA suspects from Brixton Prison in London. Second, and as a result of the first, the White Paper put security first and money was chiefly used to implement the security measures in the White Paper, not the other aspects as promoted by Woolf. As Cavadino and Dignan write (1997: 118):

> The Woolf Report was published in February 1991; by the summer, security concerns were once again in the ascendancy following the escape of two IRA suspects from Brixton prison. In the ensuing White Paper, *Custody, Care and Justice* (Home Office, 1991), the government's sense of priorities was starkly reflected in the adoption (in effect) of a two-speed approach to implementing Woolf proposals. In the fast lane was, most conspicuously, a package of measures to improve security and control, including the introduction of annual security audits and the installation of X-ray machines and metal detectors in the entrances to maximum security prisons. These were to be given first claim on the Prison Service's budget and were accompanied by the introduction (in the Prison Security Act 1992) of a new offence of mutiny,

> and increased penalties for those convicted of assisting prison escapers. In the slow lane – to be implemented only over a timescale of 20–25 years, and then only out of existing resources – were many of the reforms to which Woolf had attached particular importance.

Finally, although the White Paper and Home Secretary Baker spoke of a clear vision and continuing commitment to reform, this vision was not clarified or explicated at that time or later on. In 1991, the White Paper sent two messages: the acceptance of Woolf – which constituted reform – and yet a remaining preoccupation with security. By the end of 1993, a shift in government direction occurred as crime rose on the political agenda (Faulkner, 2001: 122). According to Faulkner (2001: 119), 'It was difficult for Ministers to express those objectives, and still more the principles, in a straightforward, unambiguous way when it was at the same time politically necessary to give an over-riding impression of being "tough on crime"'.

Nevertheless, the significance of the White Paper should not be underestimated. It formulates the ambition to search for balance as proposed by Woolf – a move that had been politically impossible to express by government before the Woolf Report was published. 'The recommendations in the "Overview" [of the Woolf Report] were entirely consistent with the Government's approach to criminal justice as it has been described in this chapter, but it is ironic that politically it would have been virtually impossible for the Government – or any recent government – to put them forward on its own account' (Faulkner, 2001: 117). The fact that events at a later stage overtook the prison service (such as the escapes from Whitemoor and Parkhurst in 1994–1995) does not negate the reformist content of the White Paper.

Riots, Crisis and Reform

From Riots to Institutional Crisis

As the disturbance in Strangeways Prison continued, the prison service came under pressure from media and MPs as they focused on the alleged malfunctioning of the prison service. The media, MPs and interest groups portrayed the prison service as unprofessional, unable to control prisons and unable to regain control once it was lost. The prison service was portrayed in such a manner in different forums. There were news reports and comments by journalists; MPs and representatives of interest groups made remarks in the media; and MPs asked questions in parliament. The media, for example, depicted the prison service as follows.

> Every extra day spent by the rioting prisoners on the roof of Strangeways jail should be an additional day of shame for the Home Office. … the

> damage to the public purse Pounds 100,000 a day for policing, Pounds 80 million to rebuild the prison is as high as the cost to public confidence in the penal system. The British penal system has shown itself unable to prevent a riot in the first place and slow to regain control thereafter. This renders hollow the claim that only in the public sector can order be maintained. The public sector is incapable of controlling its prisons. The reasons are clear: deplorable conditions, and prison officers who are as concerned with their overtime payments as they are for the welfare of those they are supposed to guard. The siege at Strangeways must be ended immediately and by force if necessary.[71]

The siege was described as 'the most flagrant failure of the system's statement of purpose'.[72] The prison service concurred with this view, when its White Paper stated that the whole episode was 'a traumatic and testing time for staff, prisoners and for the standing of the prison system' (Home Office, 1991c: 3).

MPs, media, and interest groups perceived the riots as the natural outcome of the general failure on the part of the prison service to treat prisoners properly. The bad prison living conditions, the overcrowding, the slopping out and the bad activities programme (if any) had previously been almost non-items in the news and parliament, but now appeared frequently in media and parliament as the causes of the riots. Journalists, interest groups, MPs and academics questioned the way the prison service dealt with its prisoners.

In terms of media attention, *The Guardian* and *The Times* published a large number of articles (see Figure 5.1). In April 1990 alone, 153 articles in *The Guardian* and *The Times* addressed the disturbances. Topics included the various disturbances, the statements by MPs, interest groups and policy makers, the horrors supposedly committed in Strangeways Prison and the conditions in which prisoners were held. The functioning of the prison service in dealing with the riots as well as in general was commented on in a negative way. For example, *The Guardian* wrote:

> This riot has been on such a scale and has occurred at such a stage in the development of the British prison system that it can safely be said to have undermined many of the most fundamental working assumptions of existing penal policy. It isn't just the building at Strangeways which lies in ruins. It is also the policy which has led the prison to be run in the way that it has.[73]

Another example of the negative way in which the prison service was portrayed comes from *The Times*:

> The riot at Strangeways Prison has shown, not for the first time, acute deficiencies in Britain's jails. Recent Home Office optimism that the prison service was on course to better times has been shattered. The Government's

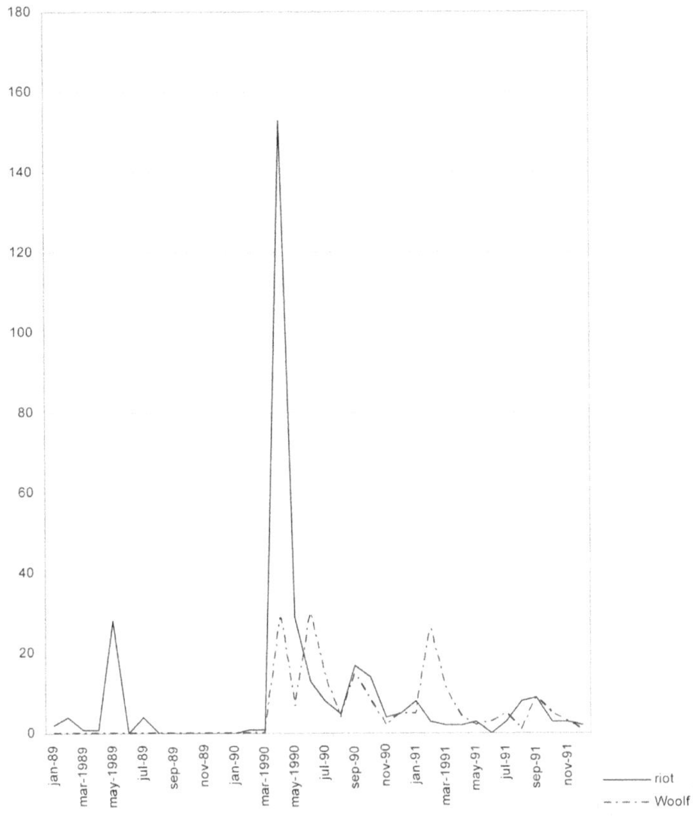

Figure 5.1 Media attention: number of articles on riots and Woolf that appeared in *The Times*, *The Sunday Times*, and *The Guardian*, 1 January 1989 to 31 December 1991

Source: Resodihardjo (2006a: 201).

> penal policy still has not achieved its main aim: to reduce the pressures which give rise to violence by prisoners, intransigence by staff and conditions which have long been a national disgrace.[74]

The highest peak in Figure 5.1 was, of course, created by the riots in April 1990. Just a year earlier, in April 1989, media paid attention to the riot in Risley remand centre, while in September 1990 articles on various topics related to the April 1990 disturbances were published. Articles in September 1990 addressed topics such as Strangeways governor O'Friel turning down a promotion and suicides in Hindley Prison that may have been caused by the high influx of prisoners evacuated from Strangeways Prison following the outbreak of the Manchester disturbance. The attention for the Woolf Inquiry fluctuated as well. In April 1990, newspapers discussed the installation of the Woolf Inquiry and what the inquiry should investigate. In June and September 1990, the proceedings of the Woolf Inquiry – including interesting remarks made during these proceedings – were followed and published by the media, while the publication of the report received ample attention in February 1991.

MPs were interested in the disturbances and the Woolf Inquiry as well. Between 1 April 1990 (when Home Secretary Waddington announced the Strangeways riot in a ministerial statement followed by debate) and 26 April 1990 (when Home Secretary Waddington announced the recapture of Strangeways Prison followed by debate), the MPs paid the following attention to the disturbances: one large debate was held on 5 April 1990; five written questions on the disturbances were tabled and answered; the question on the use of public funds to deal with the Strangeways riot was put forward when the proceeding of the Public Accounts Commission was discussed; and one question was asked to Prime Minister Thatcher during PMQs.

Though the number of written questions was not that high, the debates on 5 and 26 April and the question asked to Prime Minister Thatcher indicate that the riots were a hot item in parliament. During the debate on 5 April, MPs questions were still tepid and Home Secretary Waddington was able to deflect any difficult questions by referring to the Woolf Inquiry. The debate on 26 April, however, focused squarely on the malfunctioning prison service. MPs perceived the Strangeways riot as 'an embarrassing as well as a depressing episode … [which] is a national crisis that should be financed from national funds',[75] that top priority should be given 'to getting rid of three men being kept in a cell for 20 hours a day and slopping out, which is obviously a breeding ground for trouble'[76] and that the Home Secretary should 'feel a sense of shame about his own appalling complacency? It was 22 days before he visited the biggest prison fiasco in history, during which this so-called Government of law and order was held up to world ridicule'.[77] One of Waddington's responses was: 'what happened has been frustrating beyond measure for those of us who have had to carry the responsibility, and it has been infuriating for the public. Indeed, some members of the public have found it humiliating and I do not blame them for that.'[78] Moreover, the fact that a question (by a Conservative MP) was asked at Question Time, when MPs only have 15 minutes to talk about pressing problems, shows the importance MPs attached to the disturbances.

MPs were not only active in the House of Commons, but also in the media where they condemned the state of prisons and voiced their dissatisfaction with the functioning of the prison service. Most notably Labour's Home Affairs spokesman Sheerman who made clear that he 'blamed government complacency and prison overcrowding for the disturbances'.[79]

Policy makers face an institutional crisis when negative attention towards the functioning of their policy sector increases substantially. As the above shows, attention of the media and MPs to the prison service not only increased, but was also negative in nature. Hence, one can conclude that the prison service was in an institutional crisis. An academic described the situation as follows:

> [There was] massive publicity. What was so striking about the riots was that Strangeways is in the middle of Manchester. So TV cameras were able to catch the scene. So every night, the public got to see these images. [The prisoners] were presented as figures not as frightful for the community, but like the men who stick up two fingers to the establishment. The Director General of the prison service was made to look like a fool by the things he said. There was anger that the riots cost a lot of money and there was fear of loss of life (sex offenders being attacked). There were scare stories. So there was relief [when this was not the case]. People started to love [the prisoners]. They lost their fearfulness. It became a disruptive situation instead of sinister. The civil servants did not really look like they knew what they were doing.

When asked what the effect was of the riot on the image of the prison service, a governor involved in the Strangeways riot said:

> Very bad. We looked pretty unprofessional. ... So the early news conferences were awful or didn't happen. That led to bad news coverage and rumours. A press officer from the Home Office was sent to deal with the press. But he was a junior, his task at the Home Office had been to collect papers and arrange prison visits. Too junior. Totally swamped. So it was left to the area manager and police. And everyone speculated. We just didn't have the structure right. All boils down that we never expected to lose a big prison. Wasn't in the script.

Media and MPs Attention during the Woolf Inquiry

The prison service faced an institutional crisis during the disturbances. But what happened when the disturbances ended? When Strangeways Prison was recaptured again, attention of the media and MPs for the prison service decreased but did not disappear. Between the start of the inquiry (15 May 1990) and 1 November 1990 (when the public hearings and seminars had ended), *The Guardian* published 40 articles and *The Times* 22 articles on the proceedings of the Woolf Inquiry (see Figures 5.2 and 5.3).[80] The length of the articles ranged from 88 words to 878 words and included diverse topics (see Table 5.1 for a summing up of the topics).

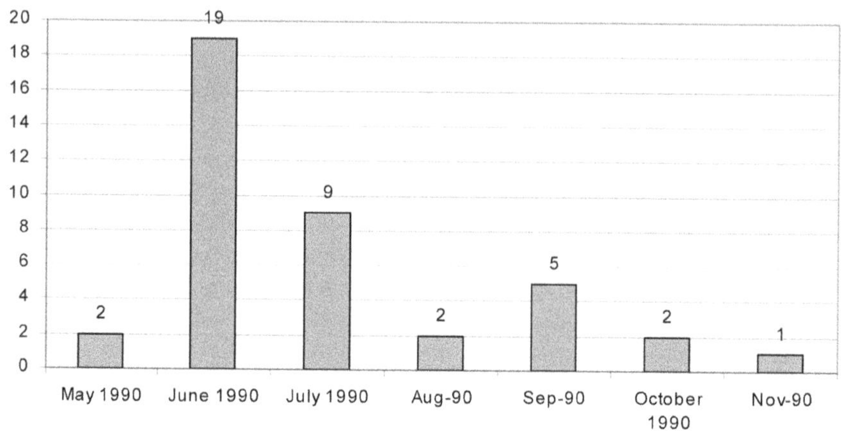

Figure 5.2 Number of articles in *The Guardian* addressing the proceedings of the Woolf Inquiry

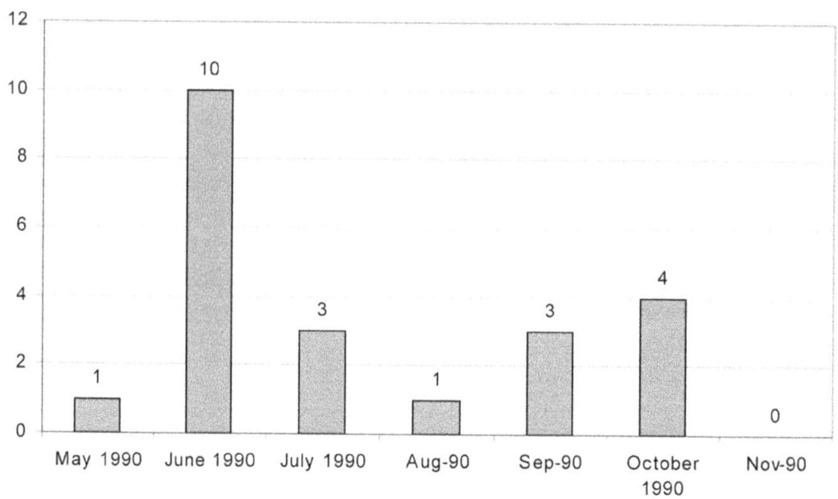

Figure 5.3 Number of articles in *The Times* addressing the proceedings of the Woolf Inquiry

Between 27 April 1990 (the first day after the end of the Strangeways riot) and 25 February 1991 (the day the Woolf Report was recommended to the House of Commons), MPs did not pay any attention to the proceedings of the Woolf Inquiry other than to inquire once when the report would be published, in accordance with the parliamentary custom to let an inquiry do its job without any questions asked in the House. But MPs did ask a large number of questions relating to the disturbances and the aftermath. During this period,

Table 5.1 Examples of topics addressed in the media during the Woolf Inquiry

The governor of Strangeways being overruled when he wanted to retake Strangeways[a]
Financial restraints had resulted in bad conditions in prisons including not enough clothes for prisoners[b]
The Woolf Inquiry had interviewed the ringleaders of the Strangeways riot[c]
The beating of prisoners by prison officers after the Dartmoor disturbance[d]
The moving of control and restraint equipment from Cardiff Prison to Dartmoor, thereby leaving the Cardiff prison short of equipment when a disturbance broke out[e]
The urging that prison officers should use CS gas by a deputy governor[f]
The 'enforced idleness' was seen as the main cause of the disturbances by the Apex Trust[g]
The deputy director general of the prison service told the inquiry that the prison service was not meeting its 'aims of treating inmates with humanity and preparing them for release'[h]

Notes:

a *The Guardian*, 12 June 1990, 'Veto on Jail Recapture "Hit Morale"'.
b *The Guardian*, 22 June 1990, 'Prison Officer Says Dress and Dignity Affected Prison Morale'.
c *The Guardian*, 27 June 1990, 'Inquiry "Consulted All Ringleaders"'.
d *The Guardian*, 12 July 1990, 'Woolf Hears Jail Beatings Charge'.
e *The Guardian*, 14 July 1990, 'Governor Tells of Riot Gear Move'.
f *The Guardian*, 18 July 1990, 'Probation Officers Protest Changes would be Wasteful'.
g *The Guardian*, 30 August 1990, 'UK News in Brief: Idleness "Main Cause of Prison Unrest"'.
h *The Guardian*, 3 October 1990, 'Prisons Chief Says Jails Fail to Meet Aims'.

23 questions were tabled and answered. In comparison, between 21 November 1989 and 1 April 1990, only five questions relating to prison conditions and disturbances were tabled.[81]

One can therefore conclude that even though attention was not as intense when compared to the April disturbances, media and MPs' attention continued. Compared to the previous months, however, this attention was almost negligible. Because an increase in negative attention from media and MPs indicates that there is an institutional crisis, one can only conclude that the worst of the institutional crisis was over once the Woolf Inquiry was under way.

The Outcome of the Events: Reform

In this study, reform is defined as intended fundamental change of the policy and/or administration of a policy sector. In this case, the question is whether the White Paper, which was the outcome of the institutional crisis, can be characterized in terms of reform. The answer to this question is 'yes'. Although the White Paper placed a larger emphasis on security than the Woolf Report, the White Paper did constitute a new prioritization whereby justice, control and security needed to be balanced. There was a shift from an almost complete focus on security (and warehousing) to a more balanced view. As such, the goals of the prison service, the fundament of the policy sector, were re-prioritized. This constitutes reform. 'The Woolf Report genuinely marked a great step forward in conceptualising what a decent prison system should be like, in a way that could command general acceptance. Its core proposition of security, control and justice all requiring to be maintained, and also to be kept in balance, may seem a very simple idea, but it caught a real truth and supported the comprehensive reform programme spelt out in the White Paper, *Custody, Care and Justice*' (Dunbar and Langdon, 1998: 33).

Linked to this shift in prioritization was the policy shift concerning slopping out and trebling (three prisoners to a cell meant for one). As one policy maker described the policy change: 'The main change, if you compare Woolf to previous policy, was better physical conditions and the end of slopping out. That was a real change. Before Woolf, it was not a priority to improve conditions.' As these changes constitute a fundamentally different approach towards the treatment of prisoners and what were considered to be humane conditions, these changes can be labelled reform as well. Other policy changes that deviated from the pre-disturbance period included, for instance, the introduction of a prison ombudsman, the development of community prisons so that prisoners did not have to travel all over the country to find a cell and as a result lose contact with friends and family, and to provide active and relevant programmes for all prisoners (Home Office, 1991c: 5–6). The policy changes in the White Paper are fundamental to the system and deviate markedly from previous policy. These changes to the prison service's policy therefore constitute reform.

Other authors agree that despite the lack of implementation later on, the White Paper in itself was progressive when published (cf. Cavadino and Dignan, 1997: 127). Although he was aware of the problematic situation in which the Woolf Report and the White Paper were conceived in terms of the law and order context and the bad relations mainly between the prison officers and headquarters, King (1994: 61) wrote that 'the Woolf package and the way it is embraced by the White Paper is comprehensive and impressively detailed. One has to suppose that its substantive programme for reform will outlast the ephemeral political and industrial relations context in which it was born'. Stern (1993: 259, cited in James et al., 1997: 59) wrote that the White Paper 'set out a programme of reform that would do credit to any prison administration in the modern world if it were implemented'. The focus of this study is on the outcome of the institutional crisis, not on the implementation of reform – a process that is riddled with its own barriers and problems. Therefore, one can conclude that the White Paper constituted reform as priorities and policies of the prison service were fundamentally changed.

Notes

1. Parts of this have been adapted from Resodihardjo (2006a; 2006b).
2. House of Lords, Disturbances, q, [518] (8.5.90) 1351–7: 1351–2.
3. House of Commons, Prison Disturbances, q, [173] (5.6.90) 412w.
4. House of Commons, Prison Security Bill, [200] (3.12.91) 167–222: 167; cf. *The Guardian*, 23 April 2004, 'Strangeways Roof-top Protester "Left to Rot". Supporters Say Inmate Still Held for Humiliating Prison Service'.
5. The prison officer, who had been at Strangeways Prison during the riot, did not die on the scene. He died from a heart attack while off duty (cf. *The Guardian*, 6 April 1990, 'Riot Inquiry to Examine Jail System: Strangeways Officers Turn Hoses on Final Protestors').
6. House of Commons, Prison Disturbances, q, [173] (5.6.90) 412w. According to the Woolf Report, 147 prison officers and 47 prisoners were injured, one prisoner died probably because of injuries received during the riot and one committed suicide later on (Woolf, 1991: 3).
7. For a detailed description of the disturbances in Manchester, Glen Parva, Dartmoor, Cardiff, Bristol and Pucklechurch Prisons, see the Woolf Report (1991).
8. *The Times*, 7 April 1990, 'Temporary Centres Considered to Reduce Jail Overcrowding'.
9. *The Sunday Times*, 8 April 1990, 'Dartmoor Inmates Loose on Rooftop Rampage'; *The Times*, 9 April 1990, 'Officers Injured at Other Prisons'.
10. The decision to use strong-arm tactics to end the Bristol riot was taken 'at a high level within the Home Office' (*The Times*, 10 April 1990, 'Use of Baton and Shield Squad Marks a Change in Tactics').
11. During the siege, prisoners surrendered until only a small group remained.
12. *The Times*, 10 April 1990, 'Use of Baton and Shield Squad Marks a Change in Tactics'.
13. *The Times*, 10 April 1990, 'Use of Baton and Shield Squad Marks a Change in Tactics'.
14. Prisoners living in cells without access to integrated sanitation had to use chamber pots. Every morning, prisoners had to slop out, that is, empty their chamber pots.
15. *The Financial Times*, 12 April 1990, 'Extra Resources Allocated to Jails'.
16. *The Times*, 21 April 1990, 'Police to Seek £2m Strangeways Cost from Waddington'; cf. *The Guardian*, 21 April 1990, 'Strangeways Riot Squad Plan "Vetoed by Prison Managers"'. For more details, see Woolf (1991).
17. *The Times*, 21 April 1990, 'Police to Seek £2m Strangeways Cost from Waddington'.

18. For details on the siege and the way the disturbance was handled, see Woolf, 1991.
19. House of Commons, Strangeways Prison, [170] (2.4.90) 903–912: 903–5.
20. House of Commons, Strangeways Prison, [170] (2.4.90) 903–912: 905.
21. *The Guardian*, 3 April 1990, 'Waddington Attacks "Orgy of Violence": Minister Highlights Improved Conditions and New Prison Building Programme'.
22. House of Commons, Strangeways Prison, [170] (2.4.90) 903–912: 904.
23. House of Commons, Strangeways Prison, [170] (2.4.90) 903–912: 905.
24. *The Times*, 2 April 1990, 'Prisoners Die in Rioting at Blazing Jail'.
25. *The Guardian*, 2 April 1990, 'Prison Erupts in Violence. 12 Feared Dead at Strangeways'.
26. *The Guardian*, 2 April 1990, 'Prison Reforms that Came too Late: Waddington's Hopes for a New Dawn in the Prison Service Dashed by Renewed Industrial Unrest and Discontent among Inmates'.
27. The Woolf Inquiry established that seven prison officers were present at the service.
28. Bartell, the chairman of the POA, cited in *The Times*, 3 April 1990, 'Warnings of Tensions Ignored, Officers Say'.
29. *The Times*, 2 April 1990, 'Prisoners Die in Rioting at Blazing Jail'.
30. House of Commons, Strangeways Prison, [171] (26.4.1990) 498–512: 510.
31. *The Times*, 10 April 1990, 'Detailed News Coverage of Prison Riots Attacked'.
32. *The Guardian*, 14 April 1990, 'Inquiry into Press Coverage of Riots'.
33. Cf. *The Guardian*, 24 April 1990, 'It Made Sense to Hold Back'.
34. *The Times*, 10 April 1990, 'Prison Officers' Dawn Raid Ends Siege at Bristol'; cf. *The Guardian*, 24 April 1990, 'Strangeways Spark Spread Protests to 19 Prisons within Three Weeks'.
35. *The Times*, 10 April 1990, 'Prison Officers' Dawn Raid Ends Siege at Bristol'; cf. *The Guardian*, 24 April 1990, 'Strangeways Spark Spread Protests to 19 Prisons within Three Weeks'.
36. Question Time is held four times a week. Prime Ministers Thatcher and Major used two of these meetings to answer MPs' questions for 15 minutes. MPs are allowed to ask any question, but not express their opinions, on any subject that the Prime Minister is responsible for. Since time is short, only the most pressing topics will be addressed. Questions on subjects that are not so high on the political agenda can be tabled for a written answer (cf. Norton, 2001a: 358–9).
37. House of Commons, Prime Minister, Engagements, [171] (26.4.90) 479–80:480.
38. House of Commons, Strangeways Prison, [171] (26.4.1990) 498–512: 500.
39. There is little information in the media and parliamentary debates on the actions of Train and Emes regarding the riots (though there is information in the Woolf Report) and no information whatsoever regarding their response to the institutional crisis. They therefore do not play a large role in this chapter.
40. *The Guardian*, 9 May 1990, 'Warders Vote for Industrial Action'.
41. The complete repair of Strangeways Prison was estimated to cost £60 million (*The Times*, 18 May 1990, 'Strangeways to be Redeveloped in £60m Plan').

42. *The Guardian*, 9 May 1990, 'Warders Vote for Industrial Action'.
43. *The Times*, 6 July 1990, 'Prison Officers to Begin Ban on Inmates Today'.
44. *The Guardian*, 23 July 1990, '400 Staff on Offer in Jail Peace Plan'.
45. *The Guardian*, 2 April 1990, 'Prison Reforms that Came too Late: Waddington's Hopes for a New Dawn in the Prison Service Dashed by Renewed Industrial Unrest and Discontent among Inmates'.
46. House of Commons, Strangeways Prison, [171] (26.4.90) 498–512: 499.
47. House of Commons, Strangeways Prison, [170] (5.4.90) 1339–47: 1345.
48. *The Guardian*, 10 April 1990, Penal reformers fail to move Waddington.
49. House of Commons, Strangeways Prison, [170] (5.4.90) 1339–47: 1340.
50. *The Guardian*, 3 September 1990, 'Battle Lines Drawn over Penal Reform: Debate Centres on Enforceable Rights for Prisoners'.
51. *The Times*, 25 September 1990, 'Prison Officers Call for Minimum Standards to Prevent More Riots'.
52. *The Guardian*, 10 May 1990, 'Second Judge Joins Inquiry into Prisons: Widening Policy Scrutiny Alarms Home Office Officials'.
53. *The Guardian*, 10 May 1990, 'Second Judge Joins Inquiry into Prisons: Widening Policy Scrutiny Alarms Home Office Officials'.
54. *The Guardian*, 3 September 1990, 'Battle Lines Drawn over Penal Reform: Debate Centres on Enforceable Rights for Prisoners'.
55. *The Times*, 25 September 1990, 'Prison Officers Call for Minimum Standards to Prevent More Riots'.
56. *The Guardian*, 3 September 1990, 'Battle Lines Drawn over Penal Reform: Debate Centres on Enforceable Rights for Prisoners'.
57. *The Guardian*, 1 November 1990, 'Prison Director Urges Minimum Jail Standards'.
58. 'The arrival of John Major at 10 Downing Street and Kenneth Baker at the Home Office is expected to move policy-making slightly to the left. All the main political parties now agree that fewer non-violent offenders should be jailed, that conditions in prisons should be improved and that police should work harder to justify increases in manpower. A Major-Baker axis on Home Office policy may increase this trend. Both also oppose capital punishment in contrast to their immediate predecessors' (*The Times*, 17 December 1990, 'Policies Move to the Left').
59. *The Times*, 1 February 1991, 'Manifesto for Prisons'.
60. *The Times*, 23 February 1991, 'Baker Ready to End Prison Slopping out a Year Early'.
61. *The Times*, 15 December 1990, 'A Mission for Mr Baker'.
62. House of Commons, Prisons (Woolf Report) [186] (25.2.91) 659–73: 660.
63. House of Commons, Prisons (Woolf Report) [186] (25.2.91) 659–73: 664.
64. Judge Tumim had been asked to investigate suicides committed in prisons.
65. On 7 July 1991, an escape occurred from Brixton Prison. Two Category A IRA prisoners shot their way out of Brixton Prison in London. It turned out that the prison service had been warned about an impending escape but that lack of communication resulted in the fact that the persons responsible for the management

of Category A prisoners and certain key staff at Brixton Prison had not been properly notified (Home Office, 1991a: 1). The media and MPs focused their attention on the apparent lack of security in the prison service. Labour MPs called for the resignation of the Home Secretary. Shadow Home Secretary Hattersley said that the Home Secretary was 'entirely unfit to occupy his office' (House of Commons, Brixton Prison (Escapes), [194] (8.7.91) 649–59: 651). Inquiries were held, including by HM Chief Inspector of Prisons Tumim, who was asked to head an inquiry into the escape, and Lakes and Hadfield, who headed an inquiry into the security of the Prison Service in general. Moreover, the governor of Brixton was asked to take a pre-retirement leave and the head of Directorate of Custody 1 (DOC1) was replaced (Home Office, 1991a: 5). The Lakes/Hadfield interim report did not recommend any policy change, but instead recommended better implementation of current policy (Home Office, 1991a: 4). Other measures were bringing forward the opening of the new high security unit for unconvicted high risk Category A prisoners at Belmarsh (originally intended to open in November 1991 (House of Commons, Brixton Prison (Escapes), [194] (8.7.91) 649–59: 650), taking a closer look at how existing security policy could be better implemented, and reviewing management performance. 'Judge Tumim's report reveals weaknesses in the management and administration of the Prison Department and its relationship with Governors in the prisons. … Mr Train, the Director General of the Prison Service, retires at the end of this month. Mr Pilling, the newly appointed Director General, will assume full responsibility for the Prison Service as from next week' (Home Office, 1991a: 6). Security measures recommended by Tumim, such as X-raying incoming parcels, were seen as 'so significant that we should both extend it to other relevant establishments and expand its scope' (Home Office, 1991a: 3; cf. Home Office, 1991b; Resodihardjo, 2002).

66. *The Times*, 17 September 1991, 'Teach Them a Lesson behind Bars' (written by Kenneth Baker).
67. House of Commons, Prison Service Review, q, [201] (16.12.91) 13w, cf. Lygo, 1991
68. House of Commons, Prison Service Review, q, [205] (11.3.92) 563w.
69. See, for example, *The Guardian*, 17 September 1991, 'Taking the Woolf Way, at a Stroll'; *The Guardian*, 17 September 1991, 'Bold Jail Reforms but no more Cash'.
70. *The Guardian*, 17 September 1991, 'Bold Jail Reforms but no more Cash'.
71. *The Times*, 21 April 1990, 'It Took a Riot'.
72. *The Guardian*, 26 April 1990, 'Longest Siege Exposed Overcrowding, Segregation and Security Failings'.
73. *The Guardian*, 6 April 1990, 'Why Woolf Needs to be the Prison Scarman'.
74. *The Times*, 3 April 1990, 'Prison Pressures'.
75. MP Hattersly, House of Commons, Strangeways Prison, [171] (26.4.90) 498–512: 499, 501.
76. MP Montgomery, House of Commons, Strangeways Prison, [171] (26.4.90) 498–512: 503.

77. MP Litherland, House of Commons, Strangeways Prison, [171] (26.4.90) 498–512: 505.
78. House of Commons, Strangeways Prison, [171] (26.4.90) 498–512: 508.
79. *The Guardian*, 9 April 1990, 'Inmate Dies as Riots Spread: Dartmoor Prisoner Found Dead in Cell, Home Office Denies System is Out of Control, 100 Rampage at Cardiff'.
80. These figures include lower numbers of articles addressing Woolf than the numbers in Figure 5.1, because the numbers in these tables refer to articles solely addressing the proceedings of the Woolf Inquiry, while Figure 5.1 includes all articles referring to the Woolf Inquiry in one way or another.
81. House of Commons, prison accommodation, q, [163] (13.12.89) 641–6w; House of Commons, Risley, q, [165] (18.1.90) 377w; House of Commons, Risley Remand Centre, q, [165] (18.1.90) 888w; House of Commons, prison accommodation, q, [167] (22.2.90) 924w; House of Commons, Category C prisoners, q, [169] (23.3.90) 796–7w.

Chapter 6
The Escapes from Whitemoor and Parkhurst (1994–1995)

Introduction[1]

Between September 1994 and January 1995, the Prison Service of England and Wales had to deal with two major escapes, a riot and the suicide of Frederick West (who was on remand for the so-called 'House of Horrors' murders). It was again a critical time for the prison service. The media portrayed the prison service as unable to maintain security, lax and as pampering prisoners and held Director General Lewis and Home Secretary Howard responsible for a failing prison service.

The events and subsequent negative attention from the media and MPs created yet another institutional crisis for the prison service. This crisis centred on two problems. First, the media and MPs raised questions about who was responsible for the failing prison service: Director General Lewis or Home Secretary Howard? According to Howard, the agency-structure of the prison service left no doubt: he was responsible for policy and Lewis for the operational side of running the prison service. Second, policy makers were under enormous pressure to do something about the perceived lax security in prisons. As a result, priorities within the prison service shifted from Woolf's balance between security, control and justice towards security as the number one, two and three priority of the prison service (Lewis, 1997: 162).

Escapes from Whitemoor and Parkhurst

Escaping from the Most Secure Prison in the Country: Whitemoor

On Friday 9 September 1994, six prisoners escaped from the Special Secure Unit (SSU) at Whitemoor Prison. Of the six prisoners, five were convicted IRA terrorists and one had previously been involved in an armed prison outbreak. Armed with two pistols, they shot one prison guard[2] on their way out. One escapee was caught just outside the prison, but the other five remained at large. A manhunt started. During this hunt, unarmed police officers ordered the five escapees to lay down. Three of them responded, while two prisoners continued to run. With the help of a thermal imager on a police helicopter, the last two escapees were captured as well (Woodcock, 1994).

The media's delight on the speedy recapture of the escapees soon gave way to a more negative stance towards the prison service. Whitemoor Prison was a relatively new prison – it had been opened in 1991 – and had been built to prevent escapes of Category A prisoners.[3] The prison 'was regarded within the service as virtually escape-proof' (Woodcock, 1994: 1) and it was described as a '£52 million showpiece prison'.[4] The fact that SSU prisoners had been able to escape was embarrassing for the prison service. Another cause for embarrassment was that the escapees had guns. 'Behind the congratulations and relief [on the recapture], however, is deep embarrassment for the prison service over how guns could be smuggled into one of its most secure units. There have been demands for heads to roll.'[5]

Before long journalists began to talk about lax security measures[6] and demanded that the Home Secretary took responsibility instead of shifting the blame to Director General Lewis by referring to operational responsibility. As *The Times* wrote: 'The creation of executive agencies, operating at a distance from ministers, was supposed to make public services more efficient and less political. In this case, it has simply made blame easier to shift around the machine.'[7] The question to be answered was therefore whether the report of the Woodcock Inquiry – installed on 10 September 1994 by the Home Secretary to investigate the escape – would prove that the Whitemoor escape was an operational or a policy failure. If the escape was classified in the former category, then Lewis would be responsible; the latter category would mean the resignation of Howard.

The media also blamed the prison service for allowing prisoners in Whitemoor's SSU to live the high life. An article in *The Sunday Times* described the luxurious five-star situation. SSU prisoners gave prison officers shopping lists for expensive goods, one spare cell was changed into a solarium with a sun bed, and there was an Astro-turf football pitch for prisoners to play on.[8] *The Daily Mirror* spoke of a 'holiday camp – except that no holiday firm could afford to treat its customers as lavishly as these vile criminals'. Howard was 'talking tough, but failing to deliver'.[9]

This escape was followed by a number of other security-related incidents. A handgun and ammunition was found at Durham prison (a high security dispersal prison) and an escape map was found in the possession of high-security prisoners at Belmarsh Prison.[10] All these incidents caught the attention of journalists who dedicated numerous articles to the incidents.

The media were not the only ones paying attention to the prison service. Prison officers and the former chairman of Whitemoor's Board of Visitors alleged that the Home Office had 'deliberately weakened security for IRA prisoners' in order to appease these prisoners.[11] Moreover, the chairman of the Boards of Prison Visitors alleged that the Home Secretary had ignored a report[12] by Judge Tumim, the Chief Inspector of Prisons, warning about prisoners conditioning prison officers at Whitemoor Prison.[13]

When approximately half a kilo (1.1lb) of Semtex was found at Whitemoor Prison on 22 September 1994 (Woodcock, 1994: 2–3), the media was quick to judge. The Semtex find was a 'deeply worrying breach of prison security which must be explained and answered for. ... No excuses can be made for this incident'.[14] The Home Secretary 'is responsible for the absurd laxity revealed by the jailbreak and easy lifestyle of prisoners there. He should have sacked the prison boss Derek Lewis and Whitemoor's governor'.[15] *The Daily Mirror* called the Home Secretary the 'serial bungler'.[16] *The Guardian* wrote 'The problem with the Prison Service security lapses is that they undermine the very basis of his claim to be the most rightwing Home Secretary for 30 years. How can you be tough on crime and [criminals] if they appear to be in control of the prisons that are supposed to be the toughest in the country? Not only in control, but reportedly ordering lobsters takeaways'.[17]

Other actors joined the choir as well. POA chairman Bartell blamed Home Secretary Howard for a 'monthly catalogue of violence against staff, drugs abuse and major security breaches'.[18] Labour prison spokeswoman Ruddock: 'It's impossible to think of a worse breach of security. We know that Michael Howard has lost control of crime on the streets. He now appears to have lost control of the prisons.'[19] Shaw, head of the Prison Reform Trust, said 'staff at Whitemoor, Howard and Lewis should "consider their positions"'.[20]

The media attacked not only the prison service, the Home Secretary and the Director General, but also the governor of Whitemoor, Clark, as well as the former governor of Whitemoor, Barclay. The media often cited Barclay's words during the opening of Whitemoor Prison that it was 'the most secure in the country'.[21]

The Daily Mirror alleged that the IRA prisoners at Whitemoor Prison had used their 60 minutes free telephone time to raise money for their cause.[22] According to *The Times*, these calls were allegedly made to Libya and Iran.[23] Labour prison spokeswoman Ruddock tabled written questions on the alleged abuse of phone privileges for the Home Secretary to answer.

The announcement that Lewis, Director General of the prison service, had received a bonus for his performance could not have come at a worse moment. This news was disclosed on 11 December 1994. A Home Office spokesman told the press that the £35,000 bonus was for the prison service's performance up to March 1994. During which time 'escapes went down 25 per cent, there was a three per cent cut in the cost per prisoner, and the practice of three people sharing a cell was virtually eliminated'.[24]

Nevertheless, the bonus did not sit well with the media and MPs because of the series of blunders in the previous months.[25] Labour Home Affairs spokesman Michael said 'it was difficult to understand which elements of Lewis's performance were related to the bonus payment'.[26] Tory MP Evans thought Lewis 'would be embarrassed to receive this money. It is certainly not the message we should be giving when many people in the public sector are receiving no increase'.[27]

The Woodcock Report

On 19 December 1994, the report of the inquiry into the Whitemoor escape was published and discussed in the House of Commons. The Woodcock Report was very critical of the practices in the SSU at Whitemoor. Physical security had lapsed, prisoners had conditioned[28] staff and prisoners had too many privileges that had resulted in an impression of pampered SSU inmates. Regarding responsibility for operational and policy matters, the report concluded that there was clear responsibility for the Director General for the day-to-day running of the prison service. There was, however, some confusion about the respective roles of all involved and it was very difficult to distinguish between operational and policy matter. Consequently, there was 'confusion as to where responsibility lies' (Woodcock, 1994: 84). The Woodcock Inquiry felt that it was beyond their remit to comment any further on this matter (Woodcock, 1994: 85).

The Woodcock Report concluded that the escape was 'a disaster waiting to happen' and the prison service had to improve the implementation of its own security measures (Woodcock, 1994: 81, 84). The report made 62 recommendations, ranging from surveillance and observation to the deployment of dogs. Most recommendations focused on improving security.

The Policy Makers' Response

The policy makers' response towards the incidents can be categorized into two steps. First, Home Secretary Howard asked Sir John Woodcock, former Chief Inspector of Constabulary, to investigate the escape on 10 September 1994;[29] establishing an inquiry into the events is a well-trusted instrument to deflect the attention of the media and MPs. Moreover, one can hope that by the time the report is published, the storm has blown over – which did not happen in this case (cf. Resodihardjo, 2006a).

Second, the Home Secretary defended himself and his actions in the media and in parliament. One way in which he did defend himself was to announce a set of measures to show the public that something was being done to prevent escapes from occurring in the future and to improve the functioning of the prison service. Moreover, Prime Minister Major backed up Howard. Senior Downing Street officials 'dismissed the calls for Mr Howard's head as hysterical and "not of the real world"'.[30]

Regarding the measures to improve security, the Home Secretary announced these measures on 18 September 1994 and on 19 December 1994. On 18 September 1994, Home Secretary Howard disclosed the restriction of prisoners' privileges[31] in response to the Whitemoor escape and the gun find in Durham. Howard said that 'I want to see privileges earned, not handed down as right'.[32]

On 19 December, Howard presented the Woodcock Report to the House of Commons. During the House of Commons debate on the Woodcock Report, Howard introduced four measures to improve overall security in the prison service and in Whitemoor particularly. First, the following measures were taken right after the Whitemoor escape: the SSU at Whitemoor was closed and physical security was improved[33] at Whitemoor, including reinforcing the perimeter, adding cameras and installing extra searching facilities such as X-ray machines. Moreover, prisons holding Category A prisoners were told to make sure that searching procedures were strictly enforced and security was reviewed in dispersal, local, and category B training prisons.[34]

Second, the Home Secretary accepted all 64 of Woodcock's recommendations, most of which 'either have been or are being implemented'.[35] Third, Howard said that it was necessary to go beyond even Woodcock's security recommendations.[36] Additional measures included: (a) introducing 'a more systematic method of recording and evaluating intelligence and security information on staff who might present a security risk';[37] (b) equipping all staff in high-security units with personal alarms; (c) reinforcing perimeter security; and (d) installing an independent inquiry headed by General Sir John Learmont, formerly Quartermaster General for the Army, into the security of the prison service in order to restore public confidence.[38]

And fourth, practices such as the abuse of telephones, the enormous amount of possessions prisoners could have, the prison officers going shopping for prisoners and the possession of luxury items were halted.[39] Prisoners would have to earn privileges instead of enjoying them 'as a matter of right'.[40] A new system of earned privileges would be in place by the end of the following year.[41]

Moreover, during the House of Commons debate, the Home Secretary defended the bonus payment made to Lewis by saying the bonus was no reward for incompetence, but reflected that the prison service had largely achieved its targets in the previous year.[42] To the amusement of the MPs, the Home Secretary told the Commons that the 'director has agreed that there is no question of a bonus during the current year'.[43] Furthermore, Home Secretary Howard responded to the calls of resignation[44] with 'I have a job to do, and I am determined to see it through'.[45] Regarding the allegations that he had ignored the Inspectorate's report on Whitemoor, he told the House of Commons that the report's recommendations were made to the Director General, the area manager and the governor, but not to the Home Secretary. The Home Secretary argued that he was therefore not responsible for the escape and did not have to resign. Moreover, 'there is not a word of criticism of policy in the Woodcock Report. Nor is there any basis for the suggestions that my policies were in any way responsible for what happened'.[46]

During the debate, the Home Secretary stressed that security was the new priority of the prison service. According to Howard, 'the first duty of the Prison Service [must be]: to keep prisoners in secure custody'.[47] Director

General Lewis supported Howard and summoned all governing governors to London where he told them that the top three priorities of the prison service were security, security and security (Lewis, 1997: 162).

> The choice we face is stark. Public confidence in the Prison Service is at a low ebb. We have done the research. There is a widely held public view that current security levels are not acceptable. I intend that *we* should take the initiative – that it should be the Prison Service that shows the way in security. It is after all our first duty. For the next twelve months security will have *not only to be our first priority but our second and third priorities also.* (Lewis, 1997: 162, italics added in last sentence)

Despite presenting all these measures during the House of Commons debate, MPs continued to criticize the Home Secretary. Shadow Home Secretary Straw (Labour), for example, concluded that

> Against that background, and given all the other disasters over which the right hon. and learned Gentleman has presided, will he now begin to acknowledge that his position is becoming increasingly untenable? Is not the truth of the situation that the report reveals a catalogue of incompetence and negligence on a truly monumental scale, which has been compounded today by buck passing by the Secretary of State [Howard], and by his failure properly to recognise his responsibility for this appalling state of affairs, in which the safety of many prison officers and the public was put at risk? Because of the Home Secretary's failure and that of the Prison Service, public confidence in the prison system has been woefully undermined.[48]

The Whitemoor Aftermath

The media spent the rest of December 1994 dissecting the Woodcock Report and contemplating whether Howard should resign and whether Lewis should be sacked.[49] Regarding the Woodcock Report, *The Guardian*, for example, stated

> Was it a Whitehall whitewash? The Woodcock Inquiry into the notorious Whitemoor Prison escape closely scrutinises one scandal – the IRA breakout from the pounds 58 million new high security prison – but completely ignores two more fundamental issues: Whitehall's accountability and the future of special secure units. ... Yet the more fundamental issue – where does the buck stop? – is ducked. The inquiry failed to discover where responsibility rests in the new system.[50]

The Times wrote 'If Michael Howard does not believe he should resign as Home Secretary over the Whitemoor affair, where does the buck stop? At present, the blame is being shifted in an unseemly way between ministers, official advisers and the Prison Service. The whole question of responsibility is blurred in ways that suit ministers in trouble like Mr Howard'.[51] *The Daily Mirror* condemned the actions of Home Secretary Howard and Director General Lewis and thought that 'the Whitemoor fiasco will not be properly resolved until heads roll'.[52]

The media, MPs and interest groups remained interested in the prison service. Nonetheless, their attention started to dwindle by the end of December 1994. Unfortunately for the prison service, however, the new year started with a series of new incidents that revived the public's attention. As a consequence, the crisis continued.

A Suicide, a Riot, and Another Escape

The new year started with a bang for the prison service. On 1 January 1995, Frederick West, who was on remand for the 'House of Horrors' murders, committed suicide. On 2 and 3 January 1995, disturbances occurred at Everthorpe Prison and on 3 January 1995 another serious escape by Category A prisoners took place.

In order to understand the fall-out created by West's suicide, some background knowledge is necessary. Frederick and Rosemary West sexually assaulted women and murdered some of them in the 1980s and 1990s in their house in Gloucester (Levi, 1997: 850). The Wests buried their victims in the garden and in the house. One of their victims included their own 16-year-old daughter; another victim had been seven months pregnant.[53] The Wests became known as the House of Horror suspects as details of their crimes became public knowledge.[54]

Fred West, who had been accused of 12 murders, was found dead on 1 January 1995 in his cell at Winson Green prison. He had committed suicide by using his own clothes to create a noose to hang himself. The condemnation both MPs and the media voiced about the prison service and Home Secretary Howard for allowing Fred West to kill himself was loud and clear. *The Times*, for example, wrote:

> After the death of Frederick West while on remand in Winson Green prison and the damning report on the IRA break-out at Whitemoor, the Everthorpe disturbances increased *the perception of a prison service with severe difficulties*. The Opposition accused Michael Howard, the Home Secretary, of running scared when neither he nor Michael Forsyth, the Prisons Minister, commented about the latest incidents. Jack Straw, the Shadow Home Secretary, said that when things were going well Mr Howard was there to take the credit, but when there were problems he could not be found.[55] (Italics added)

Howarth, a Labour MP on prisons, was quick to judge the suicide and the lack of supervision by staff.[56] Shadow Home Secretary Straw added: 'Precisely because of the horrendous nature of the charges against him, the public, and above all the victims' relatives, had a right to expect West would be kept securely until his trial.'[57] Liberal Democrat Home Affairs spokesman Beith condemned the suicide as well. 'This should never have been allowed to happen, and it may deprive grieving relatives of the chance of getting the whole truth about the dreadful murders of which he was charged.'[58]

Pressure continued to increase as others condemned the situation and tried to link the reduced cell watch of West to Home Secretary Howard. Judge Tumim, Chief Inspector of Prisons, thought 'West should have been kept under 24-hour surveillance'.[59] The POA claimed that 'ministers must have been informed that the watch on Mr West was being reduced'.[60] Tory MP French thought that West should have been on close monitoring for 24-hours a day, but that it was the prison service who made the decisions regarding monitoring.[61] *The Guardian* wrote: 'Justice thwarted is justice denied. Suicide is a highly unsatisfactory end to Fred West's role in the grim killings at 25 Cromwell Street ... Opposition MPs were right to express anger yesterday at the incompetence which allowed West to end his life.'[62] The media portrayed Home Secretary Howard as responsible for giving Fred West the opportunity to kill himself. A headline of the *Daily Mirror*, for example, read 'You let him beat justice Howard'.[63]

The pressure on the prison service intensified as disturbances broke out in Everthorpe Prison on 2 and 3 January 1995. On the first night of the disturbances, 67 inmates refused to go back to their cell. On the second night, 124 prisoners rioted in the same prison.

Moreover, on 3 January 1995 three prisoners managed to escape from Parkhurst Prison. On that day, 31 prisoners were escorted to the prison's sports hall at 6 p.m.[64] One of the two instructors present took a roll call before prisoners went to their activities. One prison officer remained in the observation box to oversee the activities, but blind spots and the crowded area hindered the observation process. As a result, three prisoners, two Category A and one Category B, were able to escape. Their escape went unnoticed as the remaining prisoners wandered around and distracted the prison officers when it was time for them to return to their cell at 7 p.m. No roll call was taken and there were no attempts to count the prisoners.

More than an hour later, a dog handler patrolling the perimeter discovered a hole in the inner perimeter. It took another 30 minutes before the absence of three prisoners could be confirmed. Parkhurst Prison, a dispersal prison, is located on the Isle of Wight. One of the prisoners was a qualified pilot and the prisoners had planned to escape from the island by stealing a plane. The prisoners had made a tool in the prison workshop so that they could use the ignition of a plane, but they had left it at the prison. The escapees then changed their plans and tried to locate a suitable boat to cross the sea to the mainland. For four days, they hid on the island in the search for a suitable boat. On 8 January, off-duty prison officers spotted the three escapees looking for a boat and recaptured them.

During the six-day hunt for the escaped prisoners more details of the escape became public knowledge. The escapees had used a copy of a master key and there were claims that the governor of Parkhurst, Marriott, had known two days before the escape of the existence of this copy key.[65] There was a sighting of one of the escapees doing a dummy run four days before their escape and parts of a prison officer's uniform went missing.[66] The PGA and POA made clear that governor Marriott had been trying to get a security alarm installed on the inner wall of the prison for more than a year, but that the Home Office had refused to strengthen security.[67] Furthermore, there was (again) a report by Tumim, Chief Inspector of Prisons. Tumim had warned the prison service about the 'serious security defects' at Parkhurst Prison in October 1994.[68]

In response to this escape, Home Secretary Howard asked Tilt, Director of Security, to conduct an internal investigation in the escape. The relationship between the POA and the prison service became strained again as Director General Lewis accused the POA of obstructing this internal inquiry. The Director General claimed that the POA had advised its members not to cooperate with Tilt's inquiry (Lewis, 1997: 167).[69] The POA hit back right away. Bartell, the POA chairman, said that Lewis' statement 'was a "total distortion of the truth"'. His members at Parkhurst had been told to provide the inquiry with a full written statement of the facts instead of giving verbal answers. "The prison department wants to have a cosy chat in a secluded room. We don't know whether they will be recorded for the record".'[70]

The media, already focused on the prison service by the West suicide and the Everthorpe disturbance, paid ample attention to the Parkhurst escape. Headlines included 'Governors "look in vain" for leadership; crisis in the prisons',[71] 'A minister who has lost all our trust'[72] and 'No escape. Howard must restore public confidence in the prisons'.[73] The article following that last headline sums up what other journalists wrote as well:

> Rarely has the Prison Service been struck by so humiliating a series of embarrassments as in the past week. On Sunday, the alleged serial murderer Frederick West was found hanged in his cell at Winson Green prison in Birmingham. There have been two riots at Everthorpe jail in Humberside. Meanwhile, three men described by the police as extremely dangerous are on the loose because of lax security at Parkhurst on the Isle of Wight. Public confidence in the prison system could scarcely be at a lower ebb.[74]

In a number of newspaper articles, the resignation of Home Secretary Howard and/or Director General Lewis was demanded. Moreover, the question was asked why nothing had been done to prevent the escape, especially as Judge Tumim, Chief Inspector of Prisons, had found 'serious security defects' at Parkhurst Prison during an inspection in October 1994.[75] The media also paid attention to the distinction between operational and policy matters.[76] *The Times* concluded that such a distinction was viable since Home Secretaries have a vast range of responsibilities, but '[a]s operational failures mount up, ministers must accept that they are failing in their primary task to maintain public faith in the criminal justice system'.[77] The media's attention also focused on the governor of Parkhurst Prison, Marriott. It did not take the tabloids long to come up with 'the Marriott Hotel' when describing the five-star treatment at Parkhurst Prison. According to the *Daily Mirror*, this included ice-cream vans and barbecues. The prison was compared with a holiday camp.[78]

Labour and Liberal Democrat MPs called for the resignation of Howard and Lewis.[79, 80] Shadow Home Secretary Straw did not exactly demand the resignation of Home Secretary Howard, but he did say that 'Howard's job was "on the line" following last year's IRA breakout from Whitemoor high security prison'.[81]

Director General Lewis emphasized that improvements had been achieved:

> There have been serious incidents. I do not wish to give any impression of complacency. But there needs to be an appreciation of the things that have been improving in the service as well. Escapes … [have] halved during the past 2½ years, with 37 per cent of the reduction coming during the past 18 months. Triple occupation of cells had been eliminated in spite of a growth in the prison population. Privately managed court escort services, although much criticised[82] when they were first introduced, had improved security by 40 per cent and were producing 25 per cent cost savings.[83]

Nevertheless, his defence did not defuse the situation as the media pointed out that the escapes from Whitemoor and Parkhurst were 'catastrophic breaches' overshadowing the previously achieved decline in the number of escapes.[84]

Home Secretary Howard came under fierce attack during the House of Commons debate on 10 January 1995, the first day after the Christmas recess.[85] Home Secretary Howard addressed the House of Commons on the incidents. He briefly addressed the West suicide and Everthorpe disturbances before turning his attention to the Parkhurst escape. Tilt had given the preliminary conclusions of the internal inquiry into the escape to the Home Secretary the night before. The report would not be published because it contained detailed information on the security of Parkhurst Prison.[86] The inquiry had shown that there were 'very serious deficiencies in procedural and physical security at Parkhurst'.[87] The Home Secretary thought that the fact that this could happen so soon after the Woodcock Report and the clear message of the Director General that security procedures had to be followed was 'a cause for dismay'.[88] Besides summing up measures to improve security at Parkhurst

Prison, Howard announced that the governor Marriott was to be removed from Parkhurst. The Learmont Inquiry would take the Parkhurst escape into account when investigating the security in the prison service; a disciplinary investigation into the Parkhurst escape would be held; and six prison officers would be transferred to other prisons. Regarding his responsibilities as Home Secretary, Howard made it clear that he was accountable to the House of Commons for the prison service and responsible for all policy decisions. He then stated that Tilt's report did not indicate that 'any policy decision of mine ... can be held to have caused in any way the breakout from Parkhurst'.[89] Nor had Tumim's report warned him of any security breaches as they had occurred during the escape. Howard concluded his statement with:

> Recent events are bound to have affected public confidence in the Prison Service and it will not be easy to repair the damage that they have done to its reputation. That damage can be repaired only by finding out exactly what went wrong in each of those events and taking all the action that is necessary to put things right. The inquiries that have been established and the general review of security under Sir John Learmont will identify what went wrong. I am determined to take the action that is needed to put things right and I am accountable to this House for that action. ...The first duty of the Prison Service is to keep prisoners in custody. That must underline all its work. We must all learn the lessons that can be learned from those events and do everything possible to prevent them happening again.[90]

During the House of Commons debate on 10 January 1995, Home Secretary Howard faced opposition MPs who critically questioned his actions. Shadow Home Secretary Straw, for instance, said: 'Does not the Secretary of State understand that he has just made a statement to the House that wholly fails to meet public anxieties about the lamentable sequence of events that have beset the Prison Service in the three short weeks since he last had to make a statement to the House on the state of that service? ... Does not the Home Secretary accept that he stands accused today of gross incompetence in the execution of his responsibilities, for the Prison Service, to the public and to the House?'[91] He questioned why the Home Secretary did not accept 'proper responsibility for this saga of ineptitude?'[92] Moreover, the events showed clearly that a distinction between policy and operations 'has no foundation whatever in reality and that, by maintaining that fiction, he continues only to evade his own responsibility?'[93]

Tory backbenchers defended the Home Secretary while attacking Director General Lewis. MP Nicholls, for example, said that 'No fair-minded or reasonable person could think that the matters that my right hon. and learned Friend explained today are a reason for resignation. It is a fact, however, that the Director General of the Prison Service has presided over a regime so lax that, in recent months, he was prepared to sanction a convicted rapist taking part in the London marathon'.[94]

The Home Affairs Committee added to the pressure by announcing that Howard and Lewis would have to appear for the Committee to answer questions. *The Financial Times* predicted that the Home Affairs Committee would 'investigate the chains of command in the Home Office and the prison service following the escape of three prisoners – all serving life sentences – from Parkhurst Prison'[95] (cf. Home Affairs Committee, 1995 and Home Affairs Committee, 1997a, b, and c).[96]

On 18 January 1995, Director General Lewis, assisted by Director of Personnel Butler and Director of Security and Services Tilt, appeared before the Home Affairs Committee, which held a one-off evidence session to question Lewis about the prison service (Home Affairs Committee, 1995: 9).[97] Lewis emphasized that although the incidents were serious and very unfortunate, they did not constitute 'symptoms of a general fall in security standards'. If they had, then a 40 per cent reduction in the number of escapes would not have been possible (Home Affairs Committee, 1995: 13). Moreover, security 'is the first of our goals as an Agency and for that reason it is at the top of our agenda' (Home Affairs Committee, 1995: 14).

As for the removal of governor Marriott, Director General Lewis explained to the Committee that members of the senior management had decided to remove the governor for operational reasons. Mullin, member of the Committee, tried to find out whether the Home Secretary had actually given the order to remove the governor that same day. Lewis responded that he had had many meetings with Howard on 10 January, but that it was during one of many telephone conversations with Drew, Director of Custody, that he was told of the transfer of governorship that day and that he had agreed with that action (Home Affairs Committee, 1995: 14–16 and 24).[98]

The Home Affairs Committee was not the only one concerned about the removal of the governor of Parkhurst. The PGA was very concerned about the treatment of Marriott as well. The PGA attacked the decision to remove Marriott as 'a premature and vindictive act by a Home Secretary intent on management by fear'.[99] The POA said that the Home Secretary had 'sacrificed the governor to save his own political skin'.[100] After a two-hour meeting with the PGA, Director General Lewis wrote a letter to all governors. In his letter, he praised Marriott's contribution to the prison service and stressed 'John Marriott has not been "sacked" or "suspended". There is no prejudgment of any disciplinary investigation, and there is no ban on John governing prisons subsequently'.[101, 102] The PGA's general secretary, Roddan, said that the letter was 'in marked contrast to the aspersions cast by the Home Secretary on Tuesday, when he inferred that there was a need for Parkhurst to have a competent governor quickly',[103] but the PGA was still considering whether to take legal action on behalf of Marriott.[104]

Newspapers critically assessed the actions of the Home Secretary. *The Financial Times* wrote that 'The placing by the home secretary of virtually all responsibility for the Parkhurst escape on the prison authorities drew fury of union leaders and is likely to lead to a further deterioration in relations'.[105] *The Daily Mirror* nicknamed the Home Secretary the artful dodger and the supreme buck-passer and stressed that he had 'committed the worst crime in the Tory Party – failing on law and order'.[106]

In the ensuing months, the media linked any incident that had to do with prisons to the already badly damaged reputation of the prison service, Director General Lewis and Home Secretary Howard. These incidents were, for example, the murder of an au pair supposedly committed by a prisoner on leave,[107] the fact that the prison service had stopped the rebuilding of Parkhurst since the escape but continued to pay the builders,[108] the finding of Parkhurst's security manual at a dog track[109] and a leaked memo stating that implementing Woodcock's security recommendations would cost £150m – almost 10 per cent of the prison service's annual budget – and that the Home Secretary would 'have to make deep cuts in the police and other emergency services to pay for the reforms'.[110] Penal reformers and prison officers expressed concern about the £150m bill for security improvements. They feared that this would halt reform.[111]

The Learmont Report

The Learmont Report was published in October 1995. The report was damning for Parkhurst Prison and the prison service as a whole. On the Parkhurst escape, the report concluded that many factors had contributed to the escape. These factors included, first, that prisoners were able to manufacture escape tools, such as a ladder, and that visitors had been able to smuggle other items in. Second, property-cluttered cells made it difficult for prison officers to conduct searches. Third, prison officers rarely did rub down searches because they were 'time-consuming, manpower-intensive and impractical in a prison undergoing major structural reorganisation' (Learmont, 1995: 22). '[A] mixture of poor planning, below standard equipment, inadequate training and confused responses', enabled the escapees to go unnoticed for so long (Learmont, 1995: 39).[112] The report concluded that the escape

> revealed a chapter of errors at every level and a naivety that defies belief. Parkhurst should never have been retained as a high security prison, with so much construction work in progress …
>
> Not only was the prison totally unsuitable for housing some of the most difficult prisoners in the system but also the procedures employed were lax and unprofessional, making it relatively easy for the escapees to achieve their objective. In addition, the Service failed to provide the prison with the benefits of technology. … The Inquiry has pinpointed a multitude of security

> lapses and unacceptable practices. … [There is] a sense of frustration over the failure of the Service to respond to and learn the lessons of previous incidents.
>
> The Inquiry recognises the commitment and bravery of many individual members of staff but the quality of leadership, from all levels of management at the prison, has to be questioned. … The escape from Parkhurst will haunt the Service for many years to come. The escape was not due to one person's folly, because many of its ingredients can be traced along the lines of communication to Prison Service Headquarters. The numerous failings identified in this Report indicate that there were many 'hands on the tiller' on this voyage to disaster. (Learmont, 1995: 72–4)

The Learmont Inquiry not only investigated the Parkhurst escape but also security in the prison service in general. Again, the report's conclusions were damning. The report advised, amongst other things, that positive and visible leadership was needed and that there was confusion over the present Statement of Purpose of the Service[113] because custody and care were competing objectives within the prison service. The report suggested changing the mission statement to make clear that the primary responsibility of the prison service is to keep people in custody (Learmont, 1995: 83).[114] The report concluded that improving security was necessary and suggested 127 ways to improve security, such as mandatory closed visits for exceptional high risk Category A prisoners and building a super maximum security prison (supermax prison) (Learmont, 1995: 169–83).

The Sacking of the Director General

On 16 October 1995, the first day after the summer recess, Home Secretary Howard made a statement on prison security in the House of Commons. The Home Secretary introduced the Learmont Report to the House of Commons by addressing the conclusions of the inquiry and the measures taken. The Home Secretary started by announcing that Parkhurst was no longer a dispersal prison, as recommended by the Learmont Inquiry.[115]

The Learmont Report contained 127 recommendations and the Home Secretary accepted the 'broad thrust of Sir John's analysis'.[116] One of the recommendations of the Learmont Report was the creation of two maximum-security prisons; one for Category A prisoners and one for disruptive prisoners (that is, those prisoners whose behaviour seriously disrupts the running of the prison and who may pose a safety risk) (Learmont, 1995: 131–46). Howard told the House of Commons that opting for such a prison would be 'a major departure in penal policy'[117] and the Home Secretary had asked the prison service to investigate this option and report in six months time.[118] Moreover, the dispersal estate was being upgraded to the standard of security as recommended by Learmont. A policy of closed visits for exceptional

Category A prisoners was already in place since June 1995 and early release would become a privilege to be earned instead of automatically granted to induce good behaviour.[119]

Home Secretary Howard disagreed with two of Learmont's recommendations. He rejected the proposal for widely available in-cell television, as that 'would not be consistent with my view that prison conditions should be decent but austere'.[120] He also rejected the proposal for more widely available home leave, because the restricted home leave which had been implemented earlier in 1995 protected the public.

Regarding his responsibility for the events, the Home Secretary made clear that the report concluded that 'responsibility for the Parkhurst escape was not confined to management and staff at Parkhurst. ... In his covering letter, Sir John Learmont makes it perfectly clear that responsibilities ultimately reach the level of the Prisons Board and that that is where criticism stops. Sir John has not found that any policy decision of mine, directly or indirectly, caused the escape'.[121]

> Those comments, coming so soon after the Woodcock Report on Whitemoor, cause me great concern. I must be able to assure the House, and through it the public, that the grave weaknesses in the service that have been disclosed will be put right.
>
> I have come to the conclusion, with some sadness, that that requires a change of leadership at the top of the prison service. The present director general has served in his post for nearly three years. I pay tribute to him for what he has achieved, but I cannot overlook the serious criticisms in the report. I believe that the service requires a change of leadership to carry forward the programme of reforms that is needed and to increase public confidence in the security of our prisons.
>
> The director general has accordingly ceased to hold his post with effect from today.[122] The director of security will take over temporarily until a successor is appointed.[123]

Shadow Home Secretary Straw condemned Howard's actions and his failure to accept responsibility. '[T]oday we have been treated to the spectacle of the Secretary of State demeaning his office, failing to acknowledge those responsibilities and instead going in for his now familiar and tawdry practice of scapegoating anybody and everybody to ensure that the buck stops anywhere but with himself.'[124]

According to Straw, the Learmont Report – like the Woodcock Report – had clearly shown a Home Secretary interfering with the daily running of the prison service. The Shadow Home Secretary also wanted to know whether Howard had told Lewis that if he did not suspend Marriott, his job would be on the line. In fact, for the first time the Shadow Home Secretary asked the Home Secretary to resign.

> In eight years on the Opposition Front Bench, I have never called for a Minister's resignation. It would be highly irresponsible for anyone to call for a Minister's resignation simply because prisoners had escaped. However, the report and the right hon. and learned Gentleman's response, highlighting as it does his stewardship of his high office, raises fundamental questions about the Secretary of State's fitness for that office. The right hon. and learned Gentleman has sought power over the prison service while continually evading his responsibilities. He was right to say that a question of leadership arises from the report – but it is his leadership. Given the state of the prison service today, the way in which it has been run ragged by continual ministerial interference and constant policy changes, will the Secretary of State not now understand that if anyone is to go, it must be him?[125]

The Home Secretary rejected the allegations of interference made by the Shadow Home Secretary, but Labour MPs were not convinced by Howard's arguments. Tory MPs supported the Home Secretary in his decision to sack Lewis and that the Learmont Report, as Tory MP Lawrence put it, placed 'absolutely no blame on my right hon. and learned Friend and which say that the buck stops with the Director General of the Prison Service'.[126]

The Prime Minister continued to support Home Secretary Howard as well. On 17 October 1995, during Question Time, Shadow Prime Minister Blair asked the Prime Minister a question on Howard's denial of interference in operational matters and the sacking of Lewis. Shadow Prime Minister Blair asked the Prime Minister three times whether Howard had interfered with operational matters. Prime Minister Major did not answer the questions but he did reply that 'I have made it entirely clear to the right hon. Gentleman that I have no doubt that whatever action my right hon. and learned Friend took was entirely proper and within his remit as Home Secretary answerable to this House'.[127]

The Fall-out

On Sunday 15 October 1995, the day before the House of Commons debate on the Learmont Report, Home Secretary Howard had asked Director General Lewis to resign at the end of the year, giving him a deadline until 5 p.m. that day to respond.[128] The Director General refused and the Home Secretary dismissed him. However, the Director General did not go quietly.[129] He hired a PR firm[130] and conducted a media blitz[131] to make public that he did not agree with his dismissal and that the Home Secretary had often interfered in daily operational matters.

In a letter to Home Secretary Howard, published in a number of newspapers, Lewis described the difficult situation the prison service was in when he arrived and the achievements of the prison service since. He acknowledged that improvements still had to be made, but Lewis was certain that the prison service was on the right track. This, combined with the support of the Prisons Board[132] for his leadership and the fact that the Learmont Report contained recommendations either already in place, about to be implemented or which had been proposed to the Learmont Inquiry by the prison service itself, Lewis was unable to accept Howard's proposal to resign. Lewis also said that the Home Secretary had 'invented a new definition of the word "operational" which now meant "difficult"' and '[t]he Learmont Report also rightly points to this very high level of ministerial involvement in operational matters'.[133] To which he added

> Whitemoor and Parkhurst have both been severe blows and embarrassments to the prison service, which the service has been determined to put right. What the service most needs at this juncture is continuity, consistency and genuine ministerial support. It is a matter of great regret that you have not chosen to give that support ...[134]

According to *The Guardian*, Lewis' decision 'not to go quietly exposes the Home Secretary to renewed pressure for his resignation'.[135] Some articles in the newspapers concurred with Howard's decision to sack Lewis and others disagreed, but they all questioned Home Secretary Howard's decision to stay in office. This pressure to resign cumulated in an emergency debate[136] in the House of Commons on 19 October 1995,[137] where Shadow Home Secretary Straw tried to prove again that Howard had interfered in operational matters. If he could prove that Howard had interfered, then Howard had misled the House of Commons, which 'is the most serious political charge that can be made against a Minister'.[138]

Shadow Home Secretary Straw tried to prove the interference by showing that the Home Secretary had been involved in replacing Marriott, governor of Parkhurst. Shadow Home Secretary Straw pointed out that 'for all the crisis which has now engulfed the Prison Service ... the Secretary of State [Howard] continues blithely to refuse to acknowledge any responsibility for this crisis',[139] before addressing Howard's interference in the day-to-day running of the service.

The debate in the House was chaotic and tumultuous as Shadow Home Secretary Straw was continuously interrupted when he tried to make his point. The discussion focused on whether the Home Secretary had exerted pressure on Lewis to suspend Marriott instead of only moving him and whether he had added the word today in the statement on Marriott's removal.

Home Secretary Howard replied that he had not insisted on removing the governor of Parkhurst that day. 'The answer is no because all the decisions that were made that day were made by the Director General of the Prison Service'[140] and 'there was no question of overruling the Director General'.[141] Nor had he insisted on the suspension of the governor. The House voted on the motion whether Home Secretary Howard had indeed acted wrongly towards

Marriott with Ayes 231 and Noes 280.[142] A majority of MPs supported Home Secretary Howard and he could stay.

Soon afterwards, the attention of both the media and the MPs focused on other topics. In the House, a small number of written questions relating, for example, to the division between operational and policy responsibility were submitted. The media did discuss the events in October, thereby focusing on the Commons debate, the distinction between policy and operation, the sacking of Lewis, the lack of additional funding to implement Learmont[143] and the costs involving the implementation of the amendments Woodcock suggested.[144] The media's attention flared up again as former Director General Lewis won his battle against the Home Office.

In response to his dismissal, Lewis had filed a High Court writ against the Home Secretary. He demanded compensation for his wrongful dismissal from office on 18 October 1995.[145] The writ cited 12 incidents. According to Lewis, these incidents showed that Howard had interfered in the day-to-day running of the prison service. The writ also contested 'Howard's claim that he did not try to force the suspension of John Marriott'.[146]

A private High Court hearing was held on 29 March 1996. The Home Office agreed to a judgement entered in Lewis' favour. After lengthy negotiations, a deal was made that 'totalled some £280,000' on 3 May 1996 (Lewis, 1997: 220).

Escapes, Crisis and Reform

From Incidents to Institutional Crisis

The Whitemoor escape and the following incidents resulted in a sharp increase in negative media attention (for the attention in the media, see Figures 6.1 and 6.2). The media portrayed the prison service as a malfunctioning organization. The media focused not on just the escape, but on every incident that happened. The following extract of an article in *The Guardian* is a good example of what was being written in the newspapers.

> As is by now familiar with John Major's banana-skin prone administration, the timing of these three incidents [the transfer of IRA prisoners, the Whitemoor escape, and the Durham find] was impeccable. Impeccably awful. This is that time of year when Tory home secretaries traditionally gear themselves up to face the hang 'em and flog 'em brigade at the Party conference. Instead, Michael Howard has been forced to deny accusations that he was going soft on ruthless criminals and terrorists.
>
> But the significance of the past two weeks goes far beyond such transient politics. The mud that is currently glued to Messrs Howard and Lewis will gradually dribble away; what will take much longer to dispel is the impression left of *a prison service in crisis*.

> Again, the timing is faultless. The three incidents occurred against a backdrop of a prison system which is already creaking at the seams; which has army camps and prison ships on standby [to deal with the growing prison population]; whose wardens are suffering from plummeting morale as they face the threat of privatisation and struggle to contain a drugs explosion among inmates; and which has a population of offenders and people on remand about to pass the 50,000 mark, the highest in Europe. (Italics added)[147]

Thus, the media linked the escape to other incidents, thereby painting a picture of a prison service unable to perform its duties, riddled with mistakes, failing security, and too lenient towards prisoners. This picture was further complemented by the so-called agency debate. The prison service had just turned into an agency and an outsider with no previous working experience in the prison service headed the prison service. The media questioned whether the new agency-structure really worked or whether it was just used as an excuse for Home Secretary Howard to deflect responsibility. A link was also made between the speeches of the Home Secretary, where he presented himself as a Home Secretary tough on law and order, and the actual functioning of the prison service. The media frequently wrote that Home Secretary Howard talked tough, but failed to deliver.

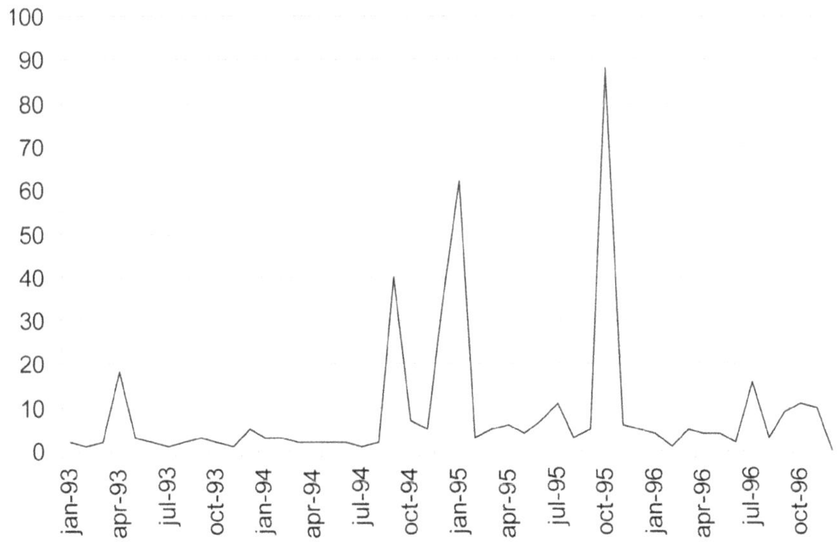

Figure 6.1 Media attention: number of articles on escapes that appeared in *The Times*, *The Sunday Times*, and *The Guardian*, 1 January 1993 to 31 December 1996

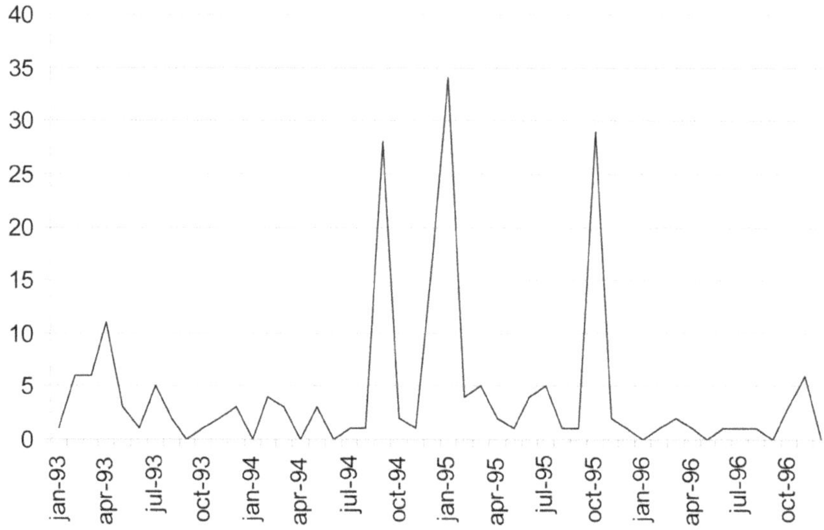

Figure 6.2 Media attention: number of articles on escapes that appeared in *The Daily Mirror* and *The Sunday Mirror*, 1 January 1993 to 31 December 1996

Figures 6.1 and 6.2 clearly show an increase in media attention. Though prisons normally do get a lot of attention in the media, especially in the tabloids, the attention was particularly intense during and after these escapes and after the publication of the subsequent reports. A policy maker described the situation as follows:

> Whitemoor incident was quite appalling. It was the first time a firearm was smuggled in. Parkhurst incident on its own, we would have survived. It was a traditional escape. But because it came so closely after Whitemoor. … After Parkhurst, we were number 1 story for 12 weeks. Quite incredible. Of course, nothing else happened at that time. When I went to Parkhurst, there were about 40 journalists with cameras standing outside, trying to get quotes from us every time we entered the prison.

A former policy maker added:

> Public was worried about rising crime, no one did anything, some people wanted harsher punishment (that'll teach them), too lax. At the same time, there were some highly publicized escapes, so it became a signal of mismanagement: management soft and not in charge. Not that Woolf was bad but current management is too soft. …

> What you had was an interplay of factors: the new story in 1990 was riot and distraction. It was easily understood as a result of the appalling conditions in the prison. Then you had an era of reform, promoted by ... people like Woolf. Ministers adopted all his objectives. The stance of government appeared liberal and reformative. That was ok for public until they realised that crime rose faster, children became murderers, police at their wit's end, care too soft, prisons had become holiday camps and escapes occurred.
>
> Something had to be done. Needed a tough speaking Home Secretary. Major was afraid to lose next election, so he was determined to see that these matters were dealt with. Major said: 'punish a little more and understand a little less', which meant: we have to get a grip and be firm. Michael Howard was set with this task to perform. So government was reacting not to the shortcomings of the system as revealed by Woolf (and still had to be corrected) but by media articles that criminals had a great time and escaped.

The media were not the only ones to question the way the prison service was functioning. MPs did that as well. Prisons, normally not a subject that draws abundant attention from MPs, was now in the limelight. Between 9 September 1994 (the Whitemoor escape) and 19 October 1995 (the House of Commons debate on the actions of Home Secretary Howard), the situation was debated in the House of Commons ten times and 61 written questions regarding the events were tabled (see Figure 6.3). Questions ranged from the number of escapes and the cost of implementing Woodcock to the hiring of Lewis as Director General. During the debates in the House of Commons, Labour MPs fiercely attacked Howard and the prison service.

In general, one can state that the media's and MPs' attention after the Whitemoor escape for the prison service was intensive and the prison service was perceived in a negative way – though this attention was not constant and was particularly apparent after each incident. The Whitemoor escape was bad for the prison service's image because, as one of the governors of Whitemoor stated, the Whitemoor escape was 'a major, major security breach, it is a reflection on the security of the state. One could put serious question marks on the competence of the state to secure'. The attention that resulted from the Parkhurst escape, however, was even worse. The damage of this second escape to 'the prison service's credibility was catastrophic' (Dunbar and Langdon, 1998: 30). Two massive breaches of security resulted in a sharp increase in negative attention by the media and MPs. In short, policy makers in the prison service faced an institutional crisis. An academic described the situation as follows:

> My impression of the escapes: they were serious offenders who had managed to escape. We were supposed to be lucky they hadn't come so far. Then came the information that they had bombs et cetera. The public saw them

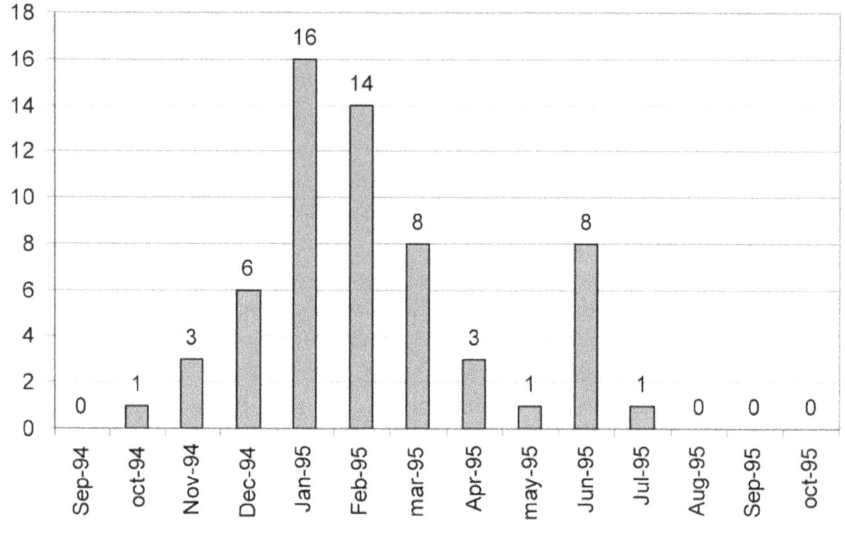

Figure 6.3 Number of written questions tabled between 9 September 1994 and 19 October 1995

> [the escapees] as dangerous. Before Learmont could start his inquiry, you had the West-case: serial killing. The Wests were involved in giving refuge to vagrant young people. They had engaged in sexual offences ultimately leading to murder. They were arrested and Fred West committed suicide. Immediately after that, you had the escapes from Parkhurst, another high security prison. So the Prison Service was seen as extremely incompetent. First, Fred West should not have been able to commit suicide, and second, the escapes should not have happened. E.g., it took two hours before anyone missed the escapees. Moreover, [this was] a huge breach of security.

The Outcome of the Events: Reform

In this study, reform is defined as intended fundamental change of the policy and/or administration of a policy sector. The question to be answered here is whether the changes following the institutional crisis can be described as reform. The answer to that question is 'yes'. In this case, the new prioritization of the prison service's goals, where the number one, two, and three priorities became security, mark a clear divergence from the post-Woolf situation. This shift in prioritization also touches the heart of the prison service, that is, this shift touches upon the ideas about the way the prison service should function and how prisoners should be treated. As such, this drastic change can be labelled reform.[148]

Though the balance proposed by Woolf was not completely rejected, the focus on security did negatively affect Woolf's search for balance in the prison service (cf. Morgan, 1996: 347–8, 350). One respondent close to the Woolf inquiry explained:

> I am not saying there weren't serious abuses. The Whitemoor escape, where IRA terrorists had a gun and escaped from a high security unit; that was serious! And if you read the report by the Inspectorate on Parkhurst, about 6-12 months before the escape, you will read that there was no safety. Prisoners were not safe in Parkhurst. Not adequate control. So of course, things needed to be looked at. But the security, security, security emphasis went too far. Learmont affected the whole system, not just high security estate. Measures were disproportionate.

When asked what the effects of the escapes were on Woolf's legacy, an academic answered:

> Lot of the Woolf agenda has been changed due to escapes. Woolf said: there are two parties involved who have a contract with each other. If you violate the contract, you can be punished. Learmont said, there are three kinds of regimes when you enter a prison. A) normal, B) less than normal, and C) more than normal, i.e. if you don't behave, you'll lose privileges. So Woolf talked about rights and Learmont talks about privileges, e.g. work, education, [and] visit. So that's a completely different approach. Things like home leave were clamped down as kind of security measure. … Howard's assistant tried to defend it, but it is indefensible. The effects of Learmont are very significant. It kind of reversed what Woolf put in place, especially regarding security, though the complaint system remained the same.

Another example of the way the focus on security was perceived is presented by the National Advisory Council of Boards of Visitors who wrote to the Home Affairs Committee:

> The reaction of the Prison Service to the serious security lapses at Whitemoor and Parkhurst were predictable responses to media and political pressure. … Scarce resources in the shape of extra staff, an increase in the annual wage bill of £2 million, additional hardware, building alterations and security equipment estimated to be in excess of £7 million; were thrown at the perceived problem. … We are pleased that all prisons have as a result of the Woodcock and Learmont Reports uprated their security awareness procedures. However, we think it essential that the correct balance is struck between security and control, and rehabilitation. We do not think it appropriate that the avoidable escapes of small numbers of, however high profile, prisoners from Parkhurst and Whitemoor should result in diverting essential resources from the rehabilitation process for the vast majority of the prison population. (Home Affairs Committee, 1997c: 222)

The PGA made it clear as well that although security was the main priority of the prison service, the focus on security had a negative side effect in terms of a reduction of the quality of regimes. Money otherwise spent on regimes was now deflected to implement security (Home Affairs Committee, 1997c: 249).

Nevertheless, the fact that the focus on security had negative effects on Woolf's balance and on regimes does not negate the fact that there was an extensive shift in prison service's priorities. '[T]here was a massive reorientation towards security throughout the prison system' (Dunbar and Langdon, 1998: 30). It was a shift that constituted reform. As Dockley, policy officer of the Howard League for Penal Reform, puts it:

> Crisis management has been another important factor in the constant change imposed on the prison system. ... All these factors have contributed to the emphasis in the prison system swinging firmly towards the needs of security, making it the Prison Service's top priority .... *This has been a marked departure from the previous, widely accepted, penal policy agenda* which promoted the principles of security, control and justice in prisons, as shaped by Lord Woolf. (Dockley, 1996: 354, italics added; cf. Morgan, 2001: 218)

Notes

1. Parts of this chapter have been adapted from Resodihardjo (2004; 2006b).
2. The guard received a flesh wound.
3. To complicate matters, a cease-fire with Northern Ireland had just been arranged. 'Security sources yesterday speculated the escape may have been part of a deliberate bid by IRA hardliners to undermine the 11–day-old ceasefire in Northern Ireland. ... But John Major yesterday appeared confident that the attempted break-out had done nothing to upset the ceasefire. After a 20–minute telephone conversation with Albert Reynolds, the Irish premier, he said the incident was a minor hiccup that would not affect the peace process' (*The Sunday Times*, 11 September 1994, 'Guns Blazing, IRA Jailbreak Prisoners Ignore Ceasefire'). The Northern Ireland situation was exacerbated by a previous row on the transfer of four IRA prisoners to Northern Ireland. Their transfer, which had been planned for a long time, accidentally occurred after the signing of the ceasefire treaty. 'Had the first incident, the transfer of four IRA prisoners, not occurred the day after the ceasefire, it would not have raised an eyebrow. As it was, it threatened to fuel Ulster Unionist suspicions that Downing Street had forged a secret deal with the Republicans' (*The Guardian*, 17 September 1994, 'Banged Up, Browned Off, Busting, Out': 'Three alarming events have exposed the crisis in our creaking prison service. Edward Pilkington and Alan Travis get the inside story from Whitemoor, scene of the armed IRA breakout').

4. *Daily Mirror*, 16 September 1994, 'Jail of the 90s. Showcase Jail Rocked by IRA Break-out Probe'.
5. 6 *The Sunday Times*, 11 September 1994, 'Guns Blazing, IRA Jailbreak Prisoners Ignore Ceasefire'.
6. See, for example, *The Times*, 14 September 1994, 'Who Goes There?'
7. *The Times*, 14 September 1994, 'Who Goes There?'
8. *The Sunday Times*, 18 September 1994, 'High Living in High-security Jails'.
9. *Daily Mirror*, 16 September 1994, Shame of IRA's soft cell. Leader on IRA break-out prison: *Daily Mirror* comment.
10. *The Sunday Times*, 18 September 1994, 'High Living in High-security Jails'.
11. *The Times*, 13 September 1994, 'Watchdog Claims Howard Eased IRA Prison Rules'. Lewis responded to these allegations by saying that 'Neither the Home Secretary nor the Prison Service has sanctioned any relaxation of security for IRA prisoners nor the provision of any special privileges.' To which he added 'Maintenance of security is the top priority for the Prison Service. It is our policy to ensure that adequate staff is available to maintain security. There have been no reductions in the number of security staff at Whitemoor which is fully staffed' (letter from Derek Lewis in *The Guardian*, 14 September 1994, 'Prison Chief Denies any Softening of Regime for IRA Inmates').
12. This report was published in July 1994.
13. *The Guardian*, 23 September 1994, 'Prison Visitors' Chief Criticises Howard'; 'We deliver reports to the Home Secretary on security but no action is taken about them'.
14. *The Times*, 24 September 1994, 'Howard's Way Out'.
15. *Daily Mirror*, 23 September 1994, 'Give us Action, not Talk. Michael Howard and Whitemoor Prison Semtex Find: *Daily Mirror* Comment'.
16. *Daily Mirror*, 26 September 1994, 'Time is Running Out for the Tory Serial Bungler. Suffolk Prison Escape Puts more Pressure on Michael Howard to Resign' (cf. 'His year-long series of climbdowns and setbacks has earned him the nickname of "Serial Bungler"' (*The Times*, 24 September 1994, 'Former Have-a-Go Hero Wanted for Questioning').).
17. *The Guardian*, 24 September 1994, 'This Way Leads to Howard's End': 'a year ago he could do no wrong. Now, writes Alan Travis, the entire criminal justice system would like to run the Home Secretary out of town.'
18. *The Times*, 24 September 1994, 'Howard's Way Out'.
19. *Daily Mirror*, 23 September 1994, 'Why are These Men Still in their Jobs. Michael Howard Urged to Quit over Whitemoor Prison Semtex Find'.
20. *Daily Mirror*, 23 September 1994, 'Why are These Men Still in their Jobs. Michael Howard Urged to Quit over Whitemoor Prison Semtex Find'.
21. *Daily Mirror*, 16 September 1994, 'Jail of the 90s. Showcase Jail Rocked by IRA Break-out Probe'.
22. *Daily Mirror*, 26 September 1994, 'Time is Running Out for the Tory Serial Bungler. Suffolk Prison Escape Puts more Pressure on Michael Howard to

Resign'; *Daily Mirror*, 26 September 1994, 'No Way Out for Howard. IRA Bomb Plots from Whitemoor Prison: *Daily Mirror* Comment'.

23. *The Times*, 27 September 1994, IRA inmates 'used prison telephones to raise money'.
24. *The Guardian*, 12 December 1994, '£35,000 Bonus for Prisons Chief'.
25. The media also paid attention to those bosses of agencies who earned more than £100,000 a year. It was made clear by the chairman of the Home Affairs Committee that it was necessary to pay top salaries in order to attract top people from outside Whitehall (cf. *The Financial Times*, 13 December 1994, 'Howard Defends Jail Chief's Bonus').
26. *The Guardian*, 12 December 1994, '£35,000 Bonus for Prisons Chief'.
27. *The Guardian*, 12 December 1994, '£35,000 Bonus for Prisons Chief'.
28. 'Staff in the SSU were prime candidates for conditioning and yet were given no special training in preparation for their role. They were made even more vulnerable by the absence of staff rotation and knowledgeable, supportive supervision' (Woodcock, 1994: 72).
29. Sir John Woodcock's terms of reference were 'To enquire into all the circumstances surrounding the escape of six prisoners from the Special Secure Unit of Whitemoor Prison on the evening of Friday 9 September 1994, to report his conclusions to the Home Secretary and to make recommendations on any action that should be taken to avoid any recurrence' (Woodcock, 1994: 2; italics removed).
30. *The Times*, 24 September 1994, 'Beleaguered Howard Wins Respite'.
31. This measure did not appear from nowhere. Director General Lewis had originally proposed the new restricted privileges plan in the prison service's second annual plan in April.
32. *The Guardian*, 19 September 1994, 'Howard Plan to Cut Prison Privileges'. See also *The Times*, 21 November 1994, 'A Liberty Too Far'.
33. House of Commons, Prison Security, [251] (19.12.94) 1397–412: 1397.
34. House of Commons, Prison Security, [251] (19.12.94) 1397–412: 1398.
35. House of Commons, Prison Security, [251] (19.12.94) 1397–412: 1398.
36. House of Commons, Prison Security, [251] (19.12.94) 1397–412: 1399.
37. House of Commons, Prison Security, [251] (19.12.94) 1397–412: 1399.
38. The terms of reference for the Learmont Inquiry were 'to review physical security procedures in the Prison Service in England and Wales, and to make recommendations' (House of Commons, Prison Security, [251] (19.12.94) 1397–412: 1399).
39. House of Commons, Prison Security, [251] (19.12.94) 1397–412: 1399.
40. House of Commons, Prison Security, [251] (19.12.94) 1397–412: 1399.
41. Howard also told the Commons that a disciplinary inquiry would be held into the escape. Sir David Yardley, former local government ombudsman, would head this inquiry (House of Commons, Prison Security, [251] (19.12.94) 1397–412: 1400).
42. *The Guardian*, 13 December 1994, 'Howard Backs £35,000 Bonus'.

43. House of Commons, Prison Security, [251] (19.12.94) 1397–412: 1405.
44. When the Home Secretary said that he had considered 'whether any change is necessary in the arrangements for the supervision of the Prison Service', he was interrupted by MPs who said 'Yes: resign' (House of Commons, Prison Security, [251] (19.12.94) 1397–412: 1400). Howard continued his statement announcing another measure: installing 'a new unit outside the Prison Service to strengthen Ministers' ability to supervise the performance of the Prison Service in accordance with the framework document' (House of Commons, Prison Security, [251] (19.12.94) 1397–412: 1400).
45. *The Times*, 24 September 1994, 'Beleaguered Howard Wins Respite'.
46. House of Commons, Prison Security, [251] (19.12.94) 1397–412: 1410.
47. House of Commons, Prison Security, [251] (19.12.94) 1397–412: 1401.
48. House of Commons, Prison Security, [251] (19.12.94) 1397–412: 1403.
49. The Conservative Government as a whole came under pressure since there were also problems in the Child Support Agency and the Student Loans Company. According to *The Guardian* 'exposing monumental ministerial incompetence. Forget Labour's best by-election result for 60 years. Consider instead how Government policies are coming apart at the seams: policies which directly affect millions of people. On a whole range of fronts – justice, education, social security – huge holes have opened up' (*The Guardian*, 22 December 1994, 'When the Killer Facts Hit Home').
50. *The Guardian*, 20 December 1994, 'There is no Escape from this Shambles'.
51. *The Times*, 21 December 1994, 'Where the Buck Stops'.
52. *The Daily Mirror*, 20 December 1994, 'Jail Farce Demands Sackings'.
53. *The Sunday Times*, 13 March 1994, Nightmare on Cromwell Street.
54. The Wests were also nicknamed the 'butchers of Gloucester' (cf. Levi, 1997: 860).
55. *The Times*, 4 January 1995, 'Inmates on Rampage at Prison for Second Night'.
56. *The Times*, 2 January 1995, 'Cromwell St Murders Case Man is Dead'.
57. *The Guardian*, 2 January 1995, 'West Found Hanged in Prison; Home Office Inquiry into Death of "House of Horror" Man Accused of 12 Murders'.
58. *The Guardian*, 2 January 1995, 'West Found Hanged in Prison; Home Office Inquiry into Death of "House of Horror" Man Accused of 12 Murders'.
59. *The Guardian*, 3 January 1995, 'Howard under Pressure over Reduced Cell Watch; The Politics'.
60. *The Guardian*, 3 January 1995, 'Howard under Pressure over Reduced Cell Watch; The Politics'.
61. *The Guardian*, 3 January 1995, 'Howard under Pressure over Reduced Cell Watch; The Politics'.
62. *The Guardian*, 3 January 1995, 'Fred West's Trail of Unanswered Questions'.
63. *Daily Mirror*, 3 January 1995, 'You Let him Beat Justice Howard. Uproar over Suicide Blunder. Death of a Monster, Michael Howard was Accused of Allowing West to Commit Suicide'.
64. For more details, see Learmont (1995).

65. *The Financial Times*, 5 January 1995, 'Pressure on Howard Increases after Jail Breakout'.
66. *The Guardian*, 6 January 1995, 'Parkhurst "Dummy Run" Warning'.
67. *Daily Mirror*, 6 January 1995, 'You're so Gullible. Now Jailbirds Drop Howard in the Mire. More Revelations about the Escape from Parkhurst Prison'.
68. *The Times*, 5 January 1995, 'No Escape. Howard Must Restore Public Confidence in the Prisons'.
69. *The Times*, 7 January 1995, 'Staff Accused of Obstructing Jail Inquiry'.
70. *The Times*, 7 January 1995, 'Staff Accused of Obstructing Jail Inquiry'.
71. *The Guardian*, 5 January 1995, 'Governors "Look in Vain" for Leadership'; 'Crisis in prisons: Chief Inspector says demoralised staff 'getting contradictory directions and bad signals right down line' * Officers allege that high-risk inmates were downgraded and moved to low-security jail through lack of space * Police guard ports after Isle of Wight escape.
72. *The Guardian*, 5 January 1995, 'A Minister who has Lost All our Trust'.
73. *The Times*, 5 January 1995, 'No Escape. Howard Must Restore Public Confidence in the Prisons'.
74. *The Times*, 5 January 1995, 'No Escape. Howard Must Restore Public Confidence in the Prisons'.
75. *The Times*, 5 January 1995, 'No Escape. Howard Must Restore Public Confidence in the Prisons'.
76. See also, for example, *The Guardian*, 6 January 1995, 'Tory Disarray "Underlines the Huge Confusion over Ministerial Accountability"'.
77. *The Times*, 5 January 1995, 'No Escape. Howard Must Restore Public Confidence in the Prisons'.
78. *Daily Mirror*, 5 January 1995, 'Welcome to the Marriott Hotel': '5-star jail boss put on ice-cream vans, rugby videos and barbecues. The atmosphere of Parkhurst Prison doesn't feel at all like a prison, more like a holiday camp'.
79. See, for example, *The Financial Times*, 5 January 1995, 'Pressure on Howard Increases after Jail Breakout', and *The Financial Times*, 6 January 1995, 'Howard to Face Questioning by MPs on Jails Crisis'.
80. According to *The Times*, there was no 'serious pressure' on Howard to resign and that Jack Straw had 'criticised Howard but has been careful not to call for his resignation, perhaps anticipating the pressures he might face if he held the office'. The article adds that 'Howard could suffer the fate of Sir Leon Brittan in 1985, who after two uneasy years trying to take a tough public line on law and order was moved sideways to Trade and Industry' (*The Times*, 6 January 1995, 'Bad Luck and Judgement Harm Howard's Prospects'). See also the article in *The Guardian*, 6 January 1995, 'Parkhurst "Dummy Run" Warning', which states that 'Even Jack Straw, the shadow home secretary, who called for an independent inquiry into the escape, stopped short of demanding Howard's resignation.'
81. *The Financial Times*, 5 January 1995, 'Pressure on Howard Increases after Jail Breakout'.

82. When Group 4 first started the prison escort service, a large number of prisoners were able to escape. Consider for instance *The Times*, 17 July 1993, 'Prisoner Fled Group 4 Jail Dressed as Girl'; or *The Times* 23 April 1993, 'Group 4 Loses its Eighth Prisoner'.
83. *The Financial Times*, 5 January 1995, 'Howard's Enemies Turn the Screw over Jails': 'As resignation calls mount, tensions in Whitehall are running as high as they are among the prisoners'.
84. *The Times*, 6 January 1995, 'Escapes Halved in Two Years'.
85. In the parliamentary session of 1994–1995, Christmas recess lasted from 21 December 1994 until 9 January 1995.
86. Learmont would have access to Tilt's report and Home Secretary Howard thought that would 'ensure that it is independently reviewed' (House of Commons, Prison Service, [252] (10.1.95) 31–46: 33).
87. House of Commons, Prison Service, [252] (10.1.95) 31–46: 32.
88. House of Commons, Prison Service, [252] (10.1.95) 31–46: 32.
89. House of Commons, Prison Service, [252] (10.1.95) 31–46: 33–4.
90. House of Commons, Prison Service, [252] (10.1.95) 31–46: 34.
91. House of Commons, Prison Service, [252] (10.1.95) 31–46: 34 -35.
92. House of Commons, Prison Service, [252] (10.1.95) 31–46: 36.
93. House of Commons, Prison Service, [252] (10.1.95) 31–46: 37.
94. House of Commons, Prison Service, [252] (10.1.95) 31–46: 42.
95. *The Financial Times*, 6 January 1995, 'Howard to Face Questioning by MPs on Jails Crisis'.
96. See also the letter sent by Shadow Home Secretary Straw to *The Times*, 9 January 1995, 'Call for External Parkhurst Inquiry'.
97. 'It is not an inquiry specifically into some of the recent events affecting the Prison Service since we would have asked to see you at this time in any event, although of course these events are very relevant' (Home Affairs Committee, 1995: 9).
98. In answer to the question 'a politician interfered with the operational matters on 10 January and that is why Marriott was treated in the disgraceful way he has been treated?', the Director General answered: 'No, that is not the case' (Home Affairs Committee, 1995: 16).
99. *The Guardian*, 11 January 1995, 'Parkhurst Governor Sacked; Six Others Go as Howard Says Inquiry Clears Him'.
100. *The Financial Times*, 11 January 1995, 'Howard Dismisses Head of Parkhurst': 'Home secretary accused of evasion – Future of prison service boss questioned/ Six other staff moved'.
101. *The Guardian*, 12 January 1995, 'Lewis Seeks to Limit Parkhurst Damage; "No Ban on Governor" Pledge Contradicts Howard'.
102. A prison service spokeswoman said: 'The way [Howard's statement to the House of Commons] is written, it is possible to interpret it in a number of ways. But the correct way is that Mr Marriott will not run a prison while the inquiries are going on' (*The Guardian*, 12 January 1995, 'Lewis Seeks to Limit Parkhurst Damage; "No Ban on Governor" Pledge Contradicts Howard').

103. *The Guardian*, 12 January 1995, ‘Lewis Seeks to Limit Parkhurst Damage; “No Ban on Governor” Pledge Contradicts Howard’.
104. *The Guardian*, 13 January 1995, ‘Governors Fight Parkhurst Sacking as Second MP Tells Jail Boss to Quit’: ‘Alan Travis on a new legal challenge to the beleaguered head of the prison service’.
105. *The Financial Times*, 11 January 1995, ‘Howard Dismisses Head of Parkhurst’: ‘Home secretary accused of evasion – Future of prison service boss questioned / Six other staff moved’.
106. *Daily Mirror*, 11 January 1995, ‘Nowhere to Run’: ‘Prison farce could yet claim ultimate sacrifice. The great survivor is on a short noose. Michael Howard’s sacking of the Parkhurst governor’.
107. *The Times*, 13 January 1995, ‘Leave Prisoner Held in Au Pair Killing’.
108. *The Times*, 16 January 1995, ‘Builders Excluded from Parkhurst Cost £200,000’.
109. *The Sunday Times*, 29 January 1995, ‘Parkhurst Manual on Prison Security Found at Dog Track’.
110. *The Sunday Times*, 29 January 1995, ‘Parkhurst Manual on Prison Security Found at Dog Track’.
111. According to *The Guardian*, ‘Leaked Home Office memos have made clear that the priority accorded the £150 million security programme will mean other areas of prison reform will have to be postponed’ (*The Guardian*, 1 March 1995, ‘Prison Officers Vote to Stick to Letter of Security Rules; Union Vows to Bring Jails to “Standstill”’).
112. For a more thorough description, see Learmont (1995).
113. ‘Her Majesty’s Prison Service serves the public by keeping in custody those committed by the courts. Our duty is to look after them with humanity and help them lead law-abiding and useful lives in custody and after release’ (Learmont, 1995: 81; italics removed).
114. ‘The primary purpose of Her Majesty’s Prison Service is to serve the public by keeping in custody those committed by the courts. It is also our duty is to look after them with humanity and help them lead law-abiding and useful lives in custody and after release’ (Learmont, 1995: 83).
115. House of Commons, Prison Service, [264] (16.10.95) 30–43: 30–31.
116. House of Commons, Prison Service, [264] (16.10.95) 30–43: 31. The Home Secretary accepted the ‘broad thrust of Sir John’s recommendations,’ but Howard did not receive additional funding from the Treasury. A leaked Treasury memo revealed that if Howard promised to implement the measures Learmont recommended as essential for the prison service, they would have to come out of his existing Home Office budgets (*The Guardian*, 20 October 1995, the Treasury tied Howard’s hands in prison row).
117. House of Commons, Prison Service, [264] (16.10.95) 30–43: 32.
118. A study group named the Supermax Feasibility Study chaired by Robin Halward investigated the supermax option. In the end, it was decided not to go through with this option. A policy maker explained why they made the decision not to go through with the supermax solution: ‘No supermax for a number of reasons:

(1) we had followed through with dispersals. If you would combine the prisoners then that would be expensive and it would create an explosive situation; (2) concentrating all problem makers in one place wouldn't make it easier to control the prison and population; (3) how to control them if you just have one prison? There were other issues, for example, human rights (family visits) plus all the money and training that had been put into dispersal prisons would be wasted. But overriding one is the expense. We never said that we wouldn't do supermax. We said we had to investigate it and then new Labour government came in. They considered it for a while and then said no. Recommendation was not accepted.'

119. House of Commons, Prison Service, [264] (16.10.95) 30–43: 32.
120. House of Commons, Prison Service, [264] (16.10.95) 30–43: 32.
121. House of Commons, Prison Service, [264] (16.10.95) 30–43: 31.
122. He was succeeded by acting Director General Tilt, previously director of security, who later became the Director General.
123. House of Commons, Prison Service, [264] (16.10.95) 30–43: 32–3.
124. House of Commons, Prison Service, [264] (16.10.95) 30–43: 33.
125. House of Commons, Prison Service, [264] (16.10.95) 30–43: 35.
126. House of Commons, Prison Service, [264] (16.10.95) 30–43: 37.
127. House of Commons, Prime Minister Engagements, [264] (17.10.95) 139–42: 140. According to the *Daily Mirror*, there were 'doubts about the strength of the Prime Minister's support for Mr Howard.' Prime Minister Major backed the Home Secretary during Question Time, 'but Downing Street later made clear that the Premier could not be expected to know the day-to-day details of the Home Secretary's business' (*The Daily Mirror*, 18 October 1995, 'Give Me a Chance to Say What I Know': 'Derek Lewis ready to tell inside story of Michael Howard's role in Parkhurst jailbreak').
128. That deadline was extended to 9 a.m. on Monday. *The Guardian*, 17 October 1995, 'Ousted Director General Condemns Howard's 'Lack of Support' for Service'; Lewis's letter: The following are extracts from yesterday's letter from Derek Lewis to the Home Secretary, Michael Howard.
129. For more details, see Lewis' book *Hidden Agendas* (1997).
130. Millbank Public Relations.
131. 'On Monday he gave interviews to the broadsheet papers, and to BBC's 6 o'clock News, Channel 4 News, Radio 4's PM and The World Tonight, and BBC's Newsnight. He followed that yesterday with appearances on Sky News at 6.45 am, GMTV at 7 am, BBC Radio 5 at 7.30 am, and BBC's Breakfast News at 7.36 am – then for a full hour on the Radio 4, Call Nick Ross phone-in programme' (*The Guardian*, 18 October 1995, 'Media Marathon Eclipses Minister').
132. 'The unanimous confidence expressed in my leadership by the whole board, including written submission to you from the non-executive directors, and their belief that what the Prison Service most needs in this difficult time is continuity' (*The Financial Times*, 17 October 1995, 'Split between Policy and Operations Confused').

133. *The Financial Times*, 17 October 1995, 'Split between policy and operations confused.'
134. *The Financial Times*, 17 October 1995, 'Split between Policy and Operations Confused'.
135. *The Guardian*, 17 October 1995, '"Disloyal" Howard under Fire; Sacked Jails Chief Unleashes Wrath'.
136. Labour had originally intended to discuss the National Lottery during its parliamentary time, but instead decided to hold a debate on prisons (*The Financial Times*, 18 October 1995, Sacked prison chief may sue Howard: Labour steps up pressure with plans for Commons debate). See also *The Daily Mirror*, 18 October 1995, 'Give Me a Chance to Say What I Know'. Derek Lewis ready to tell inside story of Michael Howard's role in Parkhurst jailbreak, and *The Times*, 18 October 1995, 'Labour Steps Up Pressure on Howard'.
137. Before this debate started, questions regarding the events were asked during Question Time (House of Commons, Prime Minister engagements, [264] (19.10.95) 478–80).
138. *The Daily Mirror*, 18 October 1995, 'Give Me a Chance to Say What I Know'. Derek Lewis ready to tell inside story of Michael Howard's role in Parkhurst jailbreak.
139. House of Commons, Home Secretary (Prison Service), [264] (19.10.95) 502–50: 505.
140. House of Commons, Home Secretary (Prison Service), [264] (19.10.95) 502–50: 517.
141. House of Commons, Home Secretary (Prison Service), [264] (19.10.95) 502–50: 520.
142. 'Resolved, That this House believes that the Home Secretary is and should be accountable to this House for all matters concerning the Prison Service; believes that he is and should be accountable and responsible for all policy decisions relating to the Service; believes that the Director General of the Prison Service is and should be responsible for the day-to- day operation of the service; and utterly rejects the very serious allegations made about the Home Secretary's conduct towards the former Governor of Parkhurst, John Marriott' (House of Commons, Home Secretary (Prison Service), [264] (19.10.95) 502–50: 547).
143. In a leaked letter, Waldegrave, Treasury Chief Secretary, warned Home Secretary Howard not to promise any measure in the House of Commons debate of 19 October 1995, that the Home Office could not afford. '[S]ignificant policy changes on prison security must be considered collectively and looked at on the basis of a proper cost benefit analysis. We are both now having to face up to the consequences of quick decisions having been taken on the Woodcock recommendations without adequate costings. It is now impractical for the Learmont recommendations and your response to it to be considered by your prior to your statement. In the circumstances you will clearly wish to avoid any actual or implied acceptance of any of the recommendations which (involve) funding, I will expect you to meet the full costs of any explicit or implicit

commitments from *within your existing provision* after taking account of the reductions currently being considered by EDX' (*The Guardian*, 20 October 1995, Waldegrave's letter; italics added). The prison service had to face serious budget cuts. The newspapers, however, do not agree on the exact figures. *The Guardian* writes that implementing Learmont's recommendations would 'have to come from within existing Home Office budgets, and only after an 8½ per cent cut has been made in the Prison Service budget over the next three years. This is being considered by the cabinet public spending committee, and the outcome will be announced in the Budget' (*The Guardian*, 20 October 1995, 'Prisons Shopping List that Shocks Treasury'). According to *The Times*, 'Senior prison managers have been told that the Government's public expenditure round has resulted in a 5 per cent budget cut next year in addition to an 8.9 per cent reduction over the three years 1995–1998' (*The Times*, 9 November 1995, 'Budget Cut may Confine Prisoners to Cells for Longer'). In contrast, *The Financial Times* writes about a 3 per cent cut (*The Financial Times*, 29 November 1995, 'Budget 95').

144. Implementing the Woodcock recommendations 'cost £150 million in capital cost and £75 million a year in running costs' (*The Guardian*, 20 October 1995, 'Prisons Shopping List that Shocks Treasury').
145. *The Times*, 19 October 1995, 'Howard Ready to Fight Back as Lewis Issues Writ'. This article also mentioned that Howard's 'troubles were compounded by the resignation of a [non-executive] Prisons Board director over his treatment of Lewis … another non-executive director is also considering standing down' (cf. Lewis, 1997: 209). Moreover, it soon became apparent that no one outside the civil service wanted the job of Director General of the prison service (cf. *The Times*, 19–2–1996, Top candidates turn down chance to be prisons chief). Acting Director General Tilt became the new Director General in March 1996.
146. *The Times*, 19 October 1995, 'Howard Ready to Fight Back as Lewis Issues Writ'.
147. *The Guardian*, 17 September 1994, 'Banged Up, Browned Off, Busting, Out': 'Three alarming events have exposed the crisis in our creaking prison service. Edward Pilkington and Alan Travis get the inside story from Whitemoor, scene of the armed IRA breakout'.
148. Some people, notably criminologists and people working in the prison service, may not be inclined to use the term reform because they would qualify the change in a negative way.

Chapter 7
Recognizing Patterns of Reform

Introduction[1]

From the very moment prisons were introduced, prison services around the world have experienced changes in their priorities, their aims and their administration: the Pennsylvania system (isolating prisoners completely) was introduced and abandoned, rehabilitation came into fashion, went out of style and is now slowly returning (though in a different form), prison services have been turned into government agencies, and a harsher climate towards crime and criminals currently prevails in most Western societies (cf. Morris and Rothman, 1998; Garland, 2001). Such changes fundamentally influence the prison service's policy or its administration and are known as reform (see Chapter 2). Political science and public administration literature usually explain the occurrence of reform in three ways. Reform is either introduced by political and bureaucratic leaders (Doig and Hargrove, 1990; 't Hart, 2000; Terry, 2003; Noll, 2005), stumbled upon through the incremental policy process as small changes add up and become reform (Lindblom, 1959, 1979; Harrison et al., 1990; Rose and Davies, 1994: 36), or crises disrupt the incremental policy-making process. This book focuses on the last explanation and combines the work of several authors (cf. Keeler, 1993; Kingdon, 1995; Cortell and Peterson, 1999) on crises-reform processes to create the crisis-reform thesis.

The authors referred to in this study can be grouped together under the single header of the crisis-reform thesis because they advocate more or less the same argument. Their line of reasoning runs as follows. During crises, the policies, paradigm (which dictates how to achieve goals and implement policies), goals, and functioning of a policy sector come under attack. The crisis poses a severe threat to the core values of a social system. Actors have to decide quickly how to deal with the crisis while the situation is highly uncertain (Rosenthal et al., 2001: 6–7). A crisis has two effects. First, actors – policy makers in this study – are under extreme pressure to find solutions to end the crisis. The media and MPs question the functioning of the policy sector and demand better performance. Their message is that policy makers either have to deal with the crisis or resign. The second effect is that questioning the policies, paradigm, goals and functioning of a policy sector results in declining support for these policies, paradigm, goals and this functioning. Normally, these policies, paradigm and goals act as constraints because they limit what policy makers can do in terms of reform. Goals, for instance, are difficult to change, and so is the paradigm that dictates how to achieve these goals. However, as support for the paradigm, policies, and goals declines, such constraints diminish. Consequently, it will be easier for people to push for reform as they can introduce new paradigms, policies, and goals that differ from the old ones. Other constraints, such as financial ones, will also diminish, as MPs will increase policy makers' budgets to deal with the crisis.

Consequently, or so the thesis suggests, policy makers looking to end the crisis will have more leeway to suggest solutions that were hitherto unacceptable or even unheard of. Moreover, so-called entrepreneurs can use the situation of lessened constraints to push for reform. Entrepreneurs can do so by either adjusting a problem definition – which will have consequences in determining the appropriate solutions to deal with the problem (cf. Rochefort and Cobb, 1994) – by suggesting solutions that link up to other steps that have already been taken to end the crisis, or they can try to get their reform measure accepted independently from other solutions introduced to end the crisis.

Though the crisis-reform thesis sounds appealing – a crisis breaks through barriers which have blocked reform for a long time – it is difficult to investigate whether this thesis holds true because the thesis lacks, for instance, a coherent use of terminology and it does neither clearly stipulate which constraints need to diminish in order to allow reform to occur nor does it give us clues on how these constraints will diminish. The aim of this study is therefore to take the first step in opening the black box of the crisis-reform process by establishing under what conditions crisis can lead to reform.

In order to accomplish this, coherency in terminology was created by opting to investigate a specific type of crisis (institutional crisis) in a clearly demarcated policy sector (prison service). Moreover, the crisis-reform thesis, which assumes that the crisis-reform process proceeds along a certain path, presents us with conditions (diminished constraints, policy makers, and entrepreneurs) that have to occur if reform is to be the outcome of a crisis. Each condition was reformulated in one or more benchmarks, thereby creating a pattern that presumably characterizes the crisis-reform process. This pattern can be compared to the actual empirical patterns in the three cases. For each condition (diminished constraints, policy makers, and entrepreneurs), it will be determined whether they occurred and interacted as predicted by theory (Table 7.1 provides an overview of institutional crises and reform in the three cases).

Constraints

The crisis-reform thesis poses that two things have to happen to constraints if reform is to occur. First, constraints should diminish. Second, a number of constraints should diminish simultaneously or one constraint should diminish significantly in order to create enough room for actors (policy makers and entrepreneurs alike) to push for reform (a so-called macro-window). However,

Table 7.1 Institutional crises and reform in three cases

Case	Incidents	Institutional crisis	Reform
Dutch escapes and cell shortage (1992–1993)	Incidents related to cell shortage combined with (violent) escapes from Special Security Units (SSUs) and other prisons.	Goals, priorities, and policies regarding double-bunking, security, and concentrating SSU prisoners in several SSUs were questioned.	Form of imprisonment (allowing double-bunking in specific instances). Security (concentration in a supermax prison, closed doors policy, new prioritization in new White Paper with a focus on security). Prison regime (standard regime).
The 1990 riots	A series of prison disturbances starting with the riot in Strangeways Prison.	Goals, priorities, and policies regarding prison conditions were questioned.	New prioritization in White Paper. Ending trebling and slopping out.
The escapes from Whitemoor and Parkhurst (1994–1995)	Escapes from supposedly escape-proof prisons combined with other security incidents.	Goals, priorities, and policies regarding prison security were questioned. Moreover, Howard was seen as failing to deliver.	New prioritization of Prison Service with security as the number one, two, and three priority.

the crisis-reform literature is not that clear cut when it comes to naming which constraints should diminish. Combining the crisis-reform literature with more general literature on policy making results in a list of constraints that may diminish at times of crisis (for a list of these constraints, see Table 7.2).

Table 7.2 Constraints

Type of constraints	Examples of constraints
Individual constraints	Vested interests
	Benefits
Organizational constraints	Rules and decision-making procedures
	Policy sector's paradigm
Political constraints	Budget
	Policy inheritance

Escapes and Cell Shortages

During the crisis, four constraints diminished. The policy inheritance and paradigm constraints diminished as MPs and media questioned the Dutch Prison Service's goals, priorities, and policies on double-bunking, security, and how to deal with SSU prisoners. Moreover, the coalition that had always blocked double-bunking crumbled. Lastly, additional money became available to build new cells and the SSU. As the diminishing of the first two constraints has been described in detail in Chapter 4, this section will focus on the latter two constraints that diminished during the institutional crisis.

Before the institutional crisis broke out an anti-reform coalition consisting of political parties and governors and prison officers unions had been able to successfully block double-bunking for many years (Franke, 1996: 312–16; cf. Boin, 1999: 25–6). Prior to the institutional crisis, the VVD was the only party in favour of double-bunking. In May 1992 the CDA joined the VVD. By the time the crisis had reached its zenith, PvdA had joined the CDA and VVD as well. As a result, the anti-reform coalition (cf. Korsten, 1993: 205) had diminished and double-bunking, though used only limitedly, became accepted policy – this seems to indicate that a reform outcome will be more likely if a politico-bureaucratic coalition is in favour of reform, that is, the reform measure is politically and bureaucratically feasible (Boin et al., 2008).

While the anti-reform coalition constraint gradually diminished as the crisis progressed, the money constraint diminished in a more chequered manner. Economic times were hard, making it especially difficult to raise extra money to end cell shortage and escapes (Singer-Dekker, 1994: 76). Consider, for instance, the parliamentary debate on 10 June 1992. During this debate, MPs submitted two motions. The motion requesting money for the Ministry of Justice so that it could do its job properly was denied.[2] The motion in which MPs demanded that government take emergency measures on a short notice to deal with cell shortage was accepted.[3] Moreover, when Kosto decided to accept the two SSUs as proposed by Hoekstra, the press release states that Kosto did not receive any additional money to build these two new prisons. Instead, he let his civil servants investigate whether money from JR-120 could be used to build the two SSUs. He wanted to make money available from JR-120 by scaling up the prisons that had to be built in this programme.[4]

When the crisis continued, however, money did become available. A civil servant explained, 'Circumstances forced and made it possible to establish the temporary SSU. Now there was money to arrange it'. A civil servant close to the study group on security said 'I experienced it [the pressure caused by the incidents] as pleasant because financial resources became available for a coherent package from training, organization, refurbishing prisons to after care'. Regarding closed doors policy, he said, 'there was a price tag attached to it. This was paid'.

In the end, Cabinet approved a huge increase of the prison building programme JR-120. 'In 1991, the cost of the [JR-120] was estimated to cost 420m–460m guilders (price level 1991). Investment costs for the 26 CAP'96 projects [the new name of the justice building programme] were almost 1.4 billion guilders (price level 1996) by mid-1997.'[5] This money was used to increase cell capacity from 8,740 cells in 1990 to about 13,500 cells in 1996.[6] Moreover, 102.4 million guilders of this budget were spent on building four new prison units in Vught – including the SSU.[7]

According to the crisis-reform thesis, one would have to speak of a macro-window. The amount of money becoming available through the Treasury given the general fiscal austerity climate was quite remarkable. Nevertheless, the crisis-reform process did not evolve as predicted by the crisis-reform thesis. Instead of a crisis leading to the diminishing of one or more constraints, which allows policy makers to take reform measures to end the crisis, the reform measure to build new SSUs was made before Kosto knew that he would get any money to build it. The same goes for the increase in cells. The policy makers promised MPs to increase the number of cells before they knew that they would get any extra money to build them. In contrast, the crisis-reform process did evolve as predicted by the crisis-reform thesis when members of the anti-reform coalition changed their alliance and started favouring double-bunking. As the anti-reform constraint diminished, the use of double-bunking in restricted situations became acceptable.

Riots

Before the crisis broke out, improving bad conditions within prisons had been high on the agenda of interest groups, academics and people working in prisons. Some prison improvements were already under way (Woolf, 1991: 1).

In Strangeways Prison, for example, living conditions had been improved (Woolf, 1991: 4). Nevertheless, overall conditions remained unsatisfactory as trebling and slopping out continued and as daily programmes were minimal. Two factors were detrimental to anyone's wish to improve the situation: the large prison population and the budget. As the prison population increased, the budget had to be used to cope with the influx of prisoners. Money used to build new prisons could not be used to improve prison conditions in existing prisons. Moreover, as the number of prisoners within prisons was higher than the certified normal accommodation (CNA), there was little time for prison officers to do more than warehouse prisoners (Cavadino and Dignan, 1997: 120).

During the institutional crisis, these two constraints diminished. However, these constraints did not always diminish as a result of the crisis. The crisis did not result in a sudden drop in prison population. Instead, this constraint had already started to diminish before the disturbances started (see Table 7.3 for the male prison population 1987–1992). As the prison population decreased, pressure on prisons to cope with the population subsided. 'Partly as a result of the new accommodations becoming available, and partly because of reductions in the prison population in 1989 and 1990, there was a paper surplus of capacity in late 1990 and early 1991 for the first time in nearly 40 years. In 1993, the CNA exceeded the prison population by 2,050' (Cavadino and Dignan, 1997: 121). The fall in the prison population resulted in the dropping of three prisons from the prison-building programme. That money could now instead be used to improve prison conditions.[8]

Table 7.3 Male prison population 1987–1992 – annual averages

	1987	1988	1989	1990	1991	1992
No. of prisoners	47,191	48,160	46,843	44,039	44,336	44,240

Source: Home Office (1993: 11) (Crown copyright material is reproduced with the permission of the Controller of HMSO and the Queen's Printer for Scotland).

The second constraint to diminish was the budget. But again the crisis was not the sole cause for the lessening of this constraint. A budget constraint diminishes if new money from the Treasury becomes available to deal with the crisis. In this case, money became available through three means: the Treasury, private finance scheme and the decrease in prison population.[9]

Regarding the first means, Home Secretary Waddington used the riots to convince Treasury to give money to refurbish prisons. *The Times* reported 'David Waddington, the Home Secretary ... won £390 million more in the Home Office budget, much of it to refurbish prisons, including Strangeways, scene of a riot earlier this year'.[10] Additional money became available through the private finance scheme to build new prisons. According to a policy maker:

> Woolf said: we need more prisons to be built. We did get money for that via the private finance scheme, i.e. building prisons with private finance. We had a big prison-rebuilding programme. Labour, although opposed to private finance scheme, didn't stop it. That was a success. So we got money for ending slopping out and building new prisons, but no new money for education or work programmes.

Thus, new money became available through the Treasury and private finance schemes to refurbish and build new prisons, but no new money became available to implement Woolf's other recommendations. The same policy maker pointed out that: 'We didn't get extra money to implement Woolf. We argued for it, but we didn't get it. Prison is just not a high priority.' Instead, money within the existing budget could be reallocated to implement Woolf because the prison population was decreasing. According to Home Secretary Waddington: 'the prison population has fallen considerably over the last year and the latest projections are much more encouraging. This enables us to scale down the new building programme and to shift resources towards continuing the programme of improving conditions in our existing prison establishments.'[11]

The policy inheritance and paradigm constraints also diminished as MPs and media questioned the prison service's goals, priorities, and policies on prison conditions and prisoners' treatment. Though some constraints (policy inheritance, paradigm, and budget) diminished (partly) as a consequence of the institutional crisis, others (prison population and budget) diminished (partly) independently from the crisis.

As pointed out in Chapter 2, diminishing policy inheritance and paradigm constraints are inherent to the nature of an institutional crisis. Consequently, a macro-window will only open if one additional constraint diminishes significantly or if more than one additional constraint diminishes at the same time.

A strict application of the crisis-reform thesis would only allow us to consider the money constraint – which diminished significantly as £390m became available. However, ignoring the decline in prison population would be to ignore the positive effect this decline had on morale as prison officers could do more than just warehouse prisoners. Consequently, it can be argued that a macro-window opened as the combined result of the significant increase in the Home Office's budget and the drop in prison numbers.

Whitemoor and Parkhurst Escapes

In this case, three constraints diminished: the policy inheritance, paradigm, and the budget. Two things stand out though. First, though the budgetary constraint diminished significantly as the Treasury offered a no-limits approach to implementing the Woodcock Report, this macro-window was only open for a very short time. Second, other constraints increased during the crisis and consequently the policy makers' leeway to deal with the crisis decreased.

Before the crisis, money had not been available to improve security. A former governor of Whitemoor explained:

> Before the escapes, I was told that there was no money available for the security measures [I wanted at Whitemoor]. After the escapes, the money poured in. Huge increase in staff, huge improvements of security and in place within months of the escapes.

After the Whitemoor escape and the publication of the Woodcock Report, money became available through the Treasury to implement Woodcock's recommendations (Lewis, 1997: 160). In other words, new money became available to improve security. This constraint, however, diminished only for a short while. The Treasury Chief Secretary had promised Howard that there would be no resource constraint present when implementing Woodcock – a decision that was soon regretted as the costs of the implementation rose. A month after the Woodcock Report had been published, a leaked civil servants' memo stated that implementing Woodcock's recommendation would cost 150m pounds.[12] As a result, people at the Treasury were reluctant to give the Home Secretary additional money to implement Learmont's recommendations. Lewis (1997: 160) writes that Howard:

> presented the Treasury with an ultimatum. The Treasury Chief Secretary, Jonathan Aitken, was caught unawares, and agreed that Howard could say that no resource constraint would inhibit implementation of [Woodcock's] recommendations. It was a mistake the Treasury soon regretted, and it poisoned future relations with the Home Office. Howard had tried one bounce too many – the price would be paid later when Aitken's successor, William Waldegrave, referring to the consequences of the Woodcock débâcle, told Howard that no more money would be available for the Learmont Report.

In a letter to Home Secretary Howard, Treasury Chief Secretary Waldegrave wrote:

> [S]ignificant policy changes on prison security must be considered collectively and looked at on the basis of a proper cost benefit analysis. We are both now having to face up to the consequences of quick decisions having been taken

> on the Woodcock recommendations without adequate costings. ... In the circumstances you will clearly wish to avoid any actual or implied acceptance of any recommendation which (involve) funding, I will expect you to meet the full costs of any explicit or implicit commitments from within your existing provision after taking account of the reductions currently being considered by [the Cabinet committee on public spending].[13]

A civil servant at the Directorate of High Security Prisons added:

> Money came from Treasury because government accepted all recommendations. When they accepted Woodcock, they had a duty to hand in the money. Cost considerable more money than they had anticipated. We normally have a £2.5 billion budget for prison service for 126 prisons. In order to upgrade security, we needed money from Treasury. So we got hundreds of millions. This was not internally funded, but externally, by the taxpayer. ... They didn't accept all Learmont recommendations; they had gotten wise.

Moreover, other constraints started to increase. Consequently, instead of increased leeway, Howard faced a situation of limited discretionary freedom. Two factors limited his freedom to act: the emphasis on law and order before and during the institutional crisis (that is, the political context of the institutional crisis) and Howard's own stance prior to the outbreak of the institutional crisis that prisons work. Howard's tough stance towards crime and punishment in the law and order debate combined with the competition between Conservatives and Labour on who was to be the party of law and order created a climate in which it was not possible for Howard to do anything but be tough where law and order was concerned (Resodihardjo, 2004).

Law and order was firmly put on the public agenda from 1993 onward. The Conservative government faced numerous problems, including problems with its leadership, the ERM exit, difficulties with handling the BSE crisis and tax increases. The Conservative Party therefore needed a populist issue to focus its attention on and law and order seemed a natural choice (cf. Faulkner, 2001: 122; Kavanagh, 2001a: 170; Kavanagh, 2001b: 235–6; Dunbar and Langdon, 1998: 99–140). The murder of Jamie Bulger by two young boys in February 1993 played an important role in this turn towards law and order as a populist issue. In response to the Jamie Bulger murder, Prime Minister Major coined the phrase 'crusade against crime'. The article's headline of Major's interview included the line 'we should condemn a little more, and understand a little less' (Dunbar and Langdon, 1998: 101–3; cf. Rutherford, 1996: 127–8; Garland, 2001: 113). By the time Howard became Home Secretary in May 1993, the tone was already set.

Howard himself had a 'discernible, socially conservative, disposition' (Richards and Smith, 1997: 72; cf. Cavadino and Dignan, 1997: 297). From the onset, Howard made clear that he was a tough minister on law and order.

Under Howard's leadership, the Home Office underwent a cultural shift towards a socially conservative approach (Richards and Smith, 1997: 72; see Figure 7.1 for prison population and policy interventions).[14]

In the months following Howard's appointment, media articles contained a 'markedly more punitive tone' (Dunbar and Langdon, 1998: 114; cf. Garland, 2001: 9). Moreover, Labour started to contest the Conservative Party's position as the traditional upholder of law and order (Downes and Morgan, 1997: 111; Garland, 2001: 111). The party who would win this contest would be able to swing votes for the next elections (cf. Jones, 2001b: 546; Downes and Morgan, 1997: 87–102; Garland, 2001: 131–2). In January 1993, Tony Blair had used the phrase 'tough on crime, tough on the causes of crime' in a BBC radio interview. Meanwhile, the political parties geared up for the 1993 autumn party conferences. During the Labour party conferences, Tony Blair declared war between Conservatives and Labour when he said 'Labour is the party of law and order in Britain today' (Dunbar and Langdon, 1998: 115). Howard responded in kind during the Conservative Party conference in October 1993. The Home Secretary declared that 'prison works' and he came up with 27 points on law and order for the legislative agenda next year.[15]

> Howard's 'Prison works' speech marks the generally recognised start of an open race between the two major parties on law and order, with the Conservative government producing ever more extreme proposals and the Labour party being sometimes equivocal, sometimes even harsher than the government, but never allowing itself to be trapped in a position of outright opposition such as might expose it, however unreasonably, to the gibe of being soft on crime. … By June 1994 public opinion polls were finding that Labour had established a lead over the Conservatives on law and order and the government soon lifted the profile of the 'Prison works' project. (Dunbar and Langdon, 1998: 115–16, 119)

The turn to a tougher stance on crime and the struggle between Labour and Conservatives to become the party of law and order forms the backdrop of the Whitemoor and Parkhurst escapes. It seems almost impossible for a Home Secretary to respond with a soft approach in these circumstances. If the soft approach is not an option, the Home Secretary is left with little discretion during the crisis. Moreover, it appears that Home Secretary's own actions prior to the institutional crisis contributed to the limited options that were available to him once the institutional crisis started. By portraying himself as a tough minister prior to the institutional crisis, Howard could do nothing but be tough once the crisis started (cf. Downes and Morgan, 2002: 297; Resodihardjo, 2004).

> These events [the escapes from Whitemoor and Parkhurst] consolidated a trend already well established since the Home Secretary's pronouncement

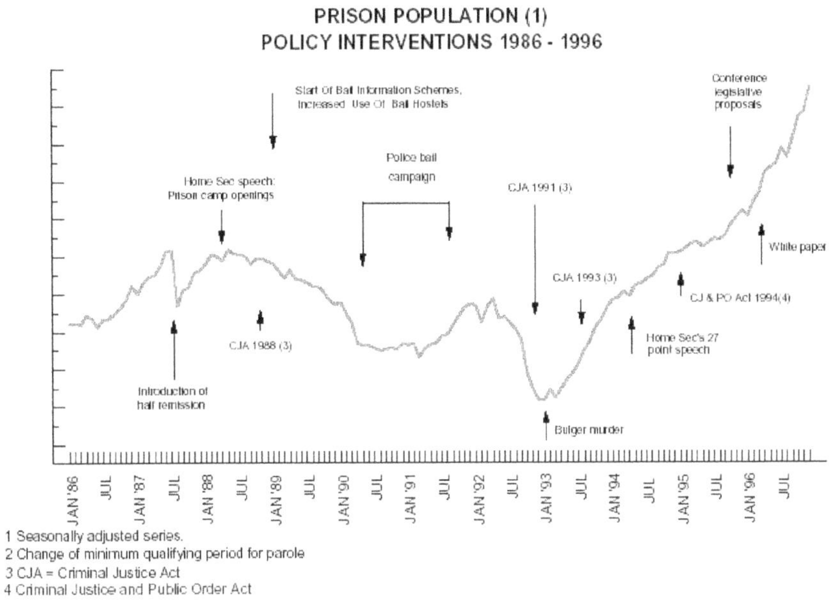

Figure 7.1 Prison population and policy interventions 1986–1996

Source: Home Office (1997: 19) (Crown copyright material is reproduced with the permission of the Controller of HMSO and the Queen's Printer for Scotland).

> at the Conservative Party Conference in October 1993 that 'prison works' and that prison regimes should be 'austere'. The Woolf reformist agenda was effectively dislodged. The prison population rose steeply and continues to do so. The Woodcock and Learmont recommendations legitimated, on security grounds, the more punitive and restrictive climate in prisons. And Woolf's emphasis on justice in prisons was no longer mentioned. Talk of prisoners' rights gave way to a focus on incentives and privileges. (Downes and Morgan, 1997: 125; cf. Morgan, 1997: 1185–7)

Furthermore, it appears that Howard was not only constrained by the law and order contest and his own actions prior to the crisis, but that these constraints were added to by the intense media scrutiny following the Whitemoor and Parkhurst escapes. The media jumped at the opportunity to attack Howard because incidents showed that he was not as tough as he had said he was. One could argue that the intense negative media attention even further limited the options Howard could choose from because the media was not going to let Howard get away with a soft approach after claiming for months that he was a tough minister on law and order. In short, Howard did not have increased discretionary powers during the crisis. Instead, the range of actions he could choose from was limited to one: acting tough (Resodihardjo, 2004).

In Short

In all three cases, policy inheritance and paradigm constraints diminished as MPs and media questioned the priorities, goals and policies on double-bunking, security and how to deal with SSU prisoners (Dutch case), on prison conditions including trebling, double-bunking and slopping out (British riots case) and on prison security (British escapes case). Other constraints that diminished were the money which became available from the Treasury to build new prisons, refurbish prisons, and increase security; the end of the anti-reform coalition as the membership of the alliance in favour of maintaining the status quo (that is, no double-bunking) declined; and the decline in the prison population during the riots.

The prison population is a constraint in prisons because a large prison population means that money is used to build new prisons instead of improving prison conditions. Moreover, prison officers will not have the time to do anything other than warehousing when dealing with a large prison population (Cavadino and Dignan, 1997: 120–22). Hence, a large prison population can act as a constraint – though it was not listed in the constraints list above. Future research should therefore include constraints that are typical of the policy sector, such as prison population in the prison service and the number of asylum seekers in the immigration sector, because they can diminish at times of crisis and can have a significant impact on the crisis-reform process.

Additionally, the Dutch case shows that policy makers can be searching for solutions without the aid of a macro-window. Two measures to end the crisis (accepting the need to build two complete new SSUs and building additional cells) were introduced at a time when constraints had not yet diminished. Both measures were introduced before policy makers even knew whether they would receive additional money to implement these measures. This is contrary to the crisis-reform thesis that states that diminished constraints will result in additional leeway for policy makers to suggest (reform) measures.

Lastly, the British escapes case shows that constraints can actually increase during an institutional crisis, thereby limiting the actions of policy makers. The combination of the political context (law and order focus plus the fight between Labour and Conservatives), Howard's actions prior to the institutional crisis, and the intense media scrutiny created a funnel: Howard could only choose one option instead of choosing from many options (Resodihardjo, 2004). Maybe if Howard had not portrayed himself as a tough Home Sectary and elections banter had been less focused on crime, Howard would have been able to weather the storm by just saying that implementation of security measures should be improved; just as Home Secretary Baker was able to do after two Category A IRA prisoners managed to escape from Brixton Prison

(Resodihardjo, 2002). In any case, this case shows us that the political context of an institutional crisis matters. An institutional crisis does not occur in a political and public vacuum. Instead, what happens in the political context can have a deciding impact on the way the institutional crisis-process evolves.

Policy Makers

Policy makers either immediately react in an entrepreneurial way to institutional crises or initially respond to institutional crises by trying to preserve the status quo. A variety of factors affect whether policy makers seek to maintain the existing situation: their need to manage the institutional crisis instead of worsening it (pushing for reform includes presenting one's own policy sector in a bad light which negatively affects relationships with stakeholders) (Boin and 't Hart, 2003), their dependence on stakeholders (Boin and 't Hart, 2003), their sunk investments (Wilson, 1989; cf. Leemans, 1976b: 88; Rose and Davies, 1994: 14; True et al., 1999: 102; Shepsle, 2001: 324), their identification with the institutional structure that they are part of (Alink and Resodihardjo, 2002: 5; Terry, 2003: 24), combined with psychological factors such as their reluctance to admit mistakes and the need to rationalize and justify prior behaviour (Staw, 1976; Fox and Staw, 1979; Staw et al., 1981).

Conservative policy makers try to preserve the status quo even when they face pressure to end an institutional crisis. If policy makers can end the institutional crisis quickly, chances are they will be able to do so without any reformist measures. The longer the institutional crisis continues and suggested solutions fail to end the institutional crisis, the more the media and MPs will put pressure on policy makers to suggest more radical solutions (cf. Rose and Davies, 1994: 105–6). Following this line of reasoning, one can assume that at some point the pressure will result in a shift in the policy makers' approach towards a reformist stance.

Escapes and Cell Shortage

The policy makers' first response to the escapes was to install an inquiry – a trusted way to try to calm things down. According to a policy maker, they installed their own inquiry 'to prevent a parliamentary inquiry. There is always a battle between policy makers and MPs. MPs love to investigate. Policy makers always want to do that first. Sometimes, you let things be investigated so that parliament does not have to do it and you want to stay ahead of parliament. Active instead of passive. Moreover, the situation really warranted an inquiry'. The policy makers' response to cell shortages was to try to find additional cells without having to spend a lot of money. Both measures stayed well within the then existing policy and paradigm framework. Policy makers' initial response to the crisis was therefore clearly conservative.

As the crisis evolved, this conservative stance slowly but steadily changed into a reformist approach. Security within prisons was improved time after time. Topping up security, however, was not sufficient to end the crisis as incidents continued to occur. The escape from SSU De Grittenborgh (Hoogeveen) on 23 October 1992 presented a turning point in policy makers' handling of the SSU escapes. Following this escape, policy makers announced that two new SSUs were going to be built – allowing for concentration of prisoners in supermax prisons. As escapes continued to occur, another reform measure was introduced: the closed doors policy.

The same path towards more radical measures can be detected where cell shortage is concerned. At first, policy makers tried to end cell shortage by creating 175 to 200 emergency cells. This measure included using containers in the Bijlmerprison (Amsterdam), using a border prison to hold illegal aliens in order to free up space in remand centres, and expediting prison cells' refurbishment to create additional cell capacity.[16] When this could not stem the tide, policy makers promised parliament that additional cells would be build. This expansion was small at first, but grew every time cell expansion was suggested. Parliament 'approved the expansion of cell capacity with 100, 600, and 1,000 cells (mainly emergency cells and replacement of old cells)'.[17] When this turned out to be insufficient as well, policy makers increased cell capacity with an additional 2,000 cells.[18]

Riots

In this case, the policy makers took a number of measures to show the public that they were taking action to prevent the occurrence of future riots. All these measures (such as extra prison officers, extra equipment, and improving security) fitted in the existing institutional structure. Policy was not adjusted. Instead, the measures were just more of the same (cf. Rose and Davies, 1994: 109). In other words, there was no change whatsoever in terms of policy. Even the 'new' policy on how to deal with prison mutiny was more of the same because the offence previously fell under a similar law, the Public Order Act 1986.[19] Hence, policy makers initially acted to preserve the status quo and their actions betrayed a conservative inclination.

Moreover, when having to decide who was to head the inquiry regarding the riots, the policy makers' decision was not focused on finding a liberal or conservative judge (Gilligan, 2002: 294–5). Instead, they were searching for a judge who was competent, had the skills to chair such an inquiry, and who had the time to preside over such a long running project. As one senior civil servant put it,

> Once the Home Secretary had decided, with advice from officials, that there had to be a judicial inquiry, he asked the Lord Chancellor to suggest possible judges, with suitable seniority, who might be appointed to take charge. The

> criteria were who could be released from their ordinary duties for long enough to do what might be quite a long job, and who had the temperament and skill to manage a complex and politically sensitive process. Not many judges met those criteria, but three or four names were put forward. ... In the event, none of them could be contacted immediately, and because of the urgency a message was left for each of them to call back and a call was then made to the next judge on the list. Lord Justice Woolf (as he then was) was not the first to be approached, but he was the first to respond and he was accordingly appointed.

As a result, the appointment of Lord Justice Woolf – who turned out to be a liberal judge – was a coincidence and cannot be construed as a wish of policy makers to either reform or conserve the policy sector.

Nevertheless, the other actions of the policy makers do betray a conservative reflex towards the management of the institutional crisis. This approach towards the crisis did not change quickly. In fact, policy makers were able to maintain their conservative stance up until the end of the crisis. Only when the crisis was almost completely over and the Woolf Inquiry was on its way did policy makers change their approach into a reformist one. This shift is indicated by the Director of Inmate Administration Dunbar's statement to the Woolf Inquiry that a minimum standard for prisoners was needed. Additionally, the newly appointed Home Secretary Baker was more committed to radical reform than his predecessors,[20] which became clear when he presented the Woolf Report to the Commons on 25 February 1991. In his speech, Baker officially announced a number of measures to improve the prison service.[21]

Whitemoor and Parkhurst

Home Secretary Howard and Director General Lewis' first response to the institutional crisis betrayed a conservative reflex on the part of the policy makers. Howard initially announced two measures. Prisoners' privileges were restricted and security in dispersal prisons and SSUs was tightened. This tightening of security consisted of strictly implementing already existing security measures and improving physical security by, for example, installing additional X-ray machines.[22] The tightening of security fell within the existing policy framework, that is, the measures were focused on better implementing of already existing policy and on improving already existing policy. In short, the tightening of security was just providing more of the same (cf. Rose and Davies, 1994: 109). These measures can therefore be labelled conservative.

The crisis-reform thesis also states that if the initial reflex of policy makers is to conserve the status quo, then the chance of reform being the outcome of the crisis will increase if policy makers change from a conservative approach to a reformist approach towards the crisis. In this case, the combination of the law and order battle, Howard's tough stance towards crime, the intense media attention, and the continuing incidents created a climate in which the Home Secretary and the Director General had to show that they were indeed tough where crime was concerned. Moreover, Howard had to show that he delivered on his promises. This change towards a tough stance shows that they did opt for a reformist approach. This shift is especially apparent after the publication of the Woodcock Report. When Home Secretary Howard presented the report to the House of Commons on 19 December 1994, he told the Commons that security was the overall aim of the prison service. This shift in priorities was also clear when Director General Lewis told his governors at a meeting that the top three priorities of the prison service were security, security and security (Lewis, 1997: 162).

In Short

In all three cases, policy makers initially responded in a way that betrays a conservative inclination. They suggested measures that remained within the perimeters of the existing institutional structure of the policy sector. Such was the case, for instance, when they stated security measures needed to be increased or that the number of prison cells should be expanded. In both escapes cases, policy makers shifted towards a reformist approach as incidents continued to occur and the crisis deepened. In contrast, policy makers in the riots case only changed their crisis-management approach once the crisis was already over. It was only during the Woolf Inquiry – which formed an integral part of the events – that policy makers shifted towards a more reformist approach. This shift was indicated by the Director of Inmate Administration Dunbar's statement to the Woolf Inquiry that a minimum standard for prisoners was needed. Moreover, the newly appointed Home Secretary Baker was more committed to radical reform than his predecessors,[23] which probably influenced the outcome of the crisis as well.[24]

Entrepreneurs

The theoretical framework states that it will be more likely that reform is the outcome of a crisis if entrepreneurs are active during a crisis. In this study, entrepreneurs are defined as people inside or outside of government who use their resources to exploit the crisis and push for reform. Policy makers can only be labelled as entrepreneurs if they have been advocating reform measures prior to the crisis and if they use the institutional crisis from the start to push for these reform measures. This restriction was added to the concept of entrepreneur in order to avoid any confusion. After all, as incidents continue and the institutional crisis deepens, policy makers can shift from a conservative inclination to a reformist inclination. The general definition would have made it difficult to decide whether to label such a change as entrepreneurial or as forced by circumstances. Moreover, theoretical and empirical evidence strongly suggests that policy makers will initially respond conservatively towards an institutional crisis. Hence, if policy makers are entrepreneurs they will act contrary to their knee-jerk reaction to conserve the status quo and push for reform right from the start. In contrast to policy makers, non-policy makers can become active as entrepreneurs at any point during the crisis. Whether entrepreneurs are policy makers or not, they can all take three paths to reach their goal. First, they can try to adjust the problem definition. The way a problem is defined determines which solution is considered the best option to deal with it. Second, they can try to let their reform measure ride along with other measures taken to end the crisis. Finally, they can try to get their reform measure accepted independently from any other measures proposed to deal with the crisis.

Escapes and Cell Shortages

In this case, a newly appointed policy maker acted as an entrepreneur working behind the scenes. Director of the Dutch Prison Service Elting was able to use the pressure created by the crisis and the resulting need to introduce a new White Paper to include his ideas on how a prison service should function in the new White Paper. In his opinion, the prison service was in need of a less fragmentized regime policy and prisoners had to work more.

Elting had just started his job as a Director – he was new to the prison service – when the crisis really broke out.[25] In order to familiarize himself with the prison service, Elting visited a number of prisons. When visiting the prisons, he 'observed that central oversight had "vanished" and that "no clear vision" was available within the Prison Section' (Boin, 1998: 147). Prison governors had enormous freedom in determining what happened in their prison[26] and regimes varied from prison to prison (Boin, 1998: 147). Elting wanted a plan to end the variety of regimes in the field, because it was necessary 'to search for integration' (Boin, 1998: 148).

Moreover, Elting also wanted to do something about the prisoners who were just hanging around in prison. According to a civil servant, Elting's starting point for the report was 'Why can't a prisoner work 40 hours a week, just like you and me!' A prison governor added 'He [Elting] was irritated with prisoners hanging around. That had to change. They had to work more and have more structure in their daily activities, including work. You had to teach prisoners a work-rhythm, this would only aid rehabilitation'. The wish to create a uniform prison policy and add more work to the daily life of prisoners, resulted in the standard regime in the new White Paper.

The prison governor also explained that prison governors were not too happy with the new White Paper (cf. Boin, 2001b). Yet, Elting was able to push his ideas through by emphasizing the threat emanating from MPs towards the prison service. According to the governor, Elting 'focused on the political side when he pushed *Effective Detention* through. That was very smart. There was a threat from MPs that the prison service was not doing very well. MPs thought that we were not doing enough. In response, Elting wrote *Effective Detention* to reassure MPs and he succeeded in that temporarily'.

According to the definition used in this study, a policy maker is an entrepreneur if he had been advocating reform measures prior to the institutional crisis and if he used the crisis from the start to push for these reform measures. Elting's actions partly correspond with this definition. The crisis had already started when Elting became director. Hence, Elting could not have advocated any reform measures prior to the institutional crisis. But once appointed, he acted as an entrepreneur by pushing for the reform of the prison regime.

In contrast, Hirsch Ballin did not act as an entrepreneur. Even though he had made it clear from the start that he was in favour of double-bunking, he did not follow through on that promise once the opportunity presented itself. The anti-double bunking coalition originally consisted of governors', prison officers' and prisoners' unions, the CDA, PvdA, Groen Links and D66. At the start of the crisis, the CDA withdrew from this coalition. Hirsch Ballin as well as CDA leader Brinkman voiced their wish to double-bunk prisoners. On 10 June 1992, during the emergency (*interpellatie*) debate, PvdA withdrew from the coalition as well. Consequently, a majority in parliament was now in favour of reform. Yet, Hirsch Ballin did not (or maybe he failed to) act on this opportunity because in September 1992, Kosto and Hirsch Ballin told Parliament that they would not opt for double-bunking. Moreover, one can wonder to what extent Hirsch Ballin's statements were part of the knee-jerk reaction of policy makers to cell shortage incidents (Franke, 1996: 312–16) or part of the elections banter to show that the CDA was tough on crime.

Riots

In this case, no one really fits the definition of entrepreneur. Still, one person stands out: Lord Justice Woolf. He deviates from the definition of entrepreneur because he did not exploit the opportunity presented by the crisis. He was not in the position to act as an entrepreneur until he became head of the inquiry. Once he was the head of the inquiry, his position allowed him to present a new way of defining the problem at hand. Instead of just perceiving it as a problem of control, he also perceived it as a problem of bad living conditions as well as control.[27] This perception was accepted by everyone involved. Consequently, one can argue that Lord Justice Woolf exploited the opportunity as head of the inquiry to change the problem definition (Resodihardjo, 2006a).[28]

Whitemoor and Parkhurst

In this case, there was only a short window of opportunity, but the opportunity was tremendous. The amount of money becoming available from the Treasury was of such a scale that one could say that a macro-window opened. Hence, there was an opportunity for an entrepreneur to push for reform. The question arises whether there was an entrepreneur present. The answer to this question is not easy to give. In the previous two cases, there were clear entrepreneurs at work. They could be identified either by their actions (Lord Justice Woolf) or – if their actions were hidden – by interviews in which respondents declared that someone was an entrepreneur (Elting). In this case, however, it is unclear whether there was an entrepreneur present. One might argue that Home Secretary Howard was an entrepreneur. After all, he had positioned himself clearly as a tough Home Secretary before the crisis broke out. Once the crisis started, he could have used the crisis to push his ideas on prisons and security. However, the Home Secretaries entrepeneurship can also be questioned. Why did he initially respond in a conservative manner towards the crisis? Why did he not jump on the opportunity to show that he was tough on law and order? Second, why did he only act reformist when the media called him out and wrote that Howard talked tough but failed to deliver? Third, there are no actions that can clearly be labelled as entrepreneurial. Although he did exert influence over the content of the Learmont Report, this cannot be labelled entrepreneurial. What happened was that the Learmont Inquiry initially recommended that there should be no closed visits in SSUs. Home Secretary Howard, however, was already planning to introduce closed visits in SSUs and he warned Learmont of his intentions. Learmont subsequently changed the recommendation in his report. One could have labelled this action entrepreneurial if Howard had used this report's recommendation to introduce closed visits. But he did not. He had already introduced the policy in June 1995, while the report was published in October 1995.[29]

Arguments can thus be made for both sides. However, seen the lack of evidence pointing towards entrepreneurial actions combined with the vehement media attention, it would be difficult to label Howard as an entrepreneur.

In Short

In two cases, an entrepreneur can be discerned – neither of which completely fit the definition of entrepreneur as used in this study. Elting – a policy maker – had not been in the employment of the prison service before the crisis started. Thus he could not have made any statements prior to the institutional crisis that he wanted to reform the prison service. Lord Justice Woolf did not use the crisis, but the inquiry to change the way riots were defined.[30] Nevertheless, considering their actions and the impact their actions had on both prison services, it is hard to argue that they are not entrepreneurs just because they do

Table 7.4 The cases and the crisis-reform thesis

Case	Diminishing constraints	Conservative reflex	Entrepreneurial action	Changes in policy makers' approach towards the crisis	Deviation from crisis-reform thesis
Dutch escapes and cell shortage	Paradigm Policy inheritance Money Anti-reform coalition	Yes	Yes: Elting	Yes, as crisis continued (Hoogeveen and Sittard escapes and murder suspect sent home).	Searching for solutions (without the aid of a macro-window).
The 1990 riots	Paradigm Policy inheritance Money Population	Yes	Yes: Woolf	Yes, during the Woolf Inquiry.	An inquiry as opportunity. Shift in policy makers' approach towards the crisis occurred when the crisis was almost over.
The escapes from Whitemoor and Parkhurst	Paradigm Policy inheritance Money	Yes	No	Yes, as pressure mounted and political context forced Howard to act tough.	No entrepreneur. Political context and media framing resulted in funnelling.

not completely fit the definition. This does seem to indicate, however, that an inquiry and newly appointed policy makers can have a remarkable influence on the crisis-reform process.

Additional Conditions

At first glance, it seems as if the crisis-reform processes evolved along predicted lines. Constraints diminished, macro-windows opened, policy makers changed their opinion on reform, and entrepreneurs were present in most cases. A closer look, however, reveals a different picture (see Table 7.4 for an overview). Institutional crises can actually lead to a situation where policy makers' discretion is limited, where policy makers are searching for solutions to end the crisis without the help of diminished constraints, and that an inquiry can be a driving force for reform. Based on the empirical findings, one can therefore conclude that even though the expected conditions did occur, the conditions did not always influence the crisis-reform process as predicted by the crisis-reform thesis. This brings us to the question whether other conditions played a role in the three cases.

In the Dutch case, no additional condition jumps out. In contrast, in both British cases conditions played a role that the crisis-reform thesis does not cover. In the riots case, the Woolf Inquiry had a decisive impact on the crisis-reform process, while the political context and media framing influenced the outcome in the British escapes case.

The Woolf Inquiry introduced a new problem definition. The political context in the British escapes case (Labour versus Conservatives) created expectations with the public that were not met – something that the media discussed in newspapers again and again. These three additional conditions will be discussed in the next chapter.

Notes

1. Parts of this chapter have been adapted from Resodihardjo (2004; 2006b).
2. TK, 1991–1992, 22 649, no. 2.
3. TK, 1991–1992, 22 649, no. 3.
4. Press release, Ministry of Justice, 3 November 1992, 'Kosto wil twee extra zwaar beveiligde inrichtingen bouwen'.
5. TK, 1998–1999, 26 385, nos 1–2: 9.
6. TK, 1998–1999, 26 385, nos 1–2: 9.
7. TK, 1998–1999, 26 385, nos 1–2: 54–5.
8. *The Financial Times*, 9 November 1990, 'The Autumn Statement; Extra Funds for Police and Prison Services – Home Office'.

9. It is very difficult to establish how much money the prison service got, from whom the money came, and why the money was given. What is certain is the following. Home Secretary Waddington received money from the Treasury to refurbish prisons in November 1990 (see for example *The Times*, 9 November 1990, 'Winners and Losers in the New Spending Settlements'). Waddington also made clear money had become available because the prison population was decreasing. As a result, the prison building programme did not have to be so extensive. Money that would otherwise have been used to build new prisons could now be used to improve prison conditions (see, for example, *The Financial Times*, 9 November 1990, 'The Autumn Statement; Extra Funds for Police and Prison Services – Home Office'). Home Secretary Baker announced on 25 February 1991 to the House of Commons that he had brought forward the deadline of ending slopping out to the end of 1994, which would cost an extra £36m over the next four years. Part of this amount would come from existing budgets, the rest 'will be provided' (House of Commons, Prisons (Woolf Report), [186] (25.2.1991) 659–73: 660). Baker did not explain what he meant with provided, but based on what the previous Home Secretary said, it can be concluded that money came available through the Treasury to refurbish prisons and that money otherwise spent on building new prisons was used to implement Woolf. Moreover, a policy maker stated that money also became available through the private finance scheme to build new prisons.
10. *The Times*, 9 November 1990, 'Winners and Losers in the New Spending Settlements'.
11. *The Financial Times*, 9 November 1990, 'The Autumn Statement; Extra Funds for Police and Prison Services – Home Office'.
12. *The Guardian*, 30 January 1995, 'Memo Leak Adds to Crisis in Orisons'.
13. *The Guardian*, 20 October 1995, Waldegrave's letter.
14. According to Dunbar and Langdon, 'the first few months of 1993 were a period of increasingly punitive and condemnatory political rhetoric, and that has certainly been a major factor in sentencing during the subsequent years' (Dunbar and Langdon, 1998: 111; cf. Sparks et al., 1996: 23–5).
15. It seems there is an error in Figure 6.3. Home Secretary Howard held his 27 points speech in October 1993 and not somewhere in 1994.
16. TK, 1991–1992, 22 649, no. 1: 2.
17. TK, 1998–1999, 26 385, nos 1–2: 9.
18. TK, 1998–1999, 26 385, nos 1–2: 9.
19. House of Lords, Prison Security Bill, 2 Rand committed to a Committee of the whole House, [535] (14.2.92) 963–78: 968–9.
20. *The Times*, 1 February 1991, 'Manifesto for Prisons'.
21. House of Commons, Prisons (Woolf Report) [186] (25.2.91) 659–73: 660.
22. House of Commons, Prison Security, [251] (19.12.94) 1397–412: 1397–8.
23. *The Times*, 1 February 1991, 'Manifesto for Prisons'.
24. House of Commons, Prisons (Woolf Report) [186] (25.2.91) 659–73: 660.

25. Elting was appointed director of the Dutch Prison Service in June 1992 (*De Telegraaf*, 7 August 1992, 'Iedere ontsnapping is er één te veel'). In comparison, the Hoekstra committee was installed on 23 March 1992 (Hoekstra, 1992: Appendix 1).
26. For a description on how prison governors responded to the new White Paper, see Boin 1998; Boin 2001b.
27. A previous report by Chief Inspector of Prisons Hennessy on prison riots which addressed the bad conditions was largely ignored by Home Office and parliament (Adams, 1994: 161).
28. One might argue that other actors such as academics and interest groups were able to present their problem definition to the inquiry and that they were therefore entrepreneurs as well. It was Lord Justice Woolf, however, who was able to get the problem definition changed.
29. See prisons minister Widdecombe's speech to the House of Commons on 19 May 1997. House of Commons, Home Affairs, [294] (19.5.1997) 397–479: 402–3.
30. Some may argue that this indicates that the institutional crisis definition should have been applied more strictly: the institutional crisis was ending (there was a decline in negative media and MP attention) while the policy makers adhered to a conservative stance. Hence, the institutional crisis did not result in reform – the Woolf Inquiry did. Nevertheless, it is important to include the Woolf Inquiry in the institutional crisis case description for two reasons. First, the analysis of the Prison Service of England and Wales shows that the Woolf Inquiry is considered by all parties involved to be an integral part of the riots and their aftermath, that is, one cannot disconnect the Woolf Inquiry from the riots. Second, though the media and MPs attention was dwindling, they were still focusing their attention on bad prison conditions. The institutional crisis had thus not completely ended but continued to simmer as the Woolf Inquiry was conducting its work.

Chapter 8
Alternative Paths to Reform

Introduction[1]

The Woolf Inquiry played a role in the riots case's crisis-reform process while media framing and political context played a role in the British escapes case. This raises the question whether inquiries played a role in the crisis-reform processes of the two escape cases and whether political context and media framing influenced the riots and Dutch escape cases. In this chapter, each case will be investigated to determine whether inquiries, media framing, and political context played a role or not (see Table 8.1 for an overview of the conditions influencing the crisis-reform thesis).

Inquiries

Four inquiries were held in the three cases investigated in this study (excluding disciplinary inquiries): the Woolf Inquiry, the Woodcock Inquiry, the Learmont Inquiry and the Hoekstra Inquiry. Each inquiry had a different impact on the policy-making process. Though the Hoekstra Report did not accelerate the reform process in the way the Woolf Inquiry had done, the report was eventually accepted and resulted in the implementation of the SSU philosophy. Consequently, the report played a role in the introduction of the super maximum-security prison (the supermax prison) in the Netherlands. In the British escapes case, two inquiries were conducted – each with its own impact on the policy process. The Woodcock Report's recommendations were all accepted right away – a decision which was most likely facilitated by the Treasury's willingness to offer unlimited funds to implement these measures – and enabled a redirection in the prison service's priorities. By contrast, the impact of Learmont's recommendations was more limited for two reasons. First, Treasury was unwilling to give Howard any additional funds to implement Learmont's recommendations, thereby limiting Howard's leeway to act. Second, even though Howard accepted a number of recommendations made by the Learmont Inquiry, these recommendations were minor. They did not involve any reform, but instead focused on improving security. Introducing the supermax prison was the only reform measure recommended in the Learmont Report. This measure, however, was not accepted. Instead, Howard told the House of Commons that opting for such a prison would be 'a major departure in penal policy'[2] and he had therefore asked the prison service to investigate this option and report in six months time.[3] In the end, it was decided not to accept the supermax recommendation mainly because of the expenses involved. A policy maker explained that they said no to the supermax for a number of reasons.[4]

> (1) We had followed through with dispersals. If you would combine the prisoners then that would be expensive and it would create an explosive situation. (2) Concentrating all problem makers in one place wouldn't make it easier to control the prison and population. (3) How to control them if you just have one prison? There were other issues, e.g. human rights (family visits) plus all the money and training that had been put into dispersal prisons would be wasted. But overriding one is the expense. We never said that we wouldn't do supermax. We said we had to investigate it and then the new Labour government came in. They considered it for a while and then said no.

The effect of the inquiry on the policy-making process differed per inquiry. This raises the question why an inquiry has a large impact in one case and not in another (Resodihardjo, 2006a). Determining the effects and success of an inquiry is difficult to achieve for a number of reasons. If recommendations are implemented years later, who is to say that the inquiry led to this implementation? Maybe other conditions played a role (Gosnell, 1934: 112; cf. Rhodes, 1975: 129–31). Moreover, a change in government can lead to a more receptive or a less receptive environment (Gosnell, 1934: 112). Cartwright (1975) also raises the question to what extent similarity between recommendations and policy is necessary if one wants to claim that an inquiry was effective. Even if there is a close similarity between recommendation and policy, the policy may still be based on arguments completely different from the arguments presented in the inquiry's report (Cartwright, 1975: 204–5). In addition to the difficulty to assess an inquiry's effects, one has to be aware that the original aim of this study was not to investigate the influence of inquiries on the policy-making process. Consequently, a thorough investigation of why one inquiry was more influential than the other cannot be undertaken because certain data may be missing. Nevertheless, combining the literature on inquiries with the data that is available does give us some insight into the factors affecting an inquiry's influence on the policy reform process.

The crisis management literature interprets inquiries from an instrumental view (Cartwright, 1975: 84). Policy makers use inquiries as an instrument to deal with a crisis. By installing an inquiry, policy makers show the public that they are in control (McConnell, 2003: 400; cf. Prasser, 1994: 6). Installing an inquiry is also a well-known and proven tactic to divert the public's attention. If any questions are asked in parliament or in the media, policy makers can refer to the ongoing inquiry and their wish to let the inquiry perform unhampered, that is, policy makers do not wish to give any answers to questions, on the basis that this could influence the inquiry's proceedings (McConnell, 2003: 403; cf. Chapman, 1973: 184; Rhodes, 1975: 50; Prasser, 1994: 8). Policy makers can also use the inquiry as a delaying tactic, hoping that by the time the inquiry publishes its report the issue is not so hot anymore (McConnell, 2003: 403; cf. Prasser, 1994: 9; Gilligan, 2002; Resodihardjo, 2006a).

The general literature on inquiries draws attention to policy makers who may try to influence the outcome of the inquiry (Rhodes, 1975: 53). They can do so in several ways. Policy makers can, for instance, select a chair and members who reflect their ideas (Cartwright, 1975: 62; Rhodes, 1975: 22; Ransley, 1994: 26) or select inappropriate members (Prasser, 1994: 13). They can also create limited terms of references (Rhodes, 1975: 22; Prasser, 1994: 13) or state in the terms of reference that only specific procedures may be used by the inquiry (Ransley, 1994: 26; cf. Rhodes, 1975: 22). Other means include influencing the way the inquiry interprets its terms of reference by outlining the inquiry's aims either orally or in writing (Cartwright, 1975: 112; Rhodes, 1975: 22), trying to determine who else is involved in the inquiry (Gilligan, 2002: 294–5), setting unreasonable deadlines, providing poor resources and setting the inquiry within a department thereby hoping that the inquiry will fall victim to bureaucratic infighting (Prasser, 1994: 13–14; cf. Resodihardjo, 2006a).

The same literature also points out that no matter how policy makers try to influence an inquiry, an inquiry can have a mind of its own. An inquiry can become more than just a fact finding inquiry, it can become a driving force for reform.[5] Several factors play a role in the process of an inquiry becoming more than just a fact finder.

First, an inquiry can introduce specific recommendations, thereby 'breaking the ice so that changes, including those not previously mentioned at all, become discussable' (Chapman, 1973: 187; Rhodes, 1975: 150).

Second, the standing of the inquiry plays a role as well. Royal commissions, for instance, supposedly have a 'neutral and regal aura' which 'can provide the intellectual, judicial or pluralist justification for that change or non-change which those agencies perceive as appropriate' (Gilligan, 2002: 303). The standing of all commissions, whether they are royal or not, is further enhanced by the procedures used during the inquiry: who can give evidence and how can they give evidence? Can anyone present evidence (written and orally) to the inquiry or only a select few who have been invited by the inquiry? The underlying assumption is that the more people are able to express their views, the larger the support base of the inquiry, and the larger the standing of the inquiry (cf. Gilligan, 2002: 303).

Third, the inquiry can become an interpretative authority by contributing 'significantly to the shaping of official discourse and public debate' (Stone, 1994: 248). An inquiry can do so by helping reform to become 'publicly acceptable and officially thinkable' (Stone, 1994: 248).

Fourth, the inquiry's tactics play a role as well. An inquiry can choose to do its work at a distance from policy makers or it can choose to work from the policy makers' point of view (Weller, 1994: 264). Both choices present advantages as well as disadvantages. While working at a distance from policy makers may add to the standing and legitimacy of the inquiry, this option may result in unfeasible recommendations as well as difficult working relations with policy makers. Working based on what is 'desirable or acceptable' (Weller, 1994: 264) from the viewpoint of policy makers has the advantage of producing results that will most likely be accepted by policy makers. The disadvantage, however, may be a more limited standing as the support base of the inquiry will be diminished because people may perceive the inquiry as a whitewash (cf. Rhodes, 1975: 22–3).

Tactics also include the use of the media to create discussion in society on the issue that the inquiry is investigating. Proper use of media, for instance by leaking information, can create a climate in which the inquiry's recommendations will be favourably met or even eagerly awaited (Cartwright, 1975: 177; cf. Rhodes, 1975: 150–51).

Fifth, an inquiry's chair can run his inquiry any way they want, though their ability to do so depends on their and the other members' personalities, their standing and position, their experience, their network and how they interact with witnesses (Cartwright, 1975: 66). A chair can decide what to focus on, which procedures to use, and who to invite to present evidence. Consequently, a chair can have a significant influence on the inquiry's direction and whether it will limit itself to fact finding or not.

Finally, the chair and members of the inquiry's first job is to interpret the terms of references. They can do so very strictly or very generously. Consequently, the interpretation may deviate from the policy makers' goals and wishes (Cartwright, 1975: 107, 111). This deviation combined with a generous interpretation opens the door for a more bold approach that includes more than just fact finding.

To this list of factors that determine whether an inquiry becomes a driving force for reform or not, another list can be added; a list of factors contributing to the acceptance of inquiry's recommendations. These factors include political feasibility as well as technical and budgetary feasibility (Gosnell, 1934: 113; Rhodes, 1975: 147), the quality of the report which should include good arguments and practical recommendations (Rhodes, 1975: 146), and recommendations should not conflict with the other aims of government (Rhodes, 1975: 147).

Considering the factors that influence whether an inquiry becomes a driving force for change, the following can be said. Lord Justice Woolf interpreted the terms of reference broadly. He did not limit the inquiry to merely establishing how the riots came about, but also investigated why the riots started (Woolf, 1991: 31). The inquiry uncovered the deeper causes of the riots (bad prison conditions and unjust treatment of prisoners). By organizing public hearings, the public became aware of these causes. Consequently, the inquiry's proceedings shaped public debate on how prisoners ought to be treated. Moreover, the inquiry acted as an interpretative authority as it shaped official discourse by stating that there should be a balance between security, control, and justice. One of the factors contributing to the inquiry's ability to shape official discourse was its standing. By operating from a distance from the policy makers and by opting for procedures that deviated from the standard operating procedures of inquiries (Woolf, 1991: 35), the inquiry's standing was enhanced. Normally, inquiries hold private sessions. Lord Justice Woolf and Judge Tumim, however, decided to hold public hearings in a non-accusatorial setting and they even introduced a new procedure, public seminars (Woolf, 1991: 35–6), which allowed people interested in the prison service to express their views and suggest improvements. Consequently, the inquiry's base of support was immense. Lastly, the inquiry's recommendations were made at a time when these recommendations had become politically, technically, and financially feasible as the prison population dropped and the bad conditions prisoners lived in were revealed (Resodihardjo, 2006a).

In short, a strong chair interpreted the terms of reference liberally, chose innovative procedures, and remained at a distance from policy makers. This resulted in the inquiry's high standing and the inquiry's ability to shape official discourse and public debate (Resodihardjo, 2006a).

In contrast, the Hoekstra Inquiry was on a fact-finding mission. The inquiry did not interpret the terms of reference liberally nor did it shape official discourse and public debate. Its standing can best be described as average: it did not have the standing of a Royal Commission or something remotely akin to the Woolf Inquiry, but neither was it perceived as a whitewash. Instead, it had the standing normally accredited to such inquiries. Despite its lack of reform-drive, the inquiry did have an impact on the policy-making process as its recommendations were accepted. This acceptance is all the more stunning because even though the recommendation to build two supermax prisons was politically and technically feasible at the time the recommendation was accepted, there was no money for it. It is likely that budgetary considerations were overruled by the need to manage the institutional crisis and stop the escapes from SSUs. In addition, recommendations are often made without knowing whether they can be funded or even to elicit their funding.

According to a policy maker interviewed for this study, Woodcock and Learmont were appointed because they were independent from the prison service. Woodcock, for example, was a former Chief Inspector of Constabulary and consequently an outsider. Woodcock did not interpret the terms of reference generously (Woodcock, 1991: 5) nor did he use public hearings. The inquiry's standing was relatively low as the inquiry demolished any support within the field by the manner in which it conducted its hearings: people were interrogated as if they were criminals (Lewis, 1997: 156). One respondent questioned by Woodcock's team described the procedure as follows. Woodcock

> was assisted by police men. This actually defined the nature of the inquiry. We were treated like suspects and interrogated. Method: desk positioned as so we were squashed between the wall and the desk. If Woodcock or someone else leaned forward on the table, we couldn't go away. Quite intimidating. No one was prepared for that.

The Woodcock Inquiry was more a police inquiry than a reform-driven inquiry, yet its effect on the policy-making process was quite significant for three reasons. First, the way in which the report was formulated was picked up by the media. This in turn influenced the public debate on the escape. The Woodcock Report, for instance, quoted a prison officer when describing the easy access to items in the hobby rooms as 'an Aladdin's cave of equipment' (Woodcock, 1991: 30). The newspapers, and especially the tabloids, were quick to use these wordings in their articles. Second, the report was published at a time when appearing to be tough towards criminals was vital for political survival. Added to this political feasibility was the budgetary feasibility as Treasury was willing to pick up the check for the recommendations' implementation.

Learmont was an outsider as well because he was a general in the army. Learmont's inquiry did not act as an interpretative authority, had an average standing, and remained well within the boundaries set by the terms of reference. Learmont remained close to the policy makers and their wishes. Consider for instance what prisons minister Widdecombe told the House of Commons. She described how Learmont changed his recommendation regarding closed visits after consultation with Home Secretary Howard who was in favour of such visits.[6] The report also broke the ice by re-introducing the concept of supermax prisons – a concept previously suggested by Lord Mountbatten in 1966 (1966: 4, 56). In so doing, the Learmont Report made the topic discussable again. In the end, however, the recommendation was not politically and budgetary feasible. Moreover, there was no money to implement any recommendation which had not yet been suggested by Woodcock. Consequently, the Learmont Report's impact on the policy process was relatively small.

The crisis-reform thesis does not consider the role inquiries can play in the crisis-reform process and it therefore lacks any theoretical thoughts on how, why, and when inquiries influence the crisis-reform process. Fortunately, the literature on inquiries helps to understand why one inquiry was more influential than the others. Moreover, the insights generated on how an inquiry can become a driving force for reform are a valuable contribution to the crisis-management literature, which tends to view inquiries as instruments for crisis managers. This instrumental view may actually undermine the efforts of crisis managers because they will be unaware of the potential dangerous effects of installing an inquiry. After all, the crisis-management literature suggests that installing an inquiry helps to appease the masses, proves that they are in control of the situation and provides them with time during which they can hope that another issue will attract the attention of the public (McConnell, 2003: 400–403). Yet, as the analysis in this book shows, an inquiry may prove to be quite an unreliable tool (Resodihardjo, 2006a).

The Media

The media play a large role in the crisis-reform process because increased negative media attention is one of the indicators showing that there is an institutional crisis. Current theory on institutional crisis and crisis-reform processes, however, neglects the influence of media once the institutional crisis has been firmly set on the agenda. The British escapes case shows, though, that the way in which the media frame the events can have a significant impact on the crisis outcome. This brings us to two questions. The first question relates to how the media can influence the policy-making process while the second asks whether the media played a role in the other two cases. Again, a reservation has to be made regarding the answers to these two questions as investigating media influence on the policy-making process was not the original intention of this study. Nevertheless, the literature on media and the policy-making process combined with the data that are available in this study does provide us with some interesting insights.

The literature on crisis and media is mainly focused on how and why media turn some events into disasters/crises and not others, how media coverage affects the political agenda-setting process and how policy makers handle the media and try to avoid being blamed (cf. Kingdon, 1995; COT, 1997; Bovens and 't Hart, 1998; Bovens et al., 1998, 1999). Literature on media framing and media influence on foreign policy does provide helpful clues to understanding how and when media directly affect the policy-making process.[7]

Though definitions on media frames vary enormously, media frames are generally understood to consist of 'fixed patterns for presenting and commenting on the news that organize the political debate in a way that is comprehensible to the public' (Auerbach and Bloch-Elkon, 2005: 85, cf. Terkildsen and Schnell, 1997: 881).[8]

In other words, the media try to make sense of events by constructing a story with the help of keywords, metaphors, concepts and symbols. These components are often drawn from existing discussions (Entman, 1991: 11). Newspapers can, for instance, frame a famine in terms of humanitarian aid, UN performance, international loans, or in terms of failing local government. Opting for a certain frame has consequences as the famine will be described in terms and concepts inherent to the selected frame while excluding the other frames at the same time. A famine framed in terms of humanitarian aid will, for instance, focus on the problems surrounding the provision of goods and the way humanitarian aid organizations function. Moreover, the cause of the famine will most likely be perceived as natural, for example, drought. Famine causes such as (civil) wars will be presented in newspaper's reporting when the humanitarian aid focus is combined with another focus, such as UN performance or failing local government. Economic causes will enter the description of the famine when newspapers opt for a frame that focuses on international loans (Resodihardjo, 2004).

This example shows that by selecting a certain frame to represent news stories (Auerbach and Bloch-Elkon, 2005: 91–3) the media determine how the public will perceive events (Entman, 1991: 7) and which solutions are viable. As a consequence, the media's frame selection affects public debate. Moreover, research shows that the way the government represents an issue (that is, the frame it uses) may correspond with the media frame and may even follow any changes made in the media frame. The similarity of government and media frames can indicate that the media influence policy makers (Auerbach and Bloch-Elkon, 2005: 93, 95–6; cf. Edwards and Wood, 1999: 328–9) and provides us with a plausible answer to the question how the media can influence the policy-making process; as a frame configures what is important, what the causes of the problem are, and what ought to be done, using the same frame as the media imposes certain courses of action upon government while rejecting others.[9]

This brings us to the second question which focuses on when the media can directly influence the policy-making process, that is, which factors create a climate in which media can influence the policy-making process. In his articles on media influence on world politics, Robinson points out that the media 'can play a key role in causing policy change' (Robinson, 2001: 531) if four factors occur simultaneously.

First, there should be *elite dissensus* which occurs when the elite have a conflict regarding a certain policy. Media may reflect this elite conflict by adopting a frame in their news reporting that corresponds with one of the elite's position in the conflict (Robinson, 2001: 531–2). Second, and to some extent related to the first, if there is *policy uncertainty*, then this policy will be susceptible to media scrutiny. Policy uncertainty exists when there is no consensus within government regarding an issue. 'If an issue suddenly arises and no policy is in place, or if there is disagreement, conflict of interest or uncertainty due to an ambiguous policy between the subsystems of the executive there can be said to be policy uncertainty' (Robinson, 2001: 534–5). Third, the *media* have to *critically report* about the policy. Lastly, the *media* have to *advocate a particular course of action* (Robinson, 2000: 615).

The combined factors can create a climate in which media can directly influence policy making in the following ways. On the one hand, disagreement between policy makers on how to deal with a policy can be solved in favour of proponents of change if critical media coverage demands change. On the other hand, critical media coverage can pressure policy makers to do something if no policy is in place. In fact, the mere existence of policy uncertainty makes policy makers vulnerable because they will not be able to defend themselves properly against critical media coverage (Robinson, 2001: 535).

In the Dutch escapes case, the media originally framed the cell shortage in terms of the double-bunking discussion, whereas the escapes were framed in terms of humane imprisonment, rehabilitation, maintaining justice, security, and a stricter regime for dangerous criminals – though reference to organized crime was infrequent and minimal. From February 1993 onwards, the media started to link the escapes with cell shortage. Articles on escapes referred to cell shortage and vice versa. Moreover, the newspaper articles on the sending away of a murder suspect referred to the tough on crime-stance of the CDA party in order to make sense of the CDA's threat to its own minister Hirsch Ballin.[10] The policy makers' frames were similar to the media frames. The only deviation is that the media started to link the two issues from February 1993 onwards, whereas the political world started to link the two from December 1992 onwards. This seems to indicate that what happened in the political arena influenced media coverage, which is in accordance with the generally accepted idea that the relation between the political world and the media is not a one-way street, but that the two influence one another (Edwards and Wood, 1999).

Though there was clear elite dissensus regarding cell shortage (Minister of Justice Hirsch Ballin favoured double-bunking while his junior minister vehemently opposed this policy option), no clear elite dissensus regarding escapes could be detected. The vague guidelines on who to send home and whom not can be construed as policy uncertainty, just as the ever-continuing escapes despite stricter security can be construed as policy failure and can consequently be labelled as policy uncertainty because there is no functioning policy in place. Finally, the media did not explicitly advocate certain courses of actions. There were no calls for resignation nor did the newspapers favour any of the solutions being pushed by the actors involved.

The similarity between the frames of media and government indicates that either the two thought alike or somehow influenced one another. At first sight it seems as if the stage was primed for direct media participation in the policy-making process: there was elite dissensus, policy uncertainty and critical media coverage. Yet, the media did not directly influence the policy-making process because they did not advocate certain courses of action – though this may have more to do with the way newspapers in the Netherlands operate. It is therefore fortunate that this study includes data on media behaviour during institutional crises in a country in which the media is much more outspoken: England.

In the riots case, the media framed the prison riots in terms of understaffing, overcrowding, and bad prison conditions. It is not clear, however, to what extent this frame was shared by policy makers. There was a common understanding with prison officers, prison governors, and civil servants at headquarters that understaffing, overcrowding, and bad prison conditions played a key role in the events. A view which opposition MPs shared in public and which policy makers, according to Faulkner (2001: 117–19), shared in private but were unable to express in public because policy makers needed to give the impression of being tough on crime.

There was no elite dissensus as everyone agreed that prison conditions had to be improved (Faulkner, 2001: 117–19) though one might argue that to an extent there was policy uncertainty regarding how to treat prisoners and the conditions they lived in. If Faulkner (2001) is correct, then policy makers acted contradictory to their own wishes because they were politically unfeasible. Consequently, this contradiction (wishing one thing while doing another), might have led to ambiguous policy. Lastly, the media did not call for the resignation of Home Secretary Waddington. Though not explicitly advocating a certain solution, the media's emphasis on overcrowding and bad conditions could be construed as an implicit call to do something about this situation.

The riots case is a clear case where media did not play an active role in the policy-making process. The media and government frames were quite similar. Moreover, there was critical media coverage and one could argue that there was to some extent policy uncertainty. Nevertheless, elite dissensus and the media's explicit call for a particular course of action – two important factors in creating a climate in which media can play an active role in policy making – were lacking. These factors, though, were clearly present in the British escapes case.

In the British escapes case, the media drew from the law and order debate to describe the situation in prisons as lax with pampered prisoners while Howard was failing to deliver. This frame was shared by the policy makers who referred to the law and order debate as well. Elite dissensus existed because Labour and Conservatives were fighting on who was to be the party on law and order. Moreover, this fight resulted in policy uncertainty as the promises made during this contest were in stark contrast to actual treatment of prisoners. The so-called five-star treatment of prisoners in Whitemoor's SSU, for instance, was described in detail in the newspapers. By claiming that Howard failed to deliver, the media effectively promoted a particular solution to end the crisis: acting tough. Moreover, the media demanded the resignation of Home Secretary Howard as well as Director General Lewis (Resodihardjo, 2004).

Again, the media and government frames were similar. In this case, however, all the factors creating a climate in which media can have an active role in policy making were present: critical media coverage, elite dissensus, policy uncertainty and policy advocacy. The presence of these factors explains why the media had such an impact on the policy-making process in this case and not in the other two cases. Because of the media activity Howard's options were limited to acting tough (Resodihardjo, 2004).

The crisis-management literature does not explain how media can influence policy making at times of crisis, but the literature on foreign policy does (cf. Kingdon, 1995; COT, 1997; Bovens and 't Hart, 1998; Bovens et al., 1998, 1999; Robinson, 2000, 2001). Using Robinson's theory (2000, 2001) on the cases investigated in this study shows that it may be time for the crisis-management literature to add another feature to its repertoire: how to minimize (or use) media's influence on the policy-making process when dealing with a crisis.

Political Context

In all three cases, the political context played a role in the crisis-reform process to some extent. Elections were coming up in both escapes cases, while a government reshuffle occurred in the riots case. Explaining why and how these events in the political context affected the crisis-reform process proves difficult because current literature does not take into account upcoming elections or government reshuffles when explaining policy change. A search for theories either results in structure-agency literature (Smith, 1999: 30–32; Hay, 2002: 94–6), the effects of upcoming elections on government spending (Tufte, 1978; Klein, 1996) or the effects of election outcomes on policy change – Keeler (1993) being a case in point as he describes how newly elected political officials can use their mandate to deal with crises. Nevertheless, based on the data available in this study and what little literature there is, ideas on how and when the political context can influence the crisis-reform process can be generated.

Government Reshuffle

Let us first consider the government reshuffle. The riots case lasted from April 1990 till February 1991 (when Lord Justice Woolf published his inquiry and Home Secretary Baker supported this report in a House of Commons debate). During this period, two government reshuffles occurred. First, prisons minister Mellor was replaced by Rumbold in July 1990. Second, and following the installation of Major as new Prime Minister, Home Secretary Waddington was replaced by Baker in November 1990.

There are three reasons underlying the initial conservative reflex of incumbent policy makers towards an institutional crisis. First, the policy maker's need to manage the institutional crisis instead of worsening it (pushing for reform includes presenting one's own policy sector in a bad light which negatively affects relationships with stakeholders) (Boin and 't Hart, 2003). Second, policy makers have invested in their policy sector and identify themselves with the institutional structure that they are part of (Wilson, 1989; cf. Leemans, 1976b: 88; Rose and Davies, 1994: 14; True et al., 1999: 102; Shepsle, 2001: 324; Alink and Resodihardjo, 2002: 5; Terry, 2003: 24). And third, psychological factors such as reluctance to admit mistakes and the need to rationalize and justify prior behaviour, will force policy makers to continue supporting existing policies (Staw, 1976; Fox and Staw, 1979; Staw et al., 1981).

Following this line of logic, one can assume that the situation of newly appointed policy makers will differ from incumbent ones when dealing with an institutional crisis. The first reason remains valid for newly appointed policy makers; they too need to tread carefully in order to establish good working relations with their stakeholders, though they may not be tied so closely to the stakeholders as incumbent policy makers because no deals have yet been struck with them. There will also be less history between the newly appointed policy maker and the stakeholders and the newly appointed policy maker will have more room to manoeuvre.

Newly appointed policy makers will not only be detached from the stakeholders, but also from the institutional structure of the policy sector – the second reason why policy makers normally adhere to a conservative crisis management stance. Because they are new to the policy sector, they have not yet become part of the norms and ways of working that are valued in the policy sector. This lack of identification with norms and ways of working creates room for manoeuvrability for newly appointed policy makers because they will not feel the urge to hold on to these norms and ways of working.

Finally, because they are newly appointed, these policy makers will not have any responsibility regarding the policy decisions that failed and subsequently resulted in an institutional crisis. They will therefore not feel reluctant to admit mistakes nor will they feel the need to justify prior behaviour (and thereby save face) by committing to existing policy.

Therefore, the introduction of a newly appointed policy maker during an institutional crisis can very well lead to reform measures being proposed and accepted because the newly appointed policy makers do not have a link with stakeholders and the policy sector, nor do they feel any responsibility/accountability regarding the failing policy. Thus, newly appointed policy makers will be more likely to propose and accept reform measures to deal with the institutional crisis.

This reasoning can explain how Home Secretary Baker affected the crisis-reform process. According to *The Times*, Major as well as Baker supported a new and more progressive direction as far as running the prison service was concerned.[11] Baker claimed to be more committed to radical reform than either Hurd or Waddington.[12] If that is correct, then Baker was willing to advocate a reformist stance. Moreover, as a newly appointed policy maker he had the autonomy to do so. Baker's willingness and ability may explain why policy makers were now willing to publicly express a reformist stance while previously, as Faulkner stated (2001: 117–19), policy makers were reluctant to do so.

Something similar happened in the Netherlands when Elting was appointed Director of the prison service. He was an outsider who was not linked in any way to the prison service – not to its institutional structure, its existing practices (fragmentized prison regimes), or its problematic relations with the prison governors (Boin, 2001b). Consequently, he did not feel obliged to uphold the existing practice which allowed prison governors to determine the regime for their own prison (cf. Boin, 2001b).

Elections

There is currently no literature on the role of upcoming elections in managing crises and making policy. Comparing the two escapes cases nevertheless gives us clues on how and when upcoming elections affect the crisis-reform process.

Although Dutch election rhetoric was nowhere near as dominant as in the British case, some similarities between the cases are present. As has already been extensively described, the British upcoming elections' rhetoric was focused on law and order and the fight between Labour and Conservatives on who was the toughest towards crime. In this election rhetoric, Howard had positioned himself as being tough on crime and criminals. The Dutch election rhetoric was focused on organized crime and problems in the public prosecution office in the Netherlands (Commissie herijking Wetboek van Strafvordering, 1993; Boin, 2001a: 337; Van de Bunt, 2004). The CDA party (Christian Democrats) and its Minister of Justice Hirsch Ballin tried to depict themselves as valuing norms and being tough on crime.[13] This tough stance towards crime was mainly focused on organized crime – not on crime in general. Incidents, such as the liquidation of mafia boss Klaas Bruinsma, were seen as proof that the Netherlands needed to fight organized crime. The feeling of anxiety within society about organized crime was reinforced by the publication in 1992 of a White Paper entitled *Organized Crime in the Netherlands*. The White Paper expressed the fear that organized crime organizations would become embedded in the legitimate world (Van de Bunt, 2004). Adding to this mixture were a number of suspects who were released by the court because the public prosecution's office had made mistakes in their subpoenas (Commissie Herijking Wetboek van Strafvordering, 1993).

At first sight, it looks as if the Dutch and British escape cases are similar as both institutional crises were preceded by law and order rhetoric. The two cases are, however, distinct from one another in two important ways. First, the British election rhetoric was much more intensive and received much more coverage in the media than the Dutch election rhetoric. Second, the Dutch tough on crime rhetoric focussed on organized crime and there was only a weak link in the media between the law and order rhetoric and the institutional crisis. As a consequence of this weak link, the media did not demand that Hirsch Ballin should keep his promises and act tough on crime.

The similarities and dissimilarities seem to indicate that whether or not upcoming elections will play an influential role in the crisis-reform process

Table 8.1 An overview of the conditions influencing the crisis-reform process

Condition	Why	How
Constraints	Constraints normally hamper reform. If there are fewer constraints, then policy makers will have additional leeway to end the crisis while entrepreneurs can push for reform.	A crisis leads to the diminishing of constraints. Further study is needed to understand how exactly a crisis can lead to a situation of diminished constraints.
Policy makers	Policy makers are the ones who suggest solutions to end the crisis. Consequently, their actions influence the crisis-reform process significantly. Policy makers' initial response will be to preserve the status quo.	Policy makers' need to manage the crisis instead of worsening it, their dependence on stakeholders, their investments in the status quo, their identification with the institutional structure that they are part of combined with psychological factors such as their reluctance to admit mistakes and the need to rationalize and justify prior behaviour result in policy makers wanting to adhere to the status quo.
	In the course of events, policy makers can shift to a reformist approach.	Policy makers can shift towards a reformist approach if (a) incidents continue and the crisis deepens; (b) an inquiry, media, and the public are in favour of reform; or (c) a new policy maker is appointed.
	Normally, a crisis will result in additional leeway for policy makers to handle the crisis. Sometimes, policy makers may face a crisis without this additional leeway. Instead of many options, they have only one option to end the crisis	Political context and media demands can create a funnel. Further research is needed to establish whether funnelling takes place in other cases as well.
Entrepreneurs	People inside or outside of government who use their resources to exploit the crisis and push for reform.	They can use the situation of diminished constraints or an inquiry to push for reform.

Table 8.1 cont'd

Condition	Why	How
Inquiry	An inquiry can have a catalytic role in the crisis-reform process instead of just an analytic one (fact finding).	• Breaking the ice. • Inquiry's standing. • Interpretative authority. • Tactics. • Role of chair. • Interpretation of the terms of reference.
Media	An increase of negative media attention is an indicator for an institutional crisis. Additionally, media may affect the policy-making process and consequently influence the crisis-outcome.	• Elite dissensus. • Policy uncertainty. • Critical media coverage. • Media advocating a particular course of action.
Political context	A crisis does not occur in a political vacuum. What has been said before the crisis broke out can have serious effects on the crisis outcome.	• Intensive election rhetoric. • Topic correspondence election rhetoric – institutional crisis. • Media pinning politicians down on their promises.

could depend on the following three factors. First, there should be *intensive election rhetoric*. Second, a *link* between election rhetoric and the institutional crisis should exist. In other words, the topics addressed in the election rhetoric have to correspond with the topics discussed in the institutional crisis. Third, the *media* have to *demand that politicians keep the promises* they made while campaigning for upcoming elections when faced with an institutional crisis.

Currently, the crisis-reform thesis emphasizes the role of actors. It is agency that matters, not context. After all, the context that usually hampers reform (that is, the barriers that limit the options to propose reform) will diminish at times of crisis, leaving room for actors to do their job and push for reform (that is, agency) (Smith, 1999: 30-2; Hay, 2002: 94–6).

If future research determines that political context played a role in other (institutional) crises as well, then the crisis-reform thesis has to incorporate the political context of events. This study has already shown that upcoming elections and a change in policy makers during an institutional crisis can have a significant impact on the crisis-outcome. If future research corroborates these findings, then two additional propositions can be added to the crisis-reform thesis. First, if elections are coming up and there is a link between the intense election rhetoric and the institutional crisis while media demand that politicians keep their promises, it will be more likely that reform will be the outcome of an institutional crisis. Second, if policy makers are replaced during an institutional crisis, it will be more likely that the outcome will include reform.

Paths to Reform

The crisis-reform thesis assumes that the process from crisis to reform evolves along a preordained path: a crisis results in diminished constraints that policy makers and entrepreneurs can use to push for reform. The findings in this study show, however, that the crisis-reform process can follow various other paths. Consequently, the crisis-reform thesis has to be adapted to incorporate these different roads to reform. Keeping in mind that further research is needed to determine whether this study's findings can explain reform outcomes in other institutional crises, the following alternative paths along which crisis can lead to reform can be sketched: searching for solutions, reform-driven inquiries, active media, upcoming elections, introducing new policy makers and funnelling.

Searching for Solutions

The first alternative path encountered in this study shows how Dutch policy makers were able to search for solutions to end the institutional crisis without the aid of a macro-window. This searching for solutions is a normal response to crises: policy makers try solutions and when these solutions fail, they will try more radical ones. As Rose and Davies point out (1994: 105–6), '[w]hen pressures for action are intense, then the technical feasibility of a new program is less important than the political infeasibility of the status quo. Almost any proposal is worth trying, however doubtful its chance of success. In such circumstances policy-making proceeds by trial and error and many new programs are likely to be found wanting, and terminated'.

This searching for solutions, however, is usually facilitated by the opening of a macro-window. In this sense, the path deviates from the preordained path: though an institutional crisis has started and policy makers are under pressure to find solutions to this crisis, no additional constraints (that is, no constraints additional to the policy inheritance and paradigm constraints) diminished.

The lack of a macro-window in the Dutch case does suggest that more factors are at play in determining the outcome of an institutional crisis than the opening of a macro-window and policy makers taking advantage of this window. What these factors are, however, is yet unknown. Future research can consider, for instance, the timing of an inquiry. Maybe if policy makers install an inquiry too early, the crisis may not be over by the time the inquiry reports its findings. If that happens and incidents continue to occur and pressure mounts, the possibility exists that policy makers are forced to accept the inquiry's radical recommendations in order to show the public that they are in control of the crisis response.

Reform-driven Inquiries

A reform-driven inquiry possesses the power to dramatically influence the crisis-outcome. The riots case shows how an inquiry that conducted its investigations at the end of an institutional crisis – a crisis that was about to end in a conservative manner – was still able to change the outcome of the institutional crisis by pushing for reform.

Two factors have to come together if an inquiry is to have such a dramatic impact on the crisis-process: an inquiry has to become a driving force for reform and its recommendations have to be accepted by policy makers. When considering the factors determining whether an inquiry will be a driving force for reform (see Table 8.2, based on the previous section), one can see that these factors are likely to influence one another: an inquiry can only recommend measures to break the ice or act as an interpretative authority if it has a certain standing. An inquiry's standing, in turn, is not only determined by being royal or not, but also by its chair, the manner in which references are interpreted, and the tactics used to investigate the problem at hand such as holding public inquiries (cf. Resodihardjo, 2006a). Based on this information, the following proposition can be generated: *an inquiry is likely to act as a driving force for reform if it has an active chair, terms of reference are interpreted broadly and hearings are held in public.*

Table 8.2 Inquiries as driving force for reform

Breaking the ice
Inquiry's standing
Interpretative authority
Tactics
Role of chair
Interpretation terms of reference

However, no matter how reform-driven an inquiry is, if its recommendations are politically, technically, and financially unfeasible (Gosnell, 1934: 113; Rhodes, 1975: 147) or if its recommendations conflict with the other aims of government (Rhodes, 1975: 147), it will be harder to have its recommendations accepted – though not completely impossible as the Dutch case shows.

Active Media

A third path to reform established in this study is the path created by media actively influencing the policy-making process. Whereas the crisis-reform thesis only considers media when a crisis is created, this study has shown that media can have an influence on the rest of the crisis-reform process as well. This influence depends on four factors (Robinson, 2000, 2001): the existence of elite dissensus and policy uncertainty, media have to critically cover the events, and the media have to advocate a particular course of action instead of just saying that a policy sector is malfunctioning and something needs to be done. In other words, the media need to propagate a specific solution to end the crisis – and this solution can either be a conservative or a reformist one. The following proposition can thus be formulated: *the media is likely to play a more active role in the crisis-reform process if there is elite dissensus, policy uncertainty, critical media coverage and a particular course of action that the media advocate.*

Upcoming Elections

Upcoming elections may open a fourth path to reform. Based on the empirical findings in the two escapes cases, three factors have been established that determine the influence of upcoming elections on the crisis-reform process. *When an institutional crisis coincides with upcoming elections the chances for reform will be enhanced if there is intensive election rhetoric which is linked with the institutional crisis while media pin down politicians on their electoral promises.*

Introducing New Policy Makers

When policy makers are replaced during an institutional crisis by new policy makers (that is, policy makers not already imbedded in the institutional structure of a policy sector), these new policy makers will be more likely to introduce reform because they neither have obligations towards stakeholders, nor any identification with norms and ways of working, nor responsibility towards failing policy. A new policy maker can steer the policy-making process into the direction of reform – again a different path to reach reform. Hence, the following proposition can be formulated: *if new policy makers replace incumbent policy makers during an institutional crisis it is more likely that the outcome of the institutional crisis will include reform.*

Funnelling

The last alternative path established in this study is the path where policy makers' discretion has been limited instead of increased, that is, funnelling. Instead of an increase in options available to policy makers to end the institutional crisis, policy makers now face a more limited selection of options – even more limited than before the institutional crisis. The available options left to policy makers may include reform (as in the British escapes case) or not (in which case the institutional crisis will not lead to reform).

Whatever these options entail, they are the result of upcoming elections, active media, or a combination of both. Upcoming elections can create a funnel as policy makers may be forced to keep their election promises, while active media can propagate specific solutions to end the crisis. Either way, other options are excluded from the equation.

As funnelling only occurred in one case, further research is necessary to establish whether this case (and the path along which the crisis led to reform) is an outlier. Moreover, even if funnelling occurs in other cases as well, it may be a phenomenon only occurring in countries where media are outspoken and election rhetoric is fierce such as in the United Kingdom.

Notes

1. Parts of this chapter have been adapted from Resodihardjo (2004; 2006a; 2006b).
2. House of Commons, Prison Service, [264] (16.10.95) 30–43: 32.
3. A study group named the *Supermax Feasibility Study* chaired by Robin Halward investigated the supermax option.
4. For a more elaborate explanation on why the British government did not opt for the supermax whereas the Dutch government did, see King and Resodihardjo, (forthcoming).

5. An inquiry that influences the policy-making process and enables reform is also known as a catalytic inquiry in the inquiries and commissions literature (Chapman, 1973: 187).
6. House of Commons, Home Affairs, [294] (19.5.1997) 397–479: 402–3.
7. For examples on how the media can indirectly influence the policy-making process, see Edwards and Wood (1999).
8. In this study, the concept frame is used to refer to the way the media construct events with the help of existing discourse. It is not used in the way the discourse and policy analysis literature uses the concept frame because this can cause unnecessary confusion in this study. See Rein and Schön (1996) for a description of the four different ways one can look at a frame in the discourse and policy analysis literature.
9. One should remain aware of the possibility that government is not just following the media's lead concerning frames, but that it may actively pursue a course of action in which it tries to manipulate the media by leaking stories in order to create a new frame of thinking within the media that will 'prime the public' to accept certain government solutions (Auerbach and Bloch-Elkon, 2005: 95; cf. Edwards and Wood, 1999; Robinson, 2001: 525).
10. See for example *Het Algemeen Dagblad*, 2 June 1993, 'Fractie velt oordeel binnen een kwartier'.
11. 'The arrival of John Major at 10 Downing Street and Kenneth Baker at the Home Office is expected to move policy-making slightly to the left. All the main political parties now agree that fewer non-violent offenders should be jailed, that conditions in prisons should be improved and that police should work harder to justify increases in manpower. A Major-Baker axis on Home Office policy may increase this trend. Both also oppose capital punishment in contrast to their immediate predecessors' (*The Times*, 17 December 1990, 'Policies Move to the Left'); cf. *The Times*, 1 February 1991, 'Manifesto for Prisons'.
12. *The Times*, 1 February 1991, 'Manifesto for Prisons'.
13. *Algemeen Dagblad*, 2 June 1993, 'Fractie velt oordeel binnen een kwartier'; cf. *NRC Handelsblad*, 3 June 1993, 'Noodverbanden'.

Appendix 1
Chronology of the Dutch Prison Service

1982	The Ministry of Justice published the White Paper *Task and Future of the Dutch Prison Service.*
1985	The Ministry of Justice published its White Paper *Society and Criminality.*
1987	The project team published its report on dangerous and escape-prone prisoners.
1990	JR-120 on expanding cell capacity published.
1990	Special Security Units became operational.
1991	National Court of Audit published its report *Fighting Crime.*
September 1992	Hoekstra Committee published its report on the escapes from SSUs.
23 October 1992	Four SSU prisoners escaped from SSU De Grittenborgh (Hoogeveen).
3 November 1992	Junior Minister of Justice Kosto accepted that building two new SSUs was necessary.
9 December 1992	Suspension of the governor of De Grittenborgh (Hoogeveen) ended.
6 January 1993	Three prisoners escaped from De Grittenborgh (Hoogeveen).
8 January 1993	Two prisoners escaped from Amsterdam Prison.
23 January 1993	Four prisoners escaped from Amsterdam Prison.
End of January 1993	Armed guards located outside Amsterdam Prison.
February 1993	One prisoner escaped from SSU De Schie (Rotterdam) armed with a gun.
30 March 1993	Two prisoners attempted to escape from SSU De Schie (Rotterdam) but failed.
3 April 1993	Six prisoners escaped from SSU De Geerhorst (Sittard).
23 April 1993	Junior Minister Kosto announced his decision to build a temporary super max/SSU.
May 1993	Murderer sent home and committed over 20 violent street robberies.
2 June 1993	Emergency debate held in Parliament.
8 July 1994	Double bunking allowed to avoid sending away category A+ prisoners.
17 July 1993	Cabinet approved Minister of Justice Hirsch Ballin's request to fund 2,000 extra cells.

August 1993	103 per cent rule implemented.
4 February 1994	The Ministry of Justice published the White Paper *Effective Detention.*

Appendix 2
Chronology of the Prison Service of England and Wales*

1 April 1990–25 April 1990	Disturbances at Strangeways Prison and other prisons.
July 1990	Rumbold appointed prisons minister.
28 November 1990	Thatcher lost leadership contest. Major chosen as new Prime Minister who selected a new Cabinet. Baker was appointed Home Secretary.
February 1991	Woolf Report published.
August 1991	Pilling appointed Director General.
September 1991	White Paper *Custody, Care, and Justice* published.
December 1991	Lygo Report published.
April 1992	Clarke appointed Home Secretary and Lloyd appointed prisons minister.
January 1993	Lewis appointed Director General. Blair used phrase 'tough on crime, tough on the causes of crime' in a BBC radio interview.
February 1993	Jamie Bulger murdered.
1 April 1993	The Prison Service became an agency.
May 1993	Howard appointed Home Secretary.
July 1993	Strangeways own prison team won market-testing competition.
October 1993	Autumn party conferences: Blair said 'Labour is the party of law and order in Britain today' (Dunbar and Langdon, 1998: 115). Home Secretary Howard declared that 'prison works' and came up with 27 points on law and order for the legislative agenda next year.
March 1994	Trebling ended.
July 1994	Forsyth appointed prisons minister.
9 September 1994	Six prisoners, including five IRA terrorists, escaped from SSU at Whitemoor Prison.
October 1994	Home secretary announced earned privileges and incentives scheme and changes in home leave and temporary leave arrangements.
19 December 1994	Woodock Report published and discussed in House of Commons.

1 January 1995	Suicide Frederick West – on remand for 'House of Horrors' murders.
2-3 January 1995	Disturbances at Everthorpe Prison.
3 January 1995	Three prisoners escaped from Parkhurst dispersal prison.
10 January 1995	House of Commons debate on recent events. Marriott, governor of Parkhurst, removed.
18 January 1995	Director General Lewis, assisted by Director of Personnel Butler, and Director of Security and services Tilt, appeared before the Home Affairs Committee that held a one-off evidence session to question Lewis about the Prison Service.
June 1995	Use of police cells to ease overcrowding ended.
August 1995	Widdecombe appointed prisons minister.
16 October 1995	Learmont Report published and discussed in House of Commons. Director General Lewis sacked. Tilt appointed acting Director General.
19 October 1995	Emergency debate held in House of Commons concerning interference of Home Secretary Howard in operational matters.
March 1996	Tilt appointed Director General.
April 1996	Slopping out ended.

* Based on and expanded from the list as presented in Home Affairs Committee (1997a: lxxxii).

References

Aberbach, J.D. and Christensen, T. (2001), 'Radical Reform in New Zealand: Crisis, Windows of Opportunity, and Rational Actors', *Public Administration* 79(2), pp. 403–22.

Adams, R. (1994), *Prison Riots in Britain and the USA*, Houndmills: Macmillan (2nd edition).

Alink, F. (2006), *Crisis als kans? Over de relatie tussen crises en hervormingen in het vreemdelingenbeleid van Nederland and Duitsland*, Amsterdam: Vossiuspers UvA – Amsterdam University Press.

Alink, F., Boin, A. and 't Hart, P. (2001), 'Institutional Crises and Reforms in Policy Sectors: The Case of Asylum Policy in Europe', *Journal of European Public Policy* 8(2), pp. 286–306.

Alink, F. and Resodihardjo, S.L. (2002), 'Conservative or Reformative – How Trigger Events Turn around Crisis Managements' Approach during Institutional Crises', conference paper *EGPA*, Potsdam (Germany).

Auerbach, Y. and Bloch-Elkon, Y. (2005), 'Media Framing and Foreign Policy: The Elite Press vis-à-vis US Policy in Bosnia, 1992–1995', *Journal of Peace Research* 42 (1), pp. 83–99.

Bachrach, P. and Baratz, M.S. (1970), 'Key Concepts: Decisions and Nondecisions', in Bachrach, P., M.S. Baratz (eds), *Power and Poverty. Theory and Practice*, New York: Oxford University Press, pp. 39–51.

Bannink, D. and Resodihardjo, S.L. (2006), 'The Myths of Reform', in Heyse, L., Resodihardjo, S.L., Lanting, T. and Lettinga, B. (eds), *Reform in Europe. Breaking the Barriers in Government*, Aldershot: Ashgate, pp. 1–20.

Baumgartner, F.R. and Jones, B.D. (1993), *Agendas and Instability in American Politics*, Chicago: University of Chicago Press.

Berg, J.T.J. van den, Elzinga, D.J. and Vis, J.J. (1984), *Parlement en politiek*, 's Gravenhage: Staatsuitgeverij (3rd revised edition).

Boeij, K. (1992), 'Nee tegen twee'. *Algemeen Politieblad* 141(13), p. 7.

Boin, A. (2001a), 'Securing Safety in the Dutch Prison System: Pros and Cons of a Supermax', *The Howard Journal* 40(4), pp. 335–46.

Boin, A. (2001b), *Crafting Public Institutions. Leadership in Two Prison Systems*, Boulder, CO: Lynne Rienner.

Boin, R.A. (1999), 'Bezuiningingen met behoud van kwaliteit; enkele lessen uit het Amerikaanse federale gevangeniswezen', *Justitiële Verkenningen* 25(1), pp. 24–33.

Boin, R.A. (1998), *Contrasts in Leadership. An Institutional Study of Two Prison Systems*, Delft: Eburon.

Boin, R.A. (1995), 'Het gevangeniswezen: naar een nieuwe balans tussen centrale controle en autonomie van inrichtingen', *Sancties* 5(3), pp. 147–61.

Boin, R.A., Dekker, S., 't Hart, P. and Resodihardjo, S.L. (2008), 'Managing Institutional Crises: Restoration and Reform in the Criminal Justice Sector', in Hermann, M. (ed.), *New Perspectives on Political Psychology*, London: Elsevier.

Boin, R.A. and 't Hart, P. (2003), 'Public Leadership in Times of Crisis: Mission Impossible?', *Public Administration Review* 63(5), pp. 544–53.

Boin, R.A. and 't Hart, P. (2000), 'Institutional Crises and Reforms in Policy Sectors', in Wagenaar, H. (ed.), *Government Institutions: Effects, Changes and Normative Foundations*, Dordrecht: Kluwer Academic Publishers, pp. 9–31.

Boin, R.A., Kuipers, S. and Otten, M. (2000), *Institutionele crises. Breuklijnen in beleidssectoren*, Alphen aan den Rijn: Samsom.

Boin, R.A. and Resodihardjo, S.L. (2000), 'Van normale incidenten tot nieuw beleid: crisis in het gevangeniswezen', in Boin, A., Kuipers, S. and Otten, M. (eds), *Institutionele crises. Breuklijnen in beleidssectoren*, Alphen aan den Rijn: Samsom, pp. 59–82.

Borst, E.J. de (1991), *Vluchten kan niet meer*, Den Haag: Beleidsinfo D&J.

Bottoms, A.E. and Stevenson, S. (1992), 'What Went Wrong? Criminal Justice Policy in England and Wales, 1945–70', in Downes, D. (ed.), *Unravelling Criminal Justice. Eleven British Studies*, Houndmills: Macmillan, pp. 1–45.

Bovens, M. and 't Hart, P. (1998), *Understanding Policy Fiascoes*, New Brunswick: Transaction Publishers.

Bovens, M., 't Hart, P. and Peters, B.G. (2001), 'The State of Public Governance', in Bovens, M., 't Hart, P. and Peters, B.G. (eds), *Success and Failure in Public Governance. A Comparative Analysis*, Cheltenham: Edward Elgar, pp. 3–11.

Bovens, M., 't Hart, P., Dekker, S., Verheuvel, G. and Vries, E. de (1998), 'The Mass Media and Policy Disasters: The IRT Disaster and The Crisis in Crime-Fighting in The Netherlands', in Gray, P. and 't Hart, P. (eds), *Public Policy Disasters in Western Europe*, London: Routledge, pp. 39–58.

Bovens, M., 't Hart, P., Dekker, S. and Verheuvel, G. (1999), 'Politics of Blame Avoidance. Defensive Tactics in a Dutch Crime-Fighting Fiasco', in Anheier, H.K. (ed.), *When Things Go Wrong. Organizational Failures and Breakdowns*, Thousand Oaks, CA: Sage Publications, pp. 123–47.

Breeman, G., Op den Kamp, K. and Zannoni, M. (2000), 'Mestproblemen en varkenspest: crisis en kansen in de landbouwsector', in Boin, A., Kuipers, S. and Otten, M. (eds), *Institutionele crises. Breuklijnen in beleidssectoren*, Alphen aan den Rijn: Samsom, pp. 114–43.

Breur, J.A. and Brekelmans, T.C.J.A. (1993), *Politie-Almanak 1993. Handboek voor de Politie in haar gehele omvang, de Rechterlijke Macht, de Gemeentebesturen en verdere Overheidsorganen*, 's-Gravenhage: VUGA.

Bunt, H. van de (2004), 'Organized Crime Policies in The Netherlands', in Fijnaut, C.J.C.F. and Paoli. L. (eds), *Organised Crime in Europe: Concepts, Patterns, and Policies in The European Union and beyond*, Deventer: Kluwer Academic Publisher, pp. 677–716.

Caiden, G.E. (1991), *Administrative Reform Comes of Age*, Berlin: Walter de Gruyter.

Cartwright, T.J. (1975), *Royal Commissions and Departmental Committees in Britain. A Case-Study in Institutional Adaptiveness and Public Participation in Government*, London: Hodder and Stoughton.

Casale, S. (1994), 'Conditions and Standards', in Player, E. and Jenkins, M. (eds), *Prisons after Woolf. Reform through Riot*, London: Routledge, pp. 66–77.

Cavadino, M. and Dignan, J. (1997), *The Penal System. An Introduction*, London: Sage Publications (2nd edition).

CBS (Centraal Bureau voor de Statistiek) (1997), *Gevangenisstatistiek 1996*, Voorburg: CBS.

Chapman, R.A. (1973), 'Commissions in Policy-Making', in Chapman, R.A. (ed.), *The Role of Commissions in Policy-Making*, London: George Allen and Unwin, pp. 174–88.

Commissie Herijking Wetboek van Strafvordering (1993), *Recht in Vorm. Een onderzoek naar vormvoorschriften in het Wetboek van Strafvordering en de gevolgen van het verzuim daarvan*, Den Haag: Commissie herijking Wetboek van Strafvordering.

Cortell, A.P. and Peterson, S. (2001), 'Limiting the Unintended Consequences of Institutional Change', *Comparative Political Studies* 34(7), pp. 768–99.

Cortell, A.P. and Peterson, S. (1999), 'Altered States: Explaining Domestic Institutional Change', *British Journal of Political Science* 29(1), pp. 77–203.

COT (Crisis Onderzoek Team Rijksuniversiteit Leiden) (1997), *Crises in het nieuws. Samenspel en tegenspel tussen overheid en media*, Alphen aan den Rijn: Samsom H.D. Tjeenk Willink.

Dekker, S., Jong, L. de and Luitwieler, S. (2000), 'Crisis in de opsporing: de complexiteit van crisismanagement', in Boin, A., Kuipers, S. and Otten, M. (eds), *Institutionele crises. Breuklijnen in beleidssectoren*, Alphen aan den Rijn: Samsom, pp. 83–113.

Dekker, S., Jongejan, R. and Spek, E. (2003), 'Crisis in het gevangeniswezen. Bolletjesslikkers en het cellentekort', *Bestuurskunde* 12(2), pp. 77–87.

Dhondt, J. (1993), '"Taak en Toekomst" op z'n kop?', *Sancties* 3(3), pp. 143–6.

Dinan, W., Ford, A., McConnell, A. and Pyper, R. (2006), 'Policy Responses to Crisis: The Case of the UK Firefighters' Dispute', *The Policy Press* 34(2), pp. 307–23.

DJI (Dienst Justitiële Inrichtingen) (2001), *Feiten in Cijfers*, Den Haag: Ministerie van Justitie.
DJI (Dienst Justitiële Inrichtingen) (1999), *Feiten in Cijfers*, Den Haag: Ministerie van Justitie.
DJI (Diens Justitiële Inrichtingen) (1998), *Gevangeniswezen*, Den Haag: Ministerie van Justitie.
Dockley, A. (1996), 'What did Learmont Say? Some "On the Ground" Views of the Learmont Report', *The Howard Journal* 35(4), pp. 353–62.
Dogan, M. and Higley, J. (1998), 'Elites, Crises, and Regimes in Comparative Analysis', in Dogan, M. and J. Higley (eds), *Elites, Crises and the Origins of Regimes*, Lanham, MD: Rowman and Littlefield, pp. 3–27.
Doig, J.W. and Hargrove, E.C. (1990), '"Leadership" and Political Analysis', in Doig, J.W. and Hargrove, E.C. (eds), *Leadership and Innovation. Entrepreneurs in Government*, Baltimore, MD: The John Hopkins University Press (abridged edition), pp. 1–22.
Downes, D. (1998), 'The Buckling of the Shields: Dutch Penal Policy 1985–1995', in Weiss, R.P. and South, N. (eds), *Comparing Prison Systems. Towards a Comparative and International Penology*, Amsterdam: OPA, pp. 143–74.
Downes, D. (1988), *Contrasts in Tolerance: Post-War Penal Policy in the Netherlands and England and Wales*, Oxford: Claredon Press.
Downes, D. and Morgan, R. (2002), 'The Skeletons in The Cupboard: The Politics of Law and Order at The Turn of The Millennium', in Maguire, M., Morgan, R. and Reiner, R. (eds), *The Oxford Handbook of Criminology*, Oxford: Oxford University Press (3rd edition), pp. 286–321.
Downes, D. and Morgan, R. (1997), 'Dumping the "Hostages to Fortune"? The Politics of Law and Order in Post-War Britain', in Maguire, M., Morgan, R. and Reiner, R. (eds), *The Oxford Handbook of Criminology*, Oxford: Oxford University Press (2nd edition), pp. 87–134.
Dunbar, I. and Langdon, A. (1998), *Tough Justice. Sentencing and Penal Policies in the 1990s*, London: Blackstone Press Limited.
Edwards III, G.C. and Wood, B.D. (1999), 'Who Influences Whom? The President, Congress, and the Media', *American Political Science Review* 93(2), pp. 327–44.
Elting, L. (1994), 'Werkzame detentie', *Justitiële Verkenningen* 20(2), pp. 84–93.
Entman, R. (1991), 'Framing US Coverage of International News: Contrasts in Narratives of the KAL and Iran Air Incidents', *Journal of Communication* 41(4), pp. 6–27.
Essen, G. van (1990), 'Een nieuw penitentiair bestel', *Sancties* 1(6), pp. 313–18.
Faulkner, D. (2001), *Crime, State and Citizen*, Winchester: Waterside Press.
Fick Commissie (1947), *Rapport van de commissie voor de verdere uitbouw van het gevangeniswezen*, 's-Gravenhage: SDU.
Fiselier, J.P.S. (1992), 'De meermanscel: de kogel door de kerk?', *Sancties* 2(4), pp. 210–17.

Fox, F.V. and Staw, B.M. (1979), 'The Trapped Administrator: Effects of Job Insecurity and Policy Resistance upon Commitment to a Course of Action', *Administrative Science Quarterly* 24(3), pp. 449–71.

Franke, H. (1996), *De Macht van het lijden. Twee eeuwen gevangenisstraf in Nederland*, Amsterdam: Balans.

Gains, F. (2006), 'Modernizing English Local Government: Voice, Loyalty, and Exit in the Demise of the Committee System', in Heyse, L., Resodihardjo, S.L., Lanting, T. and Lettinga, B. (eds), *Reform in Europe. Breaking the Barriers in Government*, Aldershot: Ashgate, pp. 127–38.

Gallagher, M., Laver, M. and Mair, P. (1992), *Representative Government in Western Europe*, New York: McGraw-Hill.

Garland, D. (2001), *The Culture of Control. Crime and Social Order in Contemporary Society*, Oxford: Oxford University Press.

George, A.L. and Bennett, A. (2004), *Case Studies and Theory Development in the Social Sciences*, Cambridge: MIT Press.

Gilligan, G. (2002), 'Royal Commissions of Inquiry', *The Australian and New Zealand Journal of Criminology* 35(3), pp. 289–307.

Goldfinch, S. and 't Hart, P. (2003), 'Leadership and Institutional Reform: Engineering Macroeconomic Policy Change in Australia', *Governance: An International Journal of Policy, Administration, and Institutions* 16(2), pp. 235–70.

Gosnell, H.F. (1934), 'British Royal Commissions of Inquiry', *Political Science Quarterly* 49(1), pp. 84–118.

Hague, R. and Harrop, M. (2001), *Comparative Government and Politics. An Introduction*, Houndmills: Palgrave.

Hall, P.A. (1993), 'Policy Paradigms, Social Learning, and the State. The Case of Economic Policymaking in Britain', *Comparative Politics* 25(3), pp. 275–96.

Hall, S., Critcher, C., Jefferson, T., Clarke, J. and Roberts, B. (1982), *Policing the Crisis. Mugging, the State, and Law and Order*, London: Macmillan.

Harrison, S., Hunter, D.J. and Pollitt, C. (1990), *The Dynamics of British Health Policy*, London: Unwin Hyman.

Hattum, W.F. van (1995), '"Celdeling" is onwettig' *Delikt en Delinkwent* 25 (3), pp. 202–221.

Hay, C. (2002), *Political Analysis. A Critical Introduction*, Houndmills: Palgrave.

Hay, C. (1999), 'Crisis and the Structural Transformation of the State: Interrogating the Process of Change', *British Journal of Politics and International Relations* 1(3), pp. 317–44.

Heffron, F. (1989), *Organization Theory and Public Organizations. The Political Connection*, Englewood Cliffs, NJ: Prentice Hall.

Heinrich, J.P. (1994), 'Doelstellingen van alternatieve sancties in de jaren negentig', *Sancties* 4(1), pp. 29–40.

Helgers, J.J.M. (1993), 'Gevangeniswezen op drift?', *Sancties* 3(6), pp. 345–55.

Heyse, L., Resodihardjo, S.L., Lanting, T. and Lettinga, B. (2006), *Reform in Europe. Breaking the Barriers in Government*, Aldershot: Ashgate.

HM Prison Service (2000), *HM Prison Service Annual Report and Accounts April 1999–March 2000,* London: The Stationery Office (Cm 622).

HM Prison Service (1993), *Prison Service Annual Report and Accounts April 1992–1993*, London: HMSO (Cm 2385).

Hoekstra Committee (1992), *Rapport Evaluatiecommissie Beveiligingsbeleid Gevangeniswezen, deel I, II and III*, Den Haag: Ministerie van Justitie.

Home Affairs Committee (1997a), *The Management of the Prison Service (Public and Private)*, Volume I, London: The Stationary Office (57–I).

Home Affairs Committee (1997b), *The Management of the Prison Service (Public and Private)*, Volume II 1/2, London: The Stationary Office (57–II).

Home Affairs Committee (1997c), *The Management of the Prison Service (Public and Private)*, Volume II 2/2, London: The Stationary Office (57–II).

Home Affairs Committee (1995), *The Operation and Performance of the Prison Service. Minutes of Evidence of Wednesday 18 January 1995*, London: HMSO.

Home Office (2001), *Prison Statistics England and Wales 2000*, London: HMSO (Cm 5250).

Home Office (1997), *The Prison Population in 1996*, Home Office Statistical Bulletins Issue 18/97, London: Home Office.

Home Office (1993), *Home Office Statistical Bulletin* Issue 7/93, London: Government Statistical Service.

Home Office (1991a), *Report of HM Inspector of Prisons into the Brixton Escape on 7 July. Statement by the Home Secretary – Statement by the Home Secretary*, London: Home Office.

Home Office (1991b), 'Inquiry by Her Majesty's Chief Inspector of Prisons into the Escape of Two Category "A" Prisoners from Her Majesty's Prison Brixton on 7 July 1991', text of parts of the report made public 5 August 1991, London: Home Office.

Home Office (1991c), *Custody, Care and Justice: The Way Ahead for the Prison Service in England and Wales*, London: HMSO (Cm 1647).

Home Office (1990a), *Report of a Review by Her Majesty's Chief Inspector of Prisons for England and Wales of Suicide and Self-harm in Prison Service Establishments in England and Wales*, London: HMSO (Cm 1383).

Home Office (1990b), *Report on the Work of the Prison Service April 1989–March 1990*, London: HMSO (Cm 1302).

Home Office (1986), *A Fresh Start*, London: Central Office of Information.

House of Commons Education, Science and Arts Committee (1991), *Prison Education, 2nd Report*, London: HMSO (HC 311–I, II).

Howlett, M. (1997), 'Issue-Attention and Punctuated Equilibria Models Reconsidered: An Empirical Examination of the Dynamics of Agenda-Setting in Canada', *Canadian Journal of Political Science* 30(1), pp. 3–29.

Hueglin, T.O. (2003), 'Majoritarianism – Consociationalism', in Axtmann, R. (ed.), *Understanding Democratic Politics. An Introduction*, London: Sage, Publications, pp. 61–71.

James, A.L., Bottomley, A.K., Liebling, A. and Clare, E. (1997), *Privatizing Prisons. Rhetoric and Reality*, London: Sage Publications.

Jones, B. (2001a), 'The Mass Media and Political Communication', in Jones, B., Kavanagh, D., Moran, M. and Norton, P. (eds), *Politics UK*, Harlow: Pearson Education, pp. 177–204.

Jones, B. (2001b), 'The Politics of Law and Order', in Jones, B., Kavanagh, D., Moran, M. and Norton, P. (eds), *Politics UK*, Harlow: Pearson Education, pp. 543–63.

Jong, H. de and Vliet, A. van (1993), 'Ontsnappingen en andere onrust in het gevangeniswezen', in Almelo, L. van, Velden, R. van der and Durieux, H. (eds), *Crimineel jaarboek uitgave 1993*, Nijmegen: Papieren Tijger, pp. 91–127.

Kaarbo, J. and Beasley, R.K. (1999), 'A Practical Guide to the Comparative Case Study Method in Political Psychology', *Political Psychology* 20(2), pp. 36–391.

Kaufman, H. (1995), *The Limits of Organizational Change*, New Brunswick, NJ: Transaction Publishers.

Kavanagh, D. (2001a), 'Voting Behaviour', in Jones, B., Kavanagh, D., Moran, M. and Norton, P. (eds), *Politics UK*, Harlow: Pearson Education, pp. 162–76.

Kavanagh, D. (2001b), 'Political Parties', in Jones, B., Kavanagh, D., Moran, M. and Norton, P. (eds), *Politics UK*, Harlow: Pearson Education, pp. 231–55.

Kavanagh, D. (2001c), 'The Cabinet and Prime Minister', in Jones, B., Kavanagh, D., Moran, M. and Norton, P. (eds), *Politics UK*, Harlow: Pearson Education, pp. 410–36.

Keeler, J.T.S. (1993), 'Opening the Window for Reform: Mandates, Crises and Extraordinary Policy-Making', *Comparative Political Studies* 25(1), pp. 433–86.

Kelk, C. (2001), 'The Netherlands', in Zyl Smit, D. van and Dünkel, F. (eds), *Imprisonment Today and Tomorrow. International Perspectives on Prisoners' Rights and Prison Conditions*, The Hague: Kluwer Law International (2nd edition), pp. 478–507.

Kelk, C. (1994), 'Sobere vooruitzichten voor het gevangeniswezen', *Delikt en Delikwent* 24(2), pp. 107–12.

King, R.D. (1994), 'Order, Disorder and Regimes in The Prison Services of Scotland, and England and Wales', in Player, E. and Jenkins, M. (eds), *Prisons after Woolf. Reform through Riot*, London: Routledge, pp. 46–65.

King, R.D. and McDermott, K. (1992), 'Security, Control, and Humane Containment in the Prison System in England and Wales', in Downes, D. (ed.), *Unravelling Criminal Justice. Eleven British Studies*, Houndmills: Macmillan, pp. 96–118.

King, R.D. and McDermott, K. (1989), 'British Prisons 1970–1987. The Ever-Deepening Crisis', *The British Journal of Criminology* 29(2), pp. 107–28.

King, R.D. and Resodihardjo, S.L. (forthcoming), 'To Max or Not to Max: Dealing with High Risk Prisoners in England and Wales and the Netherlands'.

Kingdon, J.W. (1995), *Agendas, Alternatives, and Public Policies*, New York: Longman (2nd edition).

Klein, M.W. (1996), 'Timing is All: Elections and the Duration of United States Business Cycles', *Journal of Money, Credit, and Banking* 28(1), pp. 84–101.

Korsten, A.F.A. (1993), 'Beëindiging van beleid', in Hoogerwerf, A. (ed.), *Overheidsbeleid. Een inleiding in de beleidswetenschap*, Alphen aan den Rijn: Samsom H.D. Tjeenk Wellink, pp. 198–214.

Kuipers, S.L. (2006), *The Crisis Imperative: Crisis Rhetoric and Welfare State Reform in Belgium and the Netherlands in the Early 1990s*, Amsterdam: Amsterdam University Press.

Kuipers, S.L. (2004), *Cast in Concrete? The Institutional Dynamics of Belgian and Dutch Social Policy Reform*, Delft: Eburon Academic Publishers.

Lakes, G.H. and Hadfield, R. (1991), *Interim Report of A Security Audit of Arrangements for Holding and Managing Category A Prisoners in Custody*, London: Home Office internal document.

Learmont, J. (1995), *Review of Prison Service Security in England and Wales and the escape from Parkhurst Prison on Tuesday 3rd January 1995*, London: HMSO (Cm 3020).

Leemans, A.F. (1976a), 'Overview', in Leemans, A.F. (ed.), *The Management of Change in Government*, The Hague: Martinus Nijhoff, pp. 1–62.

Leemans, A.F. (1976b), 'A Conceptual Framework for the Study of Reform of Central Government', in Leemans, A.F. (ed.), *The Management of Change in Government*, The Hague: Martinus Nijhoff, pp. 65–98.

Levi, M. (1997), 'Violent Crime', in Maguire, M., Morgan, R. and Reiner, R. (eds), *The Oxford Handbook of Criminology*, Oxford: Oxford University Press (2nd edition), pp. 841–89.

Lewis, D. (1997), *Hidden Agendas. Politics, Law and Disorder*, London: Hamish Hamilton.

Lindblom, C.E. (1979), 'Still Muddling, Not Yet Through', *Public Administration Review* 39(6), pp. 517–26.

Lindblom, C.E. (1959), 'The Science of "Muddling Through"', *Public Administration Review* 19(2), pp. 79–88.

Lygo, Admiral Sir Raymond (1991), *Management of the Prison Service*, London: Home Office internal document.

McCombs, M. (1997), 'Building Consensus: The News Media's Agenda-Setting Roles', *Political Communication* 14(4), pp. 433–43.
McConnell, A. (2003), 'Overview: Crisis Management, Influences, Responses and Evaluation', *Parliamentary Affairs* 56(3), pp. 393–409.
McDermott, K. and King, R.D. (1989), 'A Fresh Start: The Enhancement of Prison Regimes', *The Howard Journal* 28(3), pp. 161–76.
Merton, R.K. (1949), *Social Theory and Social Structure. Toward the Codification of Theory and Research*, Glencoe, IL: The Free Press of Glencoe.
Miller, D. (1999), 'Selection Processes inside Organizations. The Self-Reinforcing Consequences of Success', in Baum, J.A.C. and McKelvey, B. (eds), *Variations in Organization Science. In Honor of Donald T. Campbell*, Thousand Oaks, CA: Sage Publications, pp. 93–109.
Ministry of Justice (1994), *Werkzame Detentie*, Den Haag: Ministerie van Justitie.
Ministry of Justice (1987), *Rapport van de werkgroep Opvang Vlucht- en Gemeengevaarlijke Gedetineerden*, Den Haag: Ministerie van Justitie.
Ministry of Justice (1985), *Samenleving en Criminaliteit: Een beleidsplan voor de komende jaren*, Den Haag: Ministerie van Justitie.
Ministry of Justice (1982), *Taak en Toekomst van het Nederlandse gevangeniswezen*, Den Haag: Ministerie van Justitie.
Moerings, M. (ed.) (1994), *Hoe punitief is Nederland?*, Arnhem: Gouda Quint.
Morgan, R. (2001), 'England and Wales', in Zyl Smit, D. van and Dünkel, F. (eds), *Imprisonment Today and Tomorrow. International Perspectives on Prisoners' Rights and Prison Conditions*, The Hague: Kluwer Law International (2nd edition), pp. 211–37.
Morgan, R. (1997), 'Imprisonment: Current Concerns and a Brief History since 1945', in Maguire, M., Morgan, R. and Reiner, R. (eds), *The Oxford Handbook of Criminology*, Oxford: Oxford University Press (2nd edition), pp. 1137–94.
Morgan, R. (1996), 'Learmont: Dangerously Unbalanced', *The Howard Journal* 35(4), pp. 346–53.
Morris, N. and Rothman, D.J. (eds) (1995), *The Oxford History of the Prison. The Practice of Punishment in Western Society*, New York: Oxford University Press.
Mountbatten (Earl Mountbatten of Burma) (1966), *Report of the Inquiry into the Prison Escapes and Security*, London: HMSO.
National Court of Audit (Algemene Rekenkamer) (1991), *Criminaliteitsbestrijding*, Den Haag: SDU.
Noll, J.E. (2005), *Leadership and Institutional Reform in Consensual Democracies. Dutch and Swedish Defence Organizations after the Cold War*, Göttingen: Cuvillier Verlag.

Norton, P. (2001a), 'The House of Commons', in Jones, B., Kavanagh, D., Moran, M. and Norton, P. (eds), *Politics UK*, Harlow: Pearson Education, pp. 339–76.

Norton, P. (2001b), 'Ministers, Departments and Civil Servants', in Jones, B., Kavanagh, D., Moran, M. and Norton, P. (eds), *Politics UK*, Harlow: Pearson Education, pp. 437–57.

Patashnik, E. (2003), 'After the Public Interest Prevails: The Political Sustainability of Policy Reform', *Governance: An International Journal of Policy, Administration, and Institutions* 16(2), pp. 203–34.

Postma, A. (1985), *Nederlands parlementsrecht. Het interpellatie- en vragenrecht van de Eerste en Tweede Kamer*, Groningen: Wolters-Noordhoff.

Prasser, S. (1994), 'Royal Commissions and Public Inquiries: Scope and Uses', in Weller, P. (ed.), *Royal Commissions and the Making of Public Policy*, Melbourne: Macmillan Education Australia, pp. 1–21.

Press Council (1991), *Press at the Prison Gates. Report of the Inquiry by The Press Council into Press Coverage of the Strangeways Prison Riot and Related Matters*, Rochester: Staples Printers Rochester Limited.

Prison Service (2001), *Prison Service Order: Category A Prisoners: Reviews of Security Category* 117, London: HM Prison Service.

Prison Service (2000), *Prison Service Order: Categorisation and Allocation* 99, London: HM Prison Service.

Ransley, J. (1994), 'The Powers of Royal Commissions and Controls over Them', in Weller, P. (ed.), *Royal Commissions and the Making of Public Policy*, Melbourne: Macmillan Education Australia, pp. 22–31.

Rayner, J., Howlett, M., Wilson, J., Cashore, B. and Hoberg, G. (2001), 'Privileging the Sub-Sector: Critical Sub-Sectors and Sectoral Relationships in Forest Policy-Making', *Forest Policy and Economics* 2(3–4), pp. 319–32.

Rein, M. and Schön, D. (1996), 'Frame-critical Policy Analysis and Frame-reflective Policy Practice', *Knowledge, Technology, and Policy* 9(1), pp. 85–104.

Resodihardjo, S.L. (2006a), 'Wielding a Double-Edged Sword: The Use of Inquiries at Times of Crisis', *Journal of Contingencies and Crisis Management* 14(4), pp. 199–206.

Resodihardjo, S.L. (2006b), 'Behouden of hervormen? Crisismanagement binnen het gevangeniswezen', *Proces. Tijdschrift voor strafrechtspleging* 85(2), pp. 71–8.

Resodihardjo, S.L. (2004), 'Discourse and Funnelling: How Discourse Affected Howard's Leeway During the 1994–5 Crisis', *Journal for Crime, Conflict, and the Media* 1(3), pp. 15–27 (http://www.jc2m.co.uk/Issue3/Resodihardjo.pdf).

Resodihardjo, S.L. (2002), 'Let's Top Up Security, Shall We? Crisis Management in the Prison Service', conference paper *NWO Conference* Leiden (the Netherlands).

Rhodes, G. (1975), *Committees of Inquiry*, London: George Allen and Unwin.

Richards, D. and Smith, M.J. (1997), 'How Departments Change: Windows of Opportunity and Critical Junctures in Three Departments', *Public Policy and Administration* 12(2), pp. 62–79.

Roberts, N.C. and and King, P.J. (1996), *Transforming Public Policy. Dynamics of Policy Entrepreneurship and Innovation*, San Francisco, CA: Jossey-Bass.

Robinson, P. (2001), 'Theorizing the Influence of Media on World Politics. Models of Media Influence on Foreign Policy', *European Journal of Communication* 16(4), pp. 523–44.

Robinson, P. (2000), 'The Policy-Media Interaction Model: Measuring Media Power During Humanitarian Crisis', *Journal of Peace Research* 37(5), pp. 613–33.

Rochefort, D.A. and Cobb, R.W. (1994), 'Problem Definition: An Emerging Perspective', in Rochefort, D.A. and Cobb, R.W. (eds), *The Politics of Problem Definition. Shaping the Policy Agenda*, Lawrence, KS: University Press of Kansas, pp. 1–31.

Rose, R. and Davies, P.L. (1994), *Inheritance in Public Policy: Change without Choice in Britain*, New Haven, CT: Yale University Press.

Rosenthal, U., Boin, A. and Comfort, L.K. (2001), 'The Changing World of Crises and Crisis Management', in Rosenthal, U., Boin, A. and Comfort, L.K. (eds), *Managing Crises. Threats, Dilemmas, Opportunities*, Springfield, IL: Charles C. Thomas, pp. 5–27.

Rothman, D.J. (1998), 'Perfecting the Prison', in Morris, N. and Rothman, D.J. (eds), *The Oxford History of the Prison. The Practice of Punishment in Western Society*, New York: Oxford Univeristy Press, pp. 100–16.

Rueschemeyer, D. (2003), 'Can One or a Few Cases Yield Theoretical Gains?', in Mahoney, J. and Rueschemeyer, D. (eds), *Comparative Historical Analysis in the Social Sciences*, Cambridge: Cambridge University Press, pp. 305–36.

Rutherford, A. (1996), *Transforming Criminal Policy. Spheres of Influence in the United States, the Netherlands and England and Wales during the 1980s*, Winchester: Waterside Press.

Ryan, M. and Sim, J. (1998), 'Power, Punishment and Prisons in England and Wales 1975–1996', in Weiss, R.P. and South, N. (eds), *Comparing Prison Systems. Towards a Comparative and International Penology*, Amsterdam: OPA, pp. 175–205.

Sabatier, P.A. (1998), 'The Advocacy Coalition Framework: Revisions and Relevance for Europe', *Journal of European Public Policy* 5(1), pp. 98–130.

Sancties (1993), 'Regime in EBIs niet onrechtmatig, maar zoeken naar minder ingrijpend systeem geboden (President rechtbank 's-Gravenhage, 15 januari 1993, nr. 92/1159, mr. Van Delden)', *Sancties* 3(3), pp. 195–200.

Senior, B. (1997), *Organisational Change*, London: Pitman Publishing.

Shepsle, K.A. (2001), 'A Comment on Institutional Change', *Journal of Theoretical Politics* 13(3), pp. 321–25.

Singer-Dekker, H. (1994), 'Criminaliteitsbestrijding en verkiezingen', *Sancties* 4(2), pp. 69–76.

Singer-Dekker, H. (1992), 'De justitiebegroting 1992', *Sancties* 2(2), pp. 68–77.

Smith, M. J. (1999), *The Core Executive in Britain*, Houndmills: Macmillan.

Smith, R. (1983), 'The State of the Prisons. Crisis upon Crisis', *The British Medical Journal* 287(6400), pp. 1705–8.

Sparks, R., Bottoms, A. and Hay, W. (1996), *Prisons and the Problem of Order*, Oxford: Clarendon Press.

Staw, B.M. (1976), 'Knee-Deep in the Big Muddy: A Study of Escalating Commitment to a Chosen Course of Action', *Organizational Behavior and Human Performance* 16(1), pp. 27–44.

Staw, B.M. and Ross, J. (1987), 'Behavior in Escalation Situations: Antecedents, Prototypes, and Solutions', *Research in Organizational Behavior* 9, pp. 39–78.

Staw, B.M., Sandelands, L.E. and Dutton, J.E. (1981), 'Threat-Rigidity Effects in Organizational Behavior: A Multilevel Analysis', *Administrative Science Quarterly* 26(4), pp. 501–24.

Stone, B. (1994), 'Success in Public Inquiries: An Analysis and a Case Study', in Weller, P. (ed.), *Royal Commissions and the Making of Public Policy*, Melbourne: Macmillan Education Australia, pp. 244–58.

Suchman, M.C. (1995), 'Managing Legitimacy: Strategic and Institutional Approaches', *Academy of Management Review* 20(3), pp. 571–610.

Swaaningen, R. van and uit Beijerse, J. (1993), 'From Punishment to Diversion and Back Again: The Debate on Non-custodial Sanctions and Penal Reform in the Netherlands', *The Howard Journal* 32(2), pp. 136–56.

Swaaningen. R. van and de Jonge, G. (1995), 'The Dutch Prison System and Penal Policy in the 1990s: from Humanitarian Paternalism to Penal Business Management', in Ruggiero, V., Ryan, M. and J. Sim (eds), *Western European Penal Systems. A Critical Anatomy*, London: Sage Publications, pp. 24–45.

't Hart, P. (2001), *Verbroken verbindingen. Over de politisering van het verleden en de dreiging van een inquisitiedemocratie*, Amsterdam: De Balie.

't Hart, P. (2000), *Hervormend leiderschap. Over veranderingskunst in het openbaar bestuur*, Utrecht: Uitgeverij Lemma BV.

't Hart, P., Rosenthal, U. and Kouzmin, A. (1993), 'Crisis Decision Making The Centralization Thesis Revisted', *Administration and Society* 25(1), pp. 12–45.

Terkildsen, T. and Schnell, F. (1997), 'How Media Frames Move Public Opinion: An Analysis of the Women's Movement', *Political Research Quarterly* 50(4), pp. 879–900.

Terry, L.D. (2003), *Leadership of Public Bureaucracies. The Administrator as Conservator*, New York: M.E. Sharpe (2nd edition).

Teske, P. and Schneider, M. (1994), 'The Bureaucratic Entrepreneur: The Case of City Managers', *Public Administration Review* 54 (4), pp. 331–340.

Thomas, J.E. (1994), 'Woolf and Prison Staff: Still Looking for "Good Goalers"', in Player, E. and Jenkins, M. (eds), *Prisons after Woolf. Reform through Riot*, London: Routledge, pp. 112–24.

True, J.L., Jones, D.B. and Baumgartner, F.R. (1999), 'Punctuated-Equilibrium Theory: Explaining Stability and Change in American Policymaking', in Sabatier, P.A. (ed.), *Theories of the Policy Process*, Boulder, CO: Westview Press, pp. 97–115.

Tufte, E.R. (1978), *Political Control of the Economy*, Princeton, NJ: Princeton University Press.

Walmsley, R. (1989), *Special Security Units. A Home Office Research and Planning Unit Report* (no. 109), London: HMSO.

Weller, P. (1994), 'Royal Commissions and the Governmental System in Australia', in Weller, P. (ed.), *Royal Commissions and the Making of Public Policy*, Melbourne: Macmillan Education Australia, pp. 259–66.

Weiss, R.P. and South, N. (eds), (1998), *Comparing Prison Systems. Towards a Comparative and International Penology*, Amsterdam: Gordon and Breach Publishers.

Wiewel, P.G. (1994), 'Onwerkbare detentie. Bespreking van de beleidsnota voor het gevangeniswezen 1994: Werkzame detentie', *Sancties* 4(1), pp. 8–20.

Wilsford, D. (1994), 'Path Dependency, or Why History Makes it Difficult but not Impossible to Reform Health Care Systems in a Big Way', *Journal of Public Policy* 14(3), pp. 251–84.

Wilson, J.Q. (1989), *Bureaucracy. What Government Agencies Do and Why They Do It*, New York: BasicBooks.

WODC (1997), *Duur en volume. Ontwikkeling van de onvoorwaardelijke vrijheidsstraf tussen 1985 en 1995; feiten en verklaringen*, Den Haag: WODC.

Woodcock, J. (1994), *Report of the Enquiry into the Escape of Six prisoners from the Special Security Unit at Whitemoor Prison, Cambridgeshire, on Friday 9th September 1994*, London: HMSO.

Woolf, The Rt Hon Lord Justice (1991), *Prison Disturbances April 1990. Report of an Inquiry by the Rt Hon Lord Justice Woolf (Parts I and II) and his honour Judge Stephen Tumim (Part II)*, London: HMSO.

Yin, R.K. (2003), *Case Study Research. Design and Methods*, Thousand Oaks, CA: Sage Publications. (3rd edition).

Yin, R.K. (1993), *Applications of Case Study Research*, Thousand Oaks, CA: Sage Publications.

Zahariadis, N. (1999), 'Ambiguity, Time, and Multiple Streams', in Sabatier, P.A. (ed.), *Theories of the Policy Process*, Boulder, CO: Westview Press, pp. 73–93.

Index

For Product Safety Concerns and Information please contact our EU
representative GPSR@taylorandfrancis.com
Taylor & Francis Verlag GmbH, Kaufingerstraße 24, 80331 München, Germany

www.ingramcontent.com/pod-product-compliance
Ingram Content Group UK Ltd.
Pitfield, Milton Keynes, MK11 3LW, UK
UKHW011006180926
475701UK00004B/598

* 9 7 8 0 3 6 7 6 0 3 1 5 1 *